Crisis on the Left

The University of Massachusetts Press
Amherst 1978

Crisis on the Left

**Cold War Politics
and American Liberals,
1947–1954**

Mary Sperling McAuliffe

Copyright © 1978 by Mary Sperling McAuliffe
All rights reserved
Library of Congress Catalog Card Number 77-73479
ISBN 0-87023-241-X
Printed in the United States of America
Designed by Mary Mendell
Library of Congress Cataloging in Publication Data
appear on the last printed page of the book.

Earlier versions of material in chapters 7 and 9 originally appeared in "The Politics of Civil Liberties,"
from *The Specter: Original Essays on the Cold War and
the Origins of McCarthyism*, edited by Robert Griffith
and Athan Theoharis, copyright 1974 by Franklin
Watts, Inc.; and in "Liberals and the Communist
Control Act of 1954," *Journal of American History* 63
(September 1976), 351–67.

For Jack

Contents

Acknowledgments

Throughout this book's development from doctoral dissertation to publication, I have greatly appreciated the thoughtful advice of those who read and critiqued the manuscript. I am deeply grateful to Robert Griffith of the University of Massachusetts, for his sustained interest in the manuscript and for his invaluable counsel at every stage of revision and preparation for publication. I am indebted as well to Milton Cantor of the University of Massachusetts and Lawrence S. Wittner of the State University of New York at Albany, for reading and thoughtfully criticizing the entire manuscript. Bruce G. Laurie of the University of Massachusetts and Jon C. Teaford of Purdue University generously agreed to read portions of the manuscript and suggested improvements. My thesis adviser at the University of Maryland, Dan T. Carter, deserves special thanks for his perceptive and sympathetic guidance, as do Louis R. Harlan and Keith W. Olson, members of my thesis committee. And throughout the book's preparation, I have greatly appreciated the advice and encouragement of Malcolm L. Call, formerly editor of the University of Massachusetts Press.

I would also like to express my appreciation for the assistance I received from archivists at the manuscript divisions of the following: the State Historical Society of Wisconsin, the Princeton University library, the Library of Congress, the New York Public Library, New York University's Tamiment Library, the Catholic University of America library, and the Columbia University library and Oral History Collection. I owe thanks as well to those at the Americans for Democratic Action headquarters in Washington, D.C., the American

Civil Liberties Union headquarters in New York, and the national headquarters of the International Union of Electrical, Radio, and Machine Workers in Washington, D.C.; they readily answered my questions, allowed me to research their available historical records, and graciously helped me in many other ways.

I greatly appreciate the assistance given me by the Department of History at Iowa State University in typing the manuscript. My thanks to Susan Ulrickson for her careful and conscientious typing.

The *Journal of American History* and Franklin Watts, Inc. have kindly given me permission to use in revised form material that first appeared in their publications.

Finally, my thanks beyond measure to my understanding and supportive family—to my parents and to my husband. Without their ready encouragement I could never have undertaken and completed this study.

Crisis on the Left

Introduction

The American left has always defied neat classification and has contained, throughout its history, a turbulent mixture of overlapping political creeds of enormous diversity and complexity. Populists and progressives, liberals and radicals, Communists and Socialists have all interacted within this political tradition. Yet in spite of this diversity, and in spite of bitter and divisive conflicts, the American left was united throughout the first half of the twentieth century by a shared body of assumptions, including an identification with common people and antipathy toward big business, a faith in popular government, and a belief in progress and man's capacity for improvement, if not perfectibility.

The depression in particular drew leftists together and muted their differences by discrediting the conservative business leadership of the twenties and opening the door to social change. Sectarian divisions were never absent, but both liberals and radicals thought of themselves as members of the "left," and radicals were often viewed as "liberals in a hurry." Both liberals and radicals found employment in New Deal agencies and in the labor movement, and both seemed committed to a politics of redistributive social change. The Communist party, especially after the formation of the popular front, won new acceptability, and the Soviet Union gained considerable prestige among both liberals and radicals, although there were, of course, dissenters. Though it would be easy to exaggerate both the unity and the power of the American left (as did those who would later characterize the thirties as the "Red Decade"), it nevertheless seems clear that in the 1930s the left was more unified and exercised more influence over American politics than ever before.

The rise of Fascism and the intrusion of international events, however, shattered much of the left's unity and optimism. Many Socialists, pacifists, and old progressives feared a repetition of World War I and opposed the drift toward war, a position which drew them close to the conservative isolationists of the America First Committee. Most liberals generally supported the Roosevelt administration, joining internationalist Republicans and other moderate conservatives in advocating collective security and, ultimately, intervention. American Communists and their supporters first urged a united front against Fascism, only to reverse themselves abruptly in 1939 following the announcement of the Nazi-Soviet Pact. In 1941, following the German invasion of Russia, they reversed themselves once again. During the war liberals, Communists, and non-Communist radicals worked together once again, but the alliance was an uneasy one and did not heal the divisions of the immediate prewar period. Following the end of World War II, many liberals as well as radicals would abandon entirely the broad, united-front liberalism of the 1930s.

The war also helped to create a new and more conservative political climate. War-bred prosperity revived American business and industry, and businessmen once more enjoyed power and prestige. As Franklin D. Roosevelt increasingly relied on businessmen to administer the wartime mobilization, businessmen and conservatives supplanted the old New Dealers. In Congress the Republicans made strong gains in the off-year elections and increasingly joined with conservative Democrats to dismantle or weaken New Deal programs. Harry Truman's replacement of Henry Wallace as the Democratic vice-presidential nominee in 1944 was but one sign of this conservative trend.

The immediate postwar years of 1945 and 1946 thus found the American left still deeply divided by the bitter debates which had preceded World War II and in retreat before the conservative resurgence of the war years. The left remained, nevertheless, a large, diverse, and potentially powerful movement, with a mass base in the left-led CIO trade unions, with articulate spokesmen within the intellectual community, and with access to the government through Secretary of Commerce Henry Wallace and other old New Dealers. The growing tensions between the United States and the Soviet Union and the emergence of anti-Communist politics at home, however, would soon destroy the old left and produce in its place a new liberalism sharply different in both tone and content from the liberalism of the 1930s.

This study is an examination of the response of the left, especially liberals, to the Cold War and to the anti-Communist politics of America's second great Red Scare.

1

Liberals, Communists, and the Postwar Popular Front

$\mathbf{T}$he American left emerged from World War II with apparent strength and unity into a postwar world which many hoped would eradicate the suffering and destruction of the immediate past. Few could perceive the troubled future which lay ahead. In little more than a year, the challenges faced by the American left would be all too evident. Even during the closing months of the war powerful forces were emerging and events were taking place which would have an enormous impact upon the left and which, in retrospect, had already begun to exercise their influence as the world settled into an uneasy peace.

The wartime alliance with the Soviet Union was gradually giving way to mutual suspicion and hostility, as efforts by the United States to establish a peaceful and, in its view, beneficent postwar order were met with continued Soviet intransigence, especially in Germany, eastern Europe, and the Middle East. Soviet-American cooperation eroded, and although the United States' development of the atomic bomb gave it decisive military superiority, the possible deployment of atomic weapons added a new dimension of terror to warfare while apparently doing little to improve the United States' negotiating position on the question of Soviet influence in eastern Europe. The Soviet Union began to exercise its veto in the United Nations Security Council in early 1946 and refused to withdraw its troops from Iran. Even more alarming to Americans was the discovery in February 1946 of a Canadian spy ring charged with attempting to steal atomic information for the Soviet Union. Soon after, in March 1946, President Truman accompanied Winston Churchill to Fulton, Missouri, where the former British prime minister spoke of an "iron curtain" and said that "from what I have seen of our Russian friends and allies during the war, I am convinced that there is nothing they admire so much as strength, and there is nothing for which they have less respect than for weakness, especially military weakness." Although Truman did not formally endorse Churchill's speech, he gave every evidence of approving its hard line. Throughout the remainder of 1946 the Truman administration was careful to demonstrate toughness in its dealings with the Soviet Union. [1]

Affairs at home seemed hardly more promising. Torn between defense requirements and public clamor for rapid demobilization, the Truman administration in addition faced an unexpected and severe inflation instead of the feared postwar depression and unemployment. Confusion dogged the administration in its dealings with the economy, and the nation lurched through several months of shifting policies on price controls that resulted in economic turmoil. "Had enough?" asked the Republicans before the 1946 congressional elections, and Republican victories at the polls testified that many Americans indeed had. Conspicuous Republican use of red-baiting during the 1946 campaign added to the undercurrent of unrest and signaled that America's second great Red Scare was already beginning. [2]

In the midst of these troubles, liberals' need for national leadership was acute. In his first two years in office, Harry S. Truman had proved a disappointment and an embarrassment to those who had hoped for a continuation of the Roosevelt leadership and policies. Truman managed to irritate almost every element of the political spectrum, and despite his endorsement of New Deal legislation, he did not seem to convey the crusading, activist liberalism New Dealers had come to expect. His very dependability as a party man, even on behalf of New Deal legislation, worried liberals who feared the dominance of Southern conservatives and big city bosses in high party councils. Truman's uncertain leadership during 1945 and 1946 and his political cronyism, at the expense of leading New Dealers, reinforced fears that he was neither a liberal nor a leader and increased doubts about the future of political liberalism in America. [3]

The political figure many liberals believed most qualified to assume Roosevelt's mantle was Henry A. Wallace, former vice-president, secretary of agriculture, and, during Roosevelt's last term, secretary of commerce. He had built upon his career as a successful scientist, farm journalist, and businessman to become in Washington a successful administrator of the Department of Agriculture. Joined with his obvious abilities and his dedication to public service was a crusading belief in New Deal reforms which many liberals found attractive, particularly when he extended to the entire world the potential arena for freedom from want. Liberals saw Wallace as a man of principle and contrasted him favorably with Truman, regretting the political decision which had removed him from the Democratic party's national ticket in 1944.[4]

Wallace's abrupt dismissal from government in 1946 following his public criticism of the administration's foreign policy deeply disturbed many on the left. Already a natural rallying point for liberals and leftists dissatisfied with Truman, in particular Truman's foreign policy, Wallace now became even more attractive because of the circumstances of his dismissal. When two united-front organizations, the National Citizens Political Action Committee and the Independent Citizens Committee of the Arts, Sciences, and Professions, merged in December 1946 to form the Progressive Citizens of America, Wallace appeared as the new organization's featured speaker at its first meeting; and it quickly became evident that Wallace was in fact, if not in title, the PCA's principal leader. Talk soon arose about the possibility of a third party in support of Wallace's candidacy for president.[5]

By late 1946, however, the emerging Cold War between the United States and the Soviet Union had already created deep fissures in the left, and by early 1947 some liberals were unwilling to support any organization which openly accepted Communist membership. The 1946 congressional elections, with their severe setbacks for the Democratic party, had also shown that conservatives were hunting for "Communist influence" with devastating results, and many liberals were nervous about being labeled pro-Communist.[6] In time a "new" liberalism would give expression to this emergent mood, but at this early stage it was most frequently expressed negatively as a liberalism free from any Communist taint or ties. This alternative form of liberalism, with direct roots going back to anti-popular-front sentiment of the 1930s, had been represented during the early 1940s by the Union for Democratic Action and the Liberal party of New York, and was soon given direction, definition, and leadership by the founding of Americans for Democratic Action.

The ADA had its origins in the Union for Democratic Action, a small group founded in 1941 by liberals and by former Socialists who had disagreed with their party's reluctance to support the war against Hitler and Fascism. The prominent Protestant theologian Reinhold Niebuhr was the UDA's chairman and James Loeb its executive secretary, while Eleanor Roosevelt gave the new organization important backing. Unlike other liberal organizations of the war years, the UDA excluded Communists from membership—a prohibition which many liberals viewed with coolness and which, consequently, the UDA at first chose not to stress. During the fearful atmosphere which developed as the Cold War intensified, however, and especially following the disastrous 1946 elections, leaders of the UDA sought to mobilize and unify the anti-Communist left.[7] In January 1947, only a week after the PCA had organized, over four hundred prominent New Dealers, trade unionists, and political liberals met in Washington, D.C., in response to the UDA's call for action. These liberals concluded that a new organization, with a new name, would provide a fresher, stronger base upon which to build postwar liberalism. They named their new organization the Americans for Democratic Action and chose Wilson W. Wyatt, former housing expediter, and Leon Henderson, former price administrator, as co-chairmen. James Loeb became secretary-treasurer, a position that he would continue to fill during the ADA's formative years from 1947 through 1951.[8]

The ADA's founders thought that postwar American liberalism in general and the New Deal programs in particular were threatened by attacks from the right and by apathy from liberals themselves. They wanted the ADA to be an active, fighting organization and to provide spirited leadership for liberals. Wyatt and Henderson in their joint keynote address proclaimed, "The fight confronting liberals is long and hard," but "The fight has just begun." Loeb, in a circular sent to prospective members, asserted that the ADA believed "liberalism should amount to more than an impotent growl behind the morning paper." Instead, the ADA's liberals had "translated our impatience, our anger, our indignation into action."[9]

On the one hand, the ADA's members directed their new organization toward battling domestic conservatism and preserving and extending the New Deal. The newly elected conservative Congress, swept into office on the Republicans' "Had Enough?" campaign appeal, offered a real obstacle to such liberal domestic goals as expanded civil rights and improved levels of health, nutrition, shelter, and education. Consequently, the ADA stressed its domestic program and pointed to the necessity for comprehensive political activity from precinct level up to state and national party organizations in order to achieve its goals. "It cannot be stressed too often," the ADA national board told its local chapters, "that the basic purposes of ADA are political, and that all other activity of ADA, nationally and locally, is subordinate to political activity."[10]

On the other hand, despite its emphasis on domestic policy and politics, the ADA quickly indicated its vital interest in opposing the activities of what its leaders called the "totalitarian left" both at home and abroad. "We reject any association with Communists or sympathizers with Communism in the United States as completely as we reject any association with Fascists or their sympathizers," its first policy paper flatly stated. "Both are hostile to the principles of freedom and democracy on which this Republic has grown great." The national ADA adopted this position at its first meeting and, at its second meeting, passed a constitutional provision barring Fascists and Communists from membership.[11]

Thus two liberal organizations had been formed by early 1947, offering alternative—and competing—definitions and directions to the postwar left. Both embraced the New Deal reform program and both endeavored to save it from the attacks of the political right as well as from the bumbling and apparently half-hearted actions of the Truman administration. They differed, however, in their views of the Soviet Union and thus differed on the issue of the united left. Fundamentally, ADA liberals viewed the Soviet Union as a totalitarian regime, the headquarters of an expansionist and dangerous world Communist movement; those in the PCA, however, regarded the USSR in a more friendly light—as an ally in war against Fascism, and as the source of a remarkable and on the whole successful experiment on behalf of human welfare. While those in the ADA feared that the Soviet Union was embarked upon a program of aggressive expansion, those in the PCA believed that the Soviet Union was intent upon postwar reconstruction and national self-defense. The two organizations' assumptions about the popular front thus differed accordingly. The ADA believed it impossible to achieve liberal goals through the help of those it considered totalitarians, while the PCA advocated strengthening liberalism through uniting the entire political left and was willing to work with all those who were interested in accomplishing its program. The ADA based its anti-Communism on what it charged was the self-defeating nature of alliances with Communists, while the PCA based its acceptance of a united front on its perception of a need for unity among the left-of-center. Both had learned lessons from history: the PCA, that the American left was susceptible to splintering and self-inflicted weakness; the ADA, that Communists frequently dominated or divided united front groups in which they participated. The PCA saw liberalism as a movement of the left-of-center, whereas the ADA viewed liberalism as properly a movement of the center, operating between the "totalitarian extremes."

The PCA's and ADA's differences, however, extended far beyond opposing views on the Soviet Union and the popular front. The PCA was essentially an organization which, in the liberal as well as radical tradition, stressed the goodness and rationality of man and the possibilities for improving society. The ADA combined a striving for social reform with a certainty of human frailty and a suspicion that the ideal society was but a naive dream.[12] Those who chose between the two organizations most often did so on the basis of their feelings toward the popular front and the Soviet Union; nevertheless, the PCA and the ADA did offer philosophical as well as political alternatives, and in this sense the formation of the two organizations offered a real choice to the American left.

Liberals responded to the establishment of the two competing organizations with a certain amount of confusion, but for the most part were guided in their reactions by the issues and emotions of the Cold War. Those who approved of left-of-center unity and a continuation of the Soviet-American alliance for world peace were dismayed by the strong bid the ADA was making for liberal leadership. Joseph Loftus, political correspondent for the *New York Times*, concluded that together the PCA and ADA could have an important impact on national elections, but as separate organizations, they would have little effect. Furthermore, Loftus warned that this split might have "repercussions with awesome possibilities" in foreign affairs. The *Nation*'s editor, Freda Kirchwey, attributed the establishment of rival organizations to American liberalism's traditional spirit of independence and to a small but determined group of factionalists in both groups who were willing to sacrifice the important goal of a unified left. She clearly hoped to bring about reconciliation and maintained that the two organizations would soon come to their senses and join forces. Helen Fuller, Washington editor of the *New Republic*, underlined the closeness of ADA foreign policy views to the administration's hard-line approach, rapped the ADA for precipitating the split among liberals, and warned of the dangers of such a split "at a time when unity among liberals is desperately needed."[13]

Those liberals, however, who opposed any association with Communists and who took a wary view of the Soviet Union greeted the ADA's founding with evident relief. Robert Bendiner, associate editor of the *Nation*, praised the creation of an organization without Communists and wrote that "too many liberals, tired, discouraged, and with no place to go, have come perilously close to accepting the choice [between Fascism and Communism]. . . . The A.D.A. unequivocally rejects this choice, and in so doing it brings to an end a shoddy era in the history of American progressivism." James Loeb, from the ADA's leadership staff, asserted that his organization did not represent a split in liberal ranks but rather constituted "a broader coalition of liberal-labor leadership than has been attained in this generation."[14]

The response by the *Nation* and the *New Republic* to the ADA and PCA was important since, for many years, the two journals had been among the most prestigious of the liberal political affairs journals and continued during the Cold War to be important bellwethers for American liberalism. The *Nation* had been a potent and respected disseminator of ideas throughout the liberal community since the reforming journalist E.L. Godkin founded it in 1865. The *New Republic*, established by Willard Straight, Herbert Croly, and Walter Lippmann in 1914, had played a similar role in American political thought. Both the *New Republic* and the *Nation* suffered from declining circulation during the postwar years but, nevertheless, remained two of the most widely read and influential liberal journals.[15]

These two journals had supported united left activities in the 1930s and continued to do so. The *Nation*'s editorial staff, however, divided over Wallace, the PCA, and the ADA. Editor Freda Kirchwey's primary concern over the two potentially rival liberal political organizations was that they might widen the split among liberals and weaken the political left. Associate editor Robert Bendiner was disinterested in a united left and relieved that a movement on the left had been formed that "is free of the orthodoxies of Marxism and yet looks clearly beyond the anarchy of what . . . is called 'free enterprise'. . . ."[16]

The *New Republic* was more clearly committed to Wallace. In late 1946, as the split between liberals widened, the *New Republic*'s publisher, Michael Straight, offered the editorship to Wallace. Wallace accepted, and thus acquired a powerful platform for his views. Despite an effort on Straight's part to maintain good relations with Wallace opponents,[17] bitterness soon developed between the *New Republic* and the ADA liberals. Although shortly after the ADA's founding James Loeb was invited to make a statement in the *New Republic*, the journal's columns favored Wallace's brand of liberalism, and criticism of administration and ADA liberals soon became personal. Daniel Mebane, the *New Republic*'s treasurer, jibed the ADA for the criticism it drew from conservatives: "It's a goddam shame, Jim," he wrote, "that these Hearst writers don't appreciate the work you all are doing to thwart Russia and save our dear country from Communism! Why not give up this fruitless scholasticism and help heal the breach in liberal ranks?" Loeb replied, "Sure, this is a complicated world. But it avails nothing to give simple (and false) answers to complicated problems. . . . I hope that the *New Republic* will soon return to the liberal tradition based upon a complete dedication to the twin objectives of economic security and human freedom."[18]

| * |

The conflicts that by early 1947 were dividing liberals were also dividing the postwar American labor movement, making it impossible for the labor left to provide that support which might have averted or minimized the emerging civil war within the left. Labor unions had provided the mass constituency for the American left during the 1930s and early 1940s, for the Communist party as well as for the liberal-labor New Deal coalition. Deep-seated American fears of both radicalism and unions, however, which had surfaced during the late 1930s in the House Committee on Un-American Activities investigations and corresponding exposés, reappeared in a more vigorous form after World War II. In part, these fears stemmed from the widespread strikes of 1945 and 1946 and from the resurgence of American conservatism; to a far greater extent, however, the emerging Cold War itself created and sanctioned an American mood which was both anti-labor and anti-radical.

The Congress of Industrial Organizations, the more radical wing of American labor, was a particular target for such conservative attacks. During the late New Deal the CIO had challenged the craft-oriented American Federation of Labor by organizing workers within industries. It had attracted radicals and welcomed the hard work and dedicated organization which Communists and Socialists brought to the labor movement. John L. Lewis, the CIO's first president, made extensive use of Communist organizers and lawyers, fully confident that they could not wrest control of his organization away from him. Certain of the CIO's unions—in particular those controlled by exceptionally strong leaders, such as Lewis's own United Mine Workers, or those founded by the national CIO and organized from the top down, such as Philip Murray's Steel Workers—remained relatively free from Communist activity. Nevertheless, from the outset the CIO was, as a whole, willing to work with Communists to further labor union goals. Consequently, it participated easily with such popular-front organizations as the National Citizens Political Action Committee and found little in common with the anti-Communists in the Union for Democratic Action.[19]

The Communist question, however, constituted a potentially explosive issue for the newly formed CIO. Many of the members were devout Catholics and thus receptive to the Catholic church's animosity toward the Communist party. The Association of Catholic Trade Unionists, during the late 1930s and the 1940s, focused on fighting Communism in the trade union movement, particularly within the CIO, where Communists were most prevalent. Catholic labor schools such as the Xavier School in New York City were also deeply interested in fighting Communism in the unions. Philip Murray, Lewis's successor as president of the CIO, was a devout Catholic and, without openly opposing the Communists, managed to discourage Communist activity within his own Steel Workers Union.[20]

During the years of the Nazi-Soviet Pact, which marked the end of the popular front of the 1930s, the issue of Communists in the CIO had threatened to become a divisive one. Hitler's invasion of Russia, however, and Japan's attack on Pearl Harbor brought the United States and the Soviet Union together as allies and decreased anti-Communist animosity as the CIO experienced a renewed period of popular-front cooperation among its leadership and within its ranks. New Deal liberals and Communists, Catholics and non-Catholics—all the heterogeneous elements of the left represented within the CIO—worked together in harmony as long as the war provided a common and overriding interest. The war's end, however, dissolved this common bond and the Cold War provided the impetus for renewed and far greater internal conflict within the CIO over the Communist issue.[21]

This conflict did not surface immediately after the war. Murray, whose sympathies had never been with the Communists, had nevertheless from the beginning of his presidency of the federation attempted to play a unifying role, particularly between the CIO's radical left and its small but determined anti-Communist right. Murray thus occupied the political center in the CIO—a position equivalent to left-of-center on the American political spectrum as a whole, and one which, allied with the liberal reform politics of the New Deal, seemed to appeal to the majority of CIO members. He already had the support and admiration of the anti-Communists within his organization, particularly the Catholics, because of his reputation for anti-Communism; yet he established good relations with the left wing through personnel as well as policy decisions. Murray retained two of Lewis's top appointments to the CIO's national staff: Lee Pressman as CIO general counsel and Len DeCaux as editor of the *CIO News*, both of them Communists. Murray also attempted to establish and maintain good relations with the left-wing members of the CIO's executive board, including union presidents Harry Bridges, Mike Quill, Joe Curran, Ben Gold, and Julius Emspak. Bridges, president of the Longshoremen's and Warehousemen's Union, was one of the best known among this group. A naturalized American citizen and a radical, he faced deportation as a Communist during the 1940s, despite his denials of party membership. In 1941 Murray himself had established a defense fund for Bridges, and in 1945 the executive board agreed to advance a sizable sum in Bridges's behalf in order to take his case to the Supreme Court.[22]

Moreover, the CIO had always stressed the importance of individual union autonomy. Memories of their own expulsion from the American Federation of Labor were fresh enough to encourage CIO leaders to preserve a significant degree of freedom for the affiliates. The CIO constitution governed the federation only; it did not apply to the individual affiliates. Further, by the original arrangements, a conflict between the constitution of an individual union and that of the federation would be resolved in favor of the individual affiliate's constitution.[23]

Nevertheless, the CIO had developed quickly and from the top, so that the bulk of the federation's power was located at the national level. Several of the CIO's major affiliates, for example, most notably the unions in steel, textiles, and meat packing, were developed by the leaders of the federation.[24] Lewis had hardly been adverse to the possibilities for power which this situation offered, but as a consequence, the CIO had a built-in conflict between ideal and actuality—a conflict which remained latent until stress arose between the affiliates and the national leadership.

Such stress did not appear immediately after the war was over. Murray headed an executive board made up of a secretary-treasurer, several vice-presidents, and the presidents of each of the CIO's affiliates. Because of this structure the executive board not only gave final approval to federation policy but also reflected the mood and views of both national and affiliate leadership. In late 1945 and even early 1946, the executive board, under Murray, maintained internal unity and recommended that the Allies preserve the same spirit of unity in the interest of permanent world peace. The board continued the CIO's vigorous anti-Fascist stance and its spirit of camaraderie with Soviet workers, to whom the CIO sent a delegation in late 1945: "We in America," one delegate told the Russians, "are determined that no force within or without is ever going to turn us against your people again."[25]

Forces both within and without, however, were beginning to act on the CIO to change markedly its views on foreign and domestic policies as well as its own internal politics. Hopes for labor-management harmony dwindled as soaring inflation, together with the administration's fumbling on wage and price controls, left labor disgruntled and ready to strike. Even more significantly, the Cold War began to have its impact on the labor movement. Within the CIO, signs were distinct during 1946 that the Communist issue was becoming an important one. Walter Reuther successfully used the issue that year to combat opponents and win election as president of the United Auto Workers; although still challenged by his rivals in 1946 and 1947, Reuther would gain complete control of his union in 1948. In New York, thirty-four trade union leaders representing UAW and segments of six other CIO unions formed a CIO Committee for Democratic Trade Unionism to oppose Communist influence in the state elections. The Transport Workers Union, headed by leftist Mike Quill, contained a small but growing anti-Communist group, and anti-Communist strength within the Mine, Mill and Smelter Workers Union was by 1946 great enough to attempt a challenge of left-wing control. James B. Carey, secretary-treasurer of the CIO, who had lost his position as president of United Electrical Workers in a fight with his union's left wing, warned the Marine and Shipbuilding Workers at their 1946 convention that the Communist party wanted "to operate your international union solely as a political club in the interest of the foreign policies of Soviet Russia."[26]

At the risk of appearing to vacillate, Murray attempted to maintain harmony between the competing factions. Speaking in May 1946 before his own union, the Steel Workers, Murray said the CIO would not tolerate "outsiders" whether they were "Communists, Socialists or any other group to infiltrate, dictate, or meddle." Murray thus bid for support of the growing anti-Communist group in the CIO while attempting to appease the Communists by including Socialists in the list of forbidden meddlers; the anti-Communists, some of whom were Socialists, were not wholly pleased with Murray's tack, while the left wing was not entirely displeased. At the United Electrical Workers convention in the autumn, Murray specifically praised that union's left-wing leadership, while in a speech the following month he declared that the CIO had "no . . . use for any damn Communist coming over here meddling in our affairs. . . ."[27]

As the CIO's 1946 national convention approached, the left wing was well aware that the Communist issue was surfacing once again; it was in no position, however, to gauge accurately how dangerous this issue would prove. The stand Murray would take was particularly unpredictable, although his basic opposition to Communism was well known. His response became a matter of great interest at the executive board meeting preceding the convention.

Much of the Communist influence within the CIO was at the local and regional level, and Murray first directed the board's attention to the industrial union councils. "We have found instances," he stated, "where it was almost impossible to identify the individuals participating" in these councils, although they participated in the discussion and cast votes. Murray then proposed that those attending and voting at such meetings be accredited members of the CIO. He next recommended that local and state industrial union councils take no action or issue any statements in conflict with CIO policy, and similarly requested the end of financial support and representation from CIO industrial union councils to national organizations not endorsed by the national CIO. The purpose of these proposals, Murray said, was to divest control of local industrial union councils from "the machinations of perhaps a few people within a council bent upon the creation of dissension, confusion, or the dissemination of propaganda." Essentially, he was attempting to curb left-wing activity in the industrial councils by increasing the authority at the national level, where the left, although strong, was a minority. "There is a need of reassertion of . . . policy control over councils by national CIO," he stated. The executive board and the convention unanimously supported these proposals.[28] The first application of the new policy came quickly: the national CIO immediately directed all its industrial union councils to discontinue support of the National Negro Congress, a popular-front civil rights organization. The CIO worked with the National Association for the Advancement of Colored People instead, the councils were told, and they were also informed that the National Negro Congress duplicated much of the activity of the NAACP and "from time to time" had "policies which were opposed to those of the CIO."[29]

Murray had more to say to his executive board on the Communist question, however. "While I have you together here," he announced, "I am going to explode." What followed was a relatively restrained account of the danger Communist ties posed to the CIO's effort to be a successful organization, one capable of resisting anti-union forces. "I am not one of those who agree this is a Communistically dominated institution," he pointed out. "I do believe that there are some of our unions whose judgments on matters of political policy, particularly as they relate to international affairs, permit their judgments to be substantially influenced by the Communist Party." He told his board he had refrained from bringing this problem up earlier because he had hoped that by avoiding antagonisms, greater unity and understanding would develop within the CIO. But as affairs then stood, the CIO was building for itself "targets, targets that can be easily hit," unnecessary targets of which enemies of the CIO could take advantage. "We must be pro-American in those trade union activities of ours," he underscored, and he strongly recommended that the board unanimously approve a policy condemning Communism. Murray told the board, "We have in our family people on both sides of the fence that are extremely fanatical," many of them "irascible young men," as he called them with a fatherly tone for which he was known. But, he warned, fanaticism of any sort would endanger a responsible labor organization.[30]

Normally, such an important resolution as Murray had proposed would go to the CIO convention's committee on resolutions; the CIO, however, as Murray pointed out, could ill afford the kinds of news stories which would inevitably leak from the convention committee. Instead, Murray appointed a committee from the executive board to draw up a policy and report it back for the board's consideration and approval—with the understanding that there would be no open debate on the convention floor on the subject. He next announced that he was about to "get a group of the most contentious folks ever brought together in a meeting, and see what can be done." He appointed Emil Rieve of the Textile Workers, Milton Murray of the American Newspaper Guild, and Walter Reuther—strong anti-Communists—to meet with Abe Flaxer of the United Public Workers, Ben Gold of the Fur and Leather Workers, and Mike Quill—in Murray's term, "alleged 'Lefties.' " "They'll kill each other," someone commented. Murray suggested a breakfast meeting and requested they not bring harpoons. "Will you buy us breakfast?" one of the committee bantered. "I will buy breakfast for you," Murray replied.[31]

The committee returned with unanimous agreement that the CIO should "resent and reject efforts of the Communist Party or other political parties and their adherents to interfere in the affairs of the CIO." The committee members agreed that the CIO's goals were "to win economic security and social justice and to unite our movement against the forces of reaction and the enemies of democracy." They affirmed that these goals could be achieved for Americans through the democratic process and warned that the CIO would resist with all its might attempts from within the United States or without "to undermine or destroy our free institutions. . . . We must pledge only one national allegiance," their declaration held, "and that allegiance is to our own country, the United States of America." The board adopted the resolution unanimously, to the apparent pleasure of all present. Mike Quill, one of the members of the committee to draft the resolution and one of the most outspoken on the board, commented that he had found out for the first time "that no matter what side of the fence we are on, we are all CIO members." Reuther and the other committee members agreed with him. Board members then gave Murray and the special committee a rising vote of thanks.[32]

Murray continued to play a conciliatory role at the convention, where he stressed that the CIO would refuse to "tolerate interference from not only the Communist Party, remember, but other political parties." This appeared to be an even-handed approach and, politically, meant that the anti-Communists within the CIO had achieved considerably less than a complete victory. The convention adopted the resolution unanimously, and the left appeared pleased with the outcome.[33]

Thanks to Murray's interpretation of the resolution, the Communists and other leftists had retrieved a partial victory. The left had also avoided within the executive board and at the convention a showdown which it, as a minority, probably would have lost. The left wing had a more positive motive for accepting the resolution, however; those who were Communists or agreed with Communists did not believe their politics in any way adversely affected their contribution to the CIO. Conversely, they held strongly that the Communist party had been and continued to be the single most important force acting on the worker's behalf.[34] Such a conviction would have assured them that their activities were beneficial to labor and thus did not constitute "Communist interference" in the sense of the policy statement. Consequently, they could accept the CIO resolution in a good faith which the anti-Communists could not understand.

Although not a victory for the anti-Communists, the new CIO resolution still contained potential danger for the federation's left wing, since it could be understood to oppose unpopular political beliefs if these could be identified with the Communist party. One executive board member anticipated this possibility when he asked if the new policy might violate his union's constitution, which opposed discrimination against any member on account of race, creed, color, or political belief. Murray replied that the new policy "would not violate anything except when organizations pursue a course which violates it." He later remarked, "Every organization that conforms itself to this policy will not be susceptible to charges of violating the policy." The questioning subsided, the policy passed unanimously, and the board members applauded those responsible for the outcome.[35] The CIO's leadership, however, had approved of a policy which was both more ambiguous and more dangerous than it first appeared.

| * |

The CIO did not at first welcome the split in American liberalism symbolized by the establishment of the rival PCA and ADA in early 1947. Murray had expressed interest in the founding of the PCA and was elected—although without his knowledge—one of the PCA's vice-presidents. He had also, however, sent a representative to the founding meeting of the ADA, at which Walter Reuther and David Dubinsky, president of the International Ladies Garment Workers Union, played a prominent part.[36] Understandably, Murray was not anxious to become embroiled in a controversy which might shatter the fragile peace only recently established in the CIO. He was reluctant, he said, to engage in battles which did not directly affect labor. He declared that he was a trade unionist first and last and could not understand "why labor organizations should be beset with anything other than their fundamental trade union economic problems."[37] Taken literally, the CIO's 1946 Communist policy statement rejected interference from any political party and its adherents, and in full consistency with this statement Murray attempted to guide the CIO away from involvement with either anti-Communist or popular-front liberals. The ADA and the PCA, he told an executive board meeting in the spring of 1947, "are in a state of war, so to speak, a state of seige." He did not care what they were warring about; his responsibilities to the CIO came first. He did know that the CIO was "overcome with enough perplexities for the moment to keep us going without inviting some more, and I am not prone to invite trouble." The outcome was Murray's recommendation that officers of the CIO's member unions dissociate themselves from both the ADA and the PCA.[38]

Inevitably, those members of the board who were interested in the PCA's or ADA's future argued against the recommendation. The most provocative issue raised, however, went beyond the immediate

ADA-PCA conflict and tackled the implications of such a directive to CIO officials: "What would happen," asked Sam Wolchok of United Retail, Wholesale and Department Store Employees, "if tomorrow somebody would rise on this floor and ask that members of this Board cannot belong to the Communist Party? Do you think a resolution like that would pass? . . . I would like to see anybody bring in a resolution that a member of this Board cannot belong to the Communist Party, the Democratic Party, the Republican Party, the American Labor Party, or the Socialist Party, or anything else." Murray replied that they were not then dealing with a question of political parties. Wolchok, an ADA member, retorted that the ADA had "all the ear marks of becoming a political organization," and that if the CIO withdrew, there would be "nothing left of ADA."[39] The point was not so much the future of the ADA or PCA, or even the degree of CIO involvement in either; rather, the issue which Wolchok briefly introduced was whether the CIO could, in the name of defending its own organizational stability, prohibit members from expressing certain political beliefs and joining particular political parties, whether the Communist party or some other. Murray refused to discuss the issue at that time, and so it rested, only to explode at a later date.

At Murray's urging, the CIO board did approve a resolution recommending that CIO officers and union leaders abstain from activity in either the PCA or ADA and channel their time and attention into the CIO's own Political Action Committee. "We ought to be permitted to make our own determinations and chart our own courses without pressure from these outside groups,"[40] Murray commented.

Murray and the majority within the CIO leadership maintained this centrist position in early 1947. In one especially important instance, the national leadership acted on behalf of established labor union principles when these were threatened by a particularly disruptive form of anti-Communism which had reached a peak in the Mine, Mill and Smelter Workers union. A large proportion of the Mine, Mill and Smelter Workers, approximately one quarter of the membership, had withdrawn to form its own union. This large minority had complained of Communist interference in union affairs, particularly in the conduct and outcome of its recent election of officers, which returned Maurice Travis, a Communist, as president. The dissidents claimed that letters existed to show that Travis was receiving advice from non-union-member Communists about the administration of the union. They also claimed that his election was manipulated and did not represent union members' actual preference. Travis and his supporters, however, maintained that the dissidents were simply disgruntled because their candidate did not win, discounted any evidence of outside interference, and cited interference from the dissidents, particularly the strongly anti-Communist Association of Catholic Trade Unionists (ACTU). "I know," said one of Travis's supporters on the CIO executive board, "that if letters can be accepted as evidence sufficient to recommend the removal of a president of a union, . . . you will have many letters of that kind to depend upon as evidence." None of Travis's supporters denied that he was a Communist, but they insisted that this affiliation was political only and did not serve as evidence of outside interference. Any such evidence, they maintained, was "pretty thin."[41]

The national CIO committee investigating the dispute was convinced that Travis and other Mine, Mill leaders were allowing Communists to interfere with their union's affairs. It recommended that the CIO leadership urge the union to remove Travis from the presidency, and that Murray appoint an administrative committee to run the union temporarily. The dissidents did not win their case, however; the committee held that their action constituted secession and recommended that their leader, the secretary of an industrial union council, be removed from his office and that the dissidents return to Mine, Mill and Smelter Workers immediately.[42]

The CIO executive board was divided over the investigating committee's report. One of the board's strongest anti-Communists, Milton Murray, objected that the dissidents "felt that any seceding they were doing was a secession from the Communist Party, and on that right to secede from the Communist Party I must stand. . . ." The left-wingers on the board objected to removing Travis for Communist party interference. They spoke of anti-Communist interference in union activities, such as the work done by the ACTU. And, as one board member put it, "this business of the interference of the Communist Party—if you make that step I don't know where you will stop." Because the board did not accept the report unanimously, Murray referred a final decision to the next CIO convention, in the autumn. Just before the convention, however, the executive board agreed to re-vote and adopted the report unanimously to prevent the matter from becoming explosive on the convention floor.[43]

Although the national CIO leadership had responded to charges of "Communist interference" in Mine, Mill and Smelter Workers by recommending that actions be taken by both national CIO and the union itself to end the alleged interference, the anti-Communists received the sharpest rap: the dissidents were ordered back into their union, and their leader was expelled as secretary of his industrial union council. Murray explained the difference between the punishments given the Communist union president and the anti-Communist dissident on the basis that the national CIO had no authority over elected union officials, while industrial union councils came directly under its authority. Significantly, however, the issue of secession had appeared as important as the Communist issue in this instance, and the CIO's leadership had responded according to established trade union principles. Secession was anathema to a trade union organization, particularly one as new as the CIO, and in this dispute the CIO's leadership agreed that such action was contrary to the CIO's "fundamental law" and the "interests of all members of all international unions. . . ."[44]

Murray never appointed the administrator over Mine, Mill affairs which the CIO committee had recommended. The union rejected the report and he decided that he would push the matter no further. Despite Murray's reluctance to interfere with Mine, Mill in this instance, however, the dispute did leave unsettled the important issue of the autonomy of an individual union within the structure of the national CIO. Travis's supporters had maintained that they were carrying out the Mine, Mill constitution, which barred any discrimination on account of political beliefs. The investigating committee's report held that all member unions of the CIO were guaranteed their autonomy but added that "it must be recognized that these autonomous rights should be exercised in accordance with the fundamental policy of the CIO,"[45] and CIO policy had, since 1946, officially rejected "outside interference" in union activities. Resulting doubt about how much autonomy the individual unions actually possessed became soon after a focus for increasing internal debate.

Lastly, the Mine, Mill and Smelter Workers' dispute exacerbated the Communist question within the CIO, even though the report chastised both sides. The anti-Communists resented the fact that the dissidents had received stiff punishment while Mine, Mill's Communist president had escaped discipline. And Murray, although he had carefully observed union autonomy, showed increasing agitation over the question of Communism in the CIO. "I think we ought to quit apologizing for Communism in the CIO," he insisted during the spring 1947 executive board meeting on Mine, Mill. He stressed that lending solace and comfort to the propagation of Communism in the American trade union movement endangered the movement's life:

"Any man possesses the right to practice any damned political philosophy he believes in, . . . that is his business, but don't bring it in here. . . ." Anyone who attempted to bring Communism into the CIO was "nothing short of a God damned traitor" and "ought to be kicked the hell out of the movement."[46]

Ruptures were thus beginning to appear in the center-left coalition within the CIO, indicating that the same pressures rending organized popular-front liberalism were dividing the united labor left. The Cold War was beginning to have its impact by 1947, underscoring old rifts and creating new and far deeper divisions.

2

Liberals and the
Cold War: 1947

Conflict within the American left was intensified by increasing international conflict between the United States and the USSR. In February 1947 Britain officially informed the State Department that because of its severe postwar recovery problems it could supply economic and military aid to Greece and Turkey only through March. The Truman administration was alarmed at the prospect of sudden British withdrawal, particularly from Greece, where Communist-led guerrillas aided by Yugoslavia, Bulgaria, and Albania were rapidly gaining popular support. Assuming that the Soviet Union was directing the guerrillas, the administration's leaders concluded that the United States' role in Greece and possibly the entire Mediterranean world was at stake. To prevent this spread of Soviet influence, they agreed, the United States would have to take Britain's place in supporting the faltering Greek monarchy. Such a plan would involve a long-term and expensive United States commitment to both Greece and Turkey, however, and the administration immediately undertook to persuade congressional leaders, and then all of Congress and the American public, of the danger. Truman, in an urgent address to Congress on March 12, described a growing Soviet threat to Greece and Turkey and emphasized that, "should we fail to aid Greece and Turkey in this fateful hour, the effect will be far-reaching to the West as well as to the East. . . . Collapse of free institutions and loss of independence would be disastrous not only for them but for the world." He then proposed military and economic aid to both countries, pledging the United States' responsibility "to support free peoples who are resisting attempted subjugation by armed minorities or by outside pressures. . . ."[1]

This proposal, which became known as the Truman Doctrine, met with a mixed and highly charged reception from the American left. The doctrine particularly antagonized those who stressed the necessity for cooperating with the Soviet Union and who acknowledged its right to a protective sphere of influence in eastern Europe. They viewed the Truman Doctrine as aggressive and provocative, placing the Soviet Union on the defensive and markedly decreasing prospects for world peace. In addition, they were greatly displeased with United States intervention in Greece on behalf of the Greek monarchy and the remnants of British imperialism. The Communist party criticized the Truman Doctrine for its "unabashed imperialism [that] flows from the 'get tough' program of the biggest monopoly capitalists" and warned that the doctrine provided a base for the "possibility of eventual attack" on the Soviet Union.[2] The PCA denounced Truman's proposal as heading the United States toward war and expressed hope that the foreign policy issue would stimulate anti-administration sentiment and help revive the popular front. Henry Wallace condemned the doctrine for its militarism, its aid to reactionary governments, and its undercutting of the United Nations. In a tour of western Europe, Wallace continued to challenge Truman's foreign policy, to the consternation of many administration officials who opposed both the circumstances and the substance of Wallace's criticisms. An ensuing tour of the United States was a great success for Wallace, however, and the large crowds gathered to hear him appeared genuinely concerned over the direction of American foreign policy.[3]

There were others on the left, for the most part liberals, who viewed talk of cooperating with Soviet Russia as hopelessly naive but joined in berating the Truman Doctrine for attempting to conduct a world crusade and for unilaterally and needlessly transferring a localized conflict to a global scale. They considered that the doctrine wrongly stressed military over economic aid, bypassed the United Nations, and gave too sweeping a commitment based upon moral principle, thus tying American policy to a promise so vast that it could result only in escalating worldwide American military involvement.[4]

The CIO issued no comment on the Truman Doctrine. The ADA, itself split over the Truman Doctrine, was at first silent. A vocal minority condemned its stress on military aid and its overextended commitments. Mortimer Hays, a New York attorney and ADA member, declared that the United States' global responsibilities included not fostering democracy "by creating a world of enmity and hatred" but rather making democracy "so rich and meaningful that it will be the

preferred way of life of the majority of the peoples of the world. . . ."
Hays also pointed out that while Americans needed to prize their
liberties, they must also realize the "communities of interest which
exist between the common people of the United States and of Russia."[5]

A majority within the ADA supported the Truman Doctrine,
calling it a realistic assessment of world affairs that employed a necessary use of power in the national interest. In a foreign policy statement which predated and in many ways anticipated the Truman Doctrine, the ADA had declared that "because the interests of the United
States are the interests of free men everywhere, America must furnish
political and economic support to democratic and freedom loving
peoples the world over."[6] At its March 30 meeting, this majority was
able to win an ADA endorsement of the Truman Doctrine; continued
minority opposition, however, considerably diluted the majority
victory. In the end, the ADA agreed that the United Nations should
deal with the Greek crisis but concluded that, in the face of a probable
Russian veto, the United States in the meantime must take action "to
achieve conditions in Greece under which free institutions may
grow."[7] Evidently even this position constituted too much support of
the doctrine for the taste of many non-ADA liberals, for the ADA's
membership in early 1947 remained small and its supporters few.
Even ADA's leaders became discouraged at what seemed a risk of both
time and effort.[8] Protestant theologian and ADA leader Reinhold
Niebuhr concluded that the membership problem was directly linked
to ADA's close identification with Truman's hard-line foreign policy.
At a national board meeting in May, Niebuhr noted that the ADA was
in "rather a difficult position in regard to foreign policy." He added,
"There is nothing that dramatically presents a positive program in
contrast to the confused program of Wallace. People are worried and
we have taken a negative position."[9]

Liberals and left-liberals in Congress also expressed concern
about the Truman Doctrine and even produced some outright opposition, although in the end most voted for the aid program to Greece
and Turkey. In the Senate, the leading opponents of the aid proposal
were Democrats Claude A. Pepper of Florida and Glen Taylor of
Idaho, both strong supporters of Wallace. Together they introduced a
resolution opposing military aid to Turkey and calling for economic
aid to the Greek people through the United Nations, a proposal they
stressed as "the safest and most effective policy to protect democracy
and world peace." Both favored relief for the people of Greece but objected that unilateral aid would critically weaken the United Nations.

Both strongly opposed military aid and especially objected to any form of aid whatever to the existing governments of Greece and Turkey, which Taylor termed "tyrannical, repressive" and Pepper, "reactionary and corrupt." Each feared that such a policy would commit the United States to a policy of imperialism and would destroy any possibility for reconciliation with the Soviet Union. Taylor condemned the atmosphere of crisis which the Truman administration had created to aid the program's passage, and he warned that such tactics would have widespread and disastrous repercussions. "The Red hunt has got us all," he told the Senate. "We have got to go along here, . . . because if we do not, we will all be Communists, Republicans and Democrats alike." Further, "they will try to get us . . . face to face with Russia, snarling at each other, and they can do anything—take our civil liberties away from us, and deprive us of the very things that we claim we are going to fight for."[10]

Democratic Senator James Murray of Montana was deeply concerned that the proposed aid bill bypassed the United Nations and might lead to further commitments, resulting in national bankruptcy and the possibility of world war. Murray acknowledged the need to apply balance-of-power policies to prevent the Soviet Union from becoming a Mediterranean and Atlantic power, but admonished, "The situation calls for speed but not for reckless speed." Accordingly, he attempted—unsuccessfully—to amend the aid proposal to state that "the assistance we are rendering is wholly an emergency matter, it being the understanding of this Government that the rendering of such assistance is the continuing responsibility of the United Nations."[11]

In the House of Representatives, Vito Marcantonio, leader of the left-wing American Labor party in New York, accused the proposed aid bill of "aiding a regime . . . shot through and through with Fascists" under the guise of stopping Communism. John A. Blatnik of Minnesota, a Democrat and strong Wallace supporter, opposed the aid bill for undermining the United Nations and failing to support true democracy. Chester Holifield, a liberal California Democrat, favored economic aid to Greece through the United Nations and considered the Truman Doctrine "an undeclared declaration of war if our challenge of unilateral intervention on Russia's borders is accepted." A liberal Colorado Democrat, John A. Carroll, stressed that "there can be no peace in this world if each of the big powers arrogate to themselves the sole right to determine what is just or unjust." Adolph J. Sabath of Illinois, a long-time Democratic congressman and progressive, believed that the bill's purpose was to keep the Dardanelles as they were and quarantine the Near East oil fields, with the American people paying the bill. Helen Gahagan Douglas, the liberal California Democrat, wanted questions of national security to go first to the United Nations, before a decision for unilateral United States intervention was made. She also wanted the Greek government to agree to domestic reforms as a condition for receiving economic assistance. After both her proposed amendments were rejected, she opposed the aid bill.[12]

Other liberal and moderate Democrats, however, were ardent supporters of the administration's proposal. Senator Brien McMahon of Connecticut argued that "the test is not the kind of government which exists in a nation, but . . . whether aggression is on its way." Senator Scott Lucas of Illinois declared that Truman was "asking America to take the necessary steps to protect her safety and security from aggressors everywhere." In the House Sam Rayburn of Texas used the occasion to attack isolationism, and Henry M. Jackson of Washington argued that Russia already had unilaterally taken the same actions in eastern Europe that the United States proposed to take in Turkey and Greece. John F. Kennedy of Massachusetts defended the administration's action by arguing that if Greece and Turkey gave way to Communism, "the barriers would be down and the Red tide would flow across the face of Europe and through Asia with new power and vigor." And Lyndon B. Johnson of Texas, in a ringing address, called upon history to witness the courageous spirit of the American people ("Monroe and Jackson did not flinch"): "We will be false to our traditions, false to the American people, and false to ourselves if we falter because of fear—fear of either cost or consequences."[13]

Many of the aid bill's supporters were reluctant, however, and were swayed by patriotism, the atmosphere of national emergency, and the desire to support the president. Democratic Senator Edwin C. Johnson of Colorado commented that many senators were going to support the bill just not to "let the President down." Senator Elbert D. Thomas, a New Deal Democrat from Utah, told the Senate that "because the first thing we need in the United States, above all other things, is unity, . . . I deem it our duty to stand by the President in what he has said. . . ." Liberal Democrat Mike Mansfield of Montana told other members of the House that he was going to vote for the bill, "but not with any enthusiasm," not knowing where the policy would lead. Congressman John R. Murdock, a Democrat from Arizona, voted for the bill with a "heavy heart"; the United States must act unilaterally, he concluded, because the United Nations could not act.

And liberal Republican Jacob Javits, a New York congressman, unsuccessfully proposed several methods to involve the United Nations in the Greece-Turkey crisis; the urgency of affairs in the eastern Mediterranean, however, convinced him to support the aid bill even without such amendments, although his support gave him "a very great deal of concern."[14]

Despite anxiety from some liberals and heavy opposition from conservatives, the Greek-Turkey aid bill passed the Senate (67 to 23) and House (287 to 107) and was signed into law by Truman on May 22, 1947.[15] In the meantime, on March 23, 1947, Truman had announced Executive Order 9835, which the popular-front left soon referred to as the "domestic" Truman Doctrine. This so-called loyalty order called for the investigation of all employees of the executive branch, not just those in sensitive positions; it provided for a master index on all persons ever investigated for loyalty since 1939, and it directed the attorney general to compile a list of all subversive groups and organizations. Further, the order established procedures for loyalty hearings which did not permit confrontation or cross-examination of witnesses nor disclosure to the accused of the sources of the evidence against him.[16]

Arthur Garfield Hays, one of the leaders of the American Civil Liberties Union, called the loyalty program "the most outrageous, undemocratic measure that could possibly be conceived," and the ACLU itself responded with procedural recommendations to protect the basic rights of federal employees under the loyalty order. Henry Wallace strongly opposed the order and said that it would "threaten everything in America that is worth fighting for." The PCA urged immediate revocation and objected to the attorney general's list as well as to the order's abridgement of traditional civil liberties in the hearing procedures. Anti-Communist liberals were torn between approval of the loyalty program's objectives and concern about its procedures. Liberal historian Arthur Schlesinger, Jr., was convinced that some sort of loyalty program was necessary, and the ADA endorsed the Truman program's aim "to exclude from Government employment people who adhere to foreign governments or totalitarian political philosophies in any case where such adherence may endanger the best interests of the United States." The ADA, however, condemned those procedures of the program it deemed unfair and repressive, and Schlesinger termed the order's procedures "shocking" and "inexcusably defective," observing that they "betray[ed] a state of mind going beyond the requirements of security and entering the realm of persecution."[17]

Within Congress, Senator Glen Taylor called the president's loyalty program a "Red hunt" and noted that under this program an accused civil servant "does not have the safeguards which the accused always enjoys in American criminal trials in spite of the fact that the sanction is much greater than that in many criminal cases." Most discussion of the loyalty order, however, centered in the House of Representatives, where liberal opposition focused on a conservative-initiated House bill similar to the president's order. Estes Kefauver, a liberal Tennessee Democrat, led the fight against the House bill on the grounds that it "violates more rights that are guaranteed to the people by the Constitution, it infringes more civil liberties than any bill I have ever seen brought before the House. . . ." Congressman Emanuel Celler, a liberal New York Democrat and ranking minority member of the House Judiciary Committee, protested that the bill was unconstitutional and threatened to destroy time-honored liberties. Chester Holifield agreed with the bill's basic purpose but disliked its threat to civil liberties: the hapless federal employee, he noted, "is handed an economic death sentence" without any protection of fundamental rights. Helen Gahagan Douglas commented, "The bill strikes at the very root and fiber of democratic life." She called it, in essence, a political measure conceived by Republicans to attack the New Deal, and asked, "Are we going to make two and one-half million federal workers the whipping boy in the struggle between two political parties?"[18]

Liberals were hard pressed, however, to distinguish the Republican-sponsored House bill from Truman's executive order. As the bill's sponsor, Republican Edward H. Rees of Kansas, pointed out, "The requirements that appear under this bill and the standards set up under it also appear in the President's order." Vito Marcantonio added, "We would not have had this bill if the President had not issued his so-called loyalty order. There is very little difference, fundamentally, between the President's Executive Order 9835 and this bill. . . ." Most House Democrats avoided discussing the Truman loyalty program, although Adolph Sabath made a lone attempt to distinguish between it and the House bill. The House bill, he said, destroyed liberties, while the Truman loyalty order "preserves the American way. . . ." The Executive Order did have civil liberties drawbacks, Sabath confessed; however, it could easily be modified by the chief executive, while a bill, once enacted, "is frozen into the code of laws . . . [and] will be immensely difficult to amend or repeal. . . ."[19]

The opposition of both popular-front and anti-Communist liberals was swept aside, however, as the conservative, Republican-dominated House responded to the growing tensions of the Cold War by passing the measure on July 15, 1947, by a vote of 319 to 61. In the Senate, however, administration forces were able to bottle up the measure in committee.[20] The episode amply illustrated the dilemma which Truman's foreign and domestic anti-Communist policy presented to liberal Democratic politicians and anti-Communist liberals in general during the spring of 1947. These liberals could and did support the president's basic objectives—fighting Communism at home and abroad and protecting the New Deal from the red-baiting of the political right—but they were unable to support wholeheartedly the specific programs Truman proposed. Their dilemma was soon resolved, however, with the administration's announcement in June 1947 of the Marshall Plan.

Since the end of the war, Europe had staggered under a nearly impossible burden of reconstruction, stumbling from one economic crisis to another and facing an ever-growing threat of social upheaval. Secretary of State George C. Marshall visited western Europe during the early spring of 1947 and reported that the situation there was grave; Communist victories in France and Italy appeared imminent. Finally, in June, at Harvard University, Secretary Marshall outlined the administration's response: an offer from the United States to aid the nations of Europe in achieving economic recovery and social and political stability.[21]

Russia denounced the Marshall Plan and refused to participate in it. The Communist Party USA attacked the plan as a "cold-blooded scheme of American monopolists to establish their ruthless domination over harassed world humanity." The PCA at first ventured only cautious support, then was silent; by autumn, however, the organization denounced the Marshall Plan, together with the Truman Doctrine, as the causes for the dissolution of the wartime alliance. Wallace at first approved of the plan, which, with its stress on economic aid and apparent opportunity for Russian participation, sounded much like the reconstruction program he had been advocating. After Russia refused to participate, Wallace criticized the Soviet action but explained it as a suspicious response conditioned by the Truman Doctrine. By late July, Wallace was quoted as questioning the Marshall Plan's advisability, fearing that it would contribute further to the Cold War.[22]

The anti-Communist left, however, responded with enthusiasm to the Marshall Plan. The majority of the CIO's leadership now moved toward wholehearted support of the administration's foreign policy.

Labor, like the business community, had a special interest in the Marshall Plan, which promised an economically recovered western Europe and increased foreign markets. The issue, however, at least as Philip Murray chose to present it, was primarily that of dealing with the rising threat of international Communism. "In the distribution of relief in the fight . . . ," he told the assembled CIO members at their 1947 annual convention, "the people who absorb the food might very well refrain from becoming a part of any totalitarian government." A large majority of the CIO's membership agreed and endorsed the methods and goals of the Marshall Plan in convention, with the stipulation that "under no circumstances should food or any other aid given by our country be used as a means of coercing free but needy people in the exercise of rights of independence and self-government. . . ." Murray himself requested Secretary Marshall to address the CIO's convention in person, and Marshall agreed, receiving a warm welcome from the convention delegates. The tone of the 1947 convention was strongly anti-Communist, and those who attempted to defend the critics of Truman's foreign policy were denounced by Murray and other CIO leaders.[23]

Within Congress, liberals rapidly and enthusiastically endorsed the Marshall Plan. Among the left-of-center, only Glen Taylor in the Senate and Vito Marcantonio in the House raised serious objections. Taylor objected that the plan's goal was economic domination and that it brought the United States closer to war; he called for United Nations administration of any aid program, to keep it nonpolitical. Marcantonio made similar suggestions; United Nations management of the economic aid program would strengthen the United Nations itself and would ensure that the proposal was not just another political weapon "to maintain and preserve economic and political systems which have become satellites of our State Department. . . ."[24]

Senator Pepper agreed with his colleague Taylor that relief should be administered through the United Nations and on the basis of need rather than political considerations. But he broke significantly with Taylor by supporting the plan. "In many respects," he said, "this is the most magnificent proposal ever made by a government. . . ." He urged that instead of using the program to oppose Communism and to stop Russia, Congress should act because such action was morally correct as well as "in our own economic interest." Other congressional liberals supported the Marshall Plan without qualification. Democratic Senator Harley M. Kilgore of West Virginia supported the plan as a sound investment as well as a proper responsibility for the United States. Senator Dennis Chavez, a New Mexico Democrat, declared that such a plan was "necessary in the interest of our own country and in the interest of the world. . . ." Elbert D. Thomas stressed that Europe would collapse immediately without such an aid program, and he described the Marshall Plan as a "program of liberalism designed to promote a just and lasting peace." Senator Wayne Morse, a liberal Oregon Republican, praised the program for being in the nation's economic as well as security interest, spoke of the United States' obligation to support democracy, and charged Senator Glen Taylor with arguing on behalf of the Kremlin. In the House of Representatives, the aid plan received some opposition from liberals because the House bill also included military aid to Nationalist China. Emanuel Celler termed this "shabby politics": "In order to get what we want," he said, "we must take what we do not want." Other House liberals similarly opposed the military aid proposals but warmly endorsed the original Marshall Plan itself.[25]

The ADA united in approval of the Marshall Plan, though a minority within the organization remained opposed to the implications of the Truman Doctrine and refused to endorse the entire Truman foreign policy. In September, Schlesinger attempted to link the Truman Doctrine and the Marshall Plan in a draft ADA foreign policy report, hoping to win the membership's approval of both administration programs. Reinhold Niebuhr applauded the effort: "The Truman Doctrine and the Marshall Plan," he agreed, "are both necessary to this containment policy." The minority resisted strongly enough, however, so that Schlesinger agreed to resubmit a new policy statement the following month. Titled "A Liberal Foreign Policy for the United States," this new statement was more critical of some aspects of Truman's foreign policy, although still expressing overall approval. Its primary target was those former isolationists, now aggressive anti-Communists, who were willing to fight Communism with methods and allies unacceptable to nearly all liberals. The "Liberal Foreign Policy" statement criticized the administration for creating a "sense of crisis" in presenting the Truman Doctrine, but stressed the doctrine's continuity with past policy and linked it with Franklin D. Roosevelt, citing Roosevelt's 1937 Quarantine Speech and concluding that this speech had enunciated "the right of *all* nations to freedom from external aggression. This right must apply to all nations, whether or not we like their forms of government—not just to democratic nations. . . . If the 'Truman Doctrine' does mean unconditional support of all anti-Communists," the statement argued, "American progressives would, of course, oppose it. If it means only that the U.S. proposes to support countries menaced by external aggression, American progressives would, of course, back it up."[26]

It was precisely the Truman Doctrine's stress on military aid and its far-flung commitment of that aid, however, which its detractors stressed. Whether that commitment was to all anti-Communists or to all countries menaced by Communists was of small matter; in either case, the commitment was equally disturbing. Nevertheless, the revised draft policy statement did go so far as to say that, since the death of Roosevelt, American foreign policy had been "in important respects floundering and uncertain, . . . wander[ing] into dangerous ambiguities which it is imperative to correct." As it finally appeared, however, approved by the majority of the ADA's leadership and printed in the ADA publication *Toward Total Peace,* the foreign policy statement deleted all such critical assessment of the Truman administration's foreign policy.[27] By the autumn of 1947, when the policy expressed in *Toward Total Peace* was approved, the majority within the ADA evidently was strong enough to ignore the objections of a minority of its members.

The major factor contributing to ADA confidence was its growing membership. The PCA had benefited from opposing the Truman Doctrine and had gained substantially in membership, while the ADA remained small. The PCA's opposition to the Marshall Plan, however, did not win it new friends. It had seemed to follow the Communist party in denouncing the plan, arguing that a recovery program without Soviet participation would greatly increase the possibility of war. After October 1947, the ADA began to acquire more substantial backing among liberals. By December, James Loeb was able to report to the ADA national board that during the previous three months, "political circumstances have been greatly clarified to the advantage of the ADA's political position." The Marshall Plan provided the turning point, for "while there were many doubts about the so-called Truman Doctrine, there are no doubts among genuine liberals on the Marshall Plan."[28]

In 1947 the ADA thus scored an important victory over the rival PCA and popular-front liberalism by aligning itself closely with Truman's foreign policy. Anti-Communist liberalism was emerging quickly and already was strongly challenging the popular front for leadership of the postwar American left.

3

**Defeat for the
Popular Front: 1948**

By late 1947 anti-Communist
liberals, led by the ADA, had profited from aligning themselves closely
with Truman's foreign policy. Truman had benefited as well, attracting growing support from a constituency which had, during 1945 and
1946, grown increasingly critical of his leadership. Truman further
strengthened his support among liberals through his veto of the
Taft-Hartley Act in 1947,[1] while the report of his commission on civil
rights further established him as a liberal acting in the spirit of
Roosevelt and the New Deal.[2]

While Truman's program won increasing praise from anti-
Communist liberals, many liberals continued to consider Truman
himself personally unacceptable as a leader, particularly as a substitute for Roosevelt. Truman's style, or apparent lack of it, operated to
his disadvantage, while his inconsistent support of ongoing New
Deal programs, his inability to drive liberal programs through Congress, and his out-and-out blunders deeply disturbed New Deal liberals, who concluded that despite his increasing stature as president,
he nevertheless was not fully qualified to remain in the job. Perhaps
most important, liberals also were well aware that Truman appeared
to have little chance of winning in 1948.[3]

By rejecting the president as their leader, however, those liberals
who supported his program, particularly his foreign policy program,
seemed to have cast themselves adrift. Henry Wallace remained their
logical alternative, but by the summer of 1947 Wallace had reconsidered his original support for the Marshall Plan and by autumn he and
the PCA voiced similar objections to the plan as a political vehicle
which increased Cold War tensions. In late 1947 Wallace became the

presidential candidate of the PCA-based Progressive party; in so doing, he continued to widen the gulf existing between himself and
anti-Communist liberals. International affairs further widened the division between anti-Communist liberals and the popular-front left. In
February 1948 a Communist minority overthrew a coalition government and established a Communist regime in Czechoslovakia. In
April 1948, in response to Allied plans to unify West Germany, Soviet
authorities took steps which marked the beginning of the Berlin
blockade, restricting movement from the Western zones through the
East German corridor into Berlin. In late June, the Soviet Union
blocked all traffic from the Western zones to Berlin and Truman immediately responded with the Berlin airlift, which would last until
May 1949. By late spring of 1948, thus, there no longer was any possibility that those who supported the Truman foreign policy could accept a domestic popular-front alliance with the Communists or accept
Wallace as their leader.[4]

In searching for a candidate who could fill the role of charismatic
liberal leader and vote-getter, while maintaining the Truman administration's anti-Communist domestic and foreign policy, ADA liberals
combined political expediency with a generous amount of naiveté and
pushed wholeheartedly for the nomination of Dwight D. Eisenhower,
whose views were almost entirely unknown. General Eisenhower
was then a well-beloved war hero whose leadership abilities seemed
matched by his engaging warmth. He had so many of the qualities for
which liberals were looking that they were tempted to fill in the unknown areas with other qualities of their choice. American liberals
needed the man they hoped Eisenhower was, and needed him so
badly that they did not objectively investigate whether or not
Eisenhower was indeed that man.[5]

In April 1948 the ADA called for an open convention, boosted the
candidacies of both Eisenhower and Supreme Court Justice William
O. Douglas, and prepared itself to offer evidence in support of the
general's candidacy. The evidence was thin, however, as even ADA
members admitted privately. One example the ADA stressed was
Eisenhower's 1946 speech before the CIO annual convention; another
was an address in London at the close of the war; and a third was a
brief statement on desegregation in the armed services. The CIO
speech, in which Eisenhower had said, "There is no need for me to
expound upon the importance of American labor to our position before the world, and to our own future happiness and prosperity,"
served to establish his support of organized labor. The London

speech, in which Eisenhower had said, "Neither London nor Abilene, sisters under the skin, will sell her birthright for physical safety, her liberty for mere existence," pointed up his internationalism. Finally, the statement, "We are giving Negro troops equal status in the military field. We must give them the same consideration in their personal relationships," established Eisenhower as a friend of civil rights. The ADA knew little more about his views. "In response to your letter of April 1st on background for Eisenhower," the ADA's director of organizations wrote to the secretary of the Cleveland chapter, "we may be able to fill in for you within a few days but, as you indicated, not much can be found out at this moment on where 'Ike stands.' "[6]

Most important to Eisenhower's liberal supporters was the question of his availability. In January 1948 he issued a statement that he was unavailable as a candidate but wished to uphold his duties as a citizen and placed "no limitations upon [my] readiness to serve in any designated capacity." This was interpreted as a cautious testing of the political waters before joining the swim, and, thus encouraged, election talk which Eisenhower did nothing more to discourage continued to surround his name. On April 27, 1948, the ADA concluded that "in the right circumstances, General Eisenhower could be drafted for the Democratic nomination." Those circumstances, the ADA stressed, consisted of "a genuine and practically unanimous draft."[7]

Other anti-Wallace liberals hurried to get on the Eisenhower bandwagon. In late March, New York's Liberal party—an anti-Communist political off-shoot of New York's American Labor party—announced its endorsement of Eisenhower. Liberal party leader David Dubinsky, president of the International Ladies Garment Workers Union and a former Socialist party member, played a prominent role in the ADA. Shortly after the Liberal party's endorsement, the *New York Times* reported that CIO secretary-treasurer James B. Carey had spoken in favor of Eisenhower and that "those who know the relationship between [Carey and Murray] are well aware that Mr. Carey must have spoken with the foreknowledge of the CIO president."[8] At the same time, change was occurring at the *New Republic* where, in July, Wallace resigned as editor. Publisher Michael Straight had from the outset opposed Wallace's third-party candidacy. He also took issue with Wallace on the Marshall Plan. The Czechoslovakian coup of February 1948 immensely disturbed him and turned him away from popular-front politics. As a result,

Straight rejected the Progressive party but, like many other liberals, hoped that there was an alternative to Truman and considered both Eisenhower and Douglas as possible Democratic presidential candidates.[9]

In the time remaining before the Democratic convention, the ADA did its best to promote an open convention and Eisenhower's nomination. State and local political leaders, linked with the ADA, who had been fighting Wallace in the name of supporting the Democratic party and Truman, began to change their slogans. In Minnesota Hubert H. Humphrey switched from a "support Truman" theme to one urging Minnesotans "to participate in the precinct caucuses in the interest of any [Democratic] national ticket other than the Wallace that they might desire." Humphrey, who had already won solid anti-Communist credentials and attracted national attention as the young mayor of Minneapolis, was in fact, if not in name, the real leader of the Democratic-Farmer-Labor party in Minnesota. Within the Minnesota state DFL convention in June, Humphrey and his supporters successfully opposed the effort of Truman supporters to instruct Minnesota's Democratic national convention delegation for Truman. The ADA's national staff worked both to influence state nominating conventions and to establish liaisons with those state delegations already selected. At first receiving only slight response, the campaign began to pick up momentum, supported by liberals and conservatives, by Northern big city bosses and Southern states'-righters. Eisenhower's all-things-to-all-people image did not seem to concern either his liberal or his conservative backers, who joined happily to support him.[10]

Then, after weeks of silence on the movement to nominate him, Eisenhower announced that he had not changed his mind and would not accept any nomination for public office. Liberals, however, were not yet ready to give up. The ADA's Leon Henderson continued to hope that the Democratic convention would ignore Eisenhower's statement and draft him anyway. Franklin D. Roosevelt's oldest son, James Roosevelt, concluded that Eisenhower "will not serve as a partisan President but will answer a call to national duty" and promptly re-issued the call for a caucus of draft-Eisenhower forces. Frank Hague, Democratic boss of New Jersey, flatly refused to reverse his delegation's support for Eisenhower. Then, in response to a telegram from Senator Claude Pepper which was intended to ease the general's way back into the political ring, Eisenhower issued his third and most pointed statement: "no matter under what terms, conditions or premises a proposal might be couched," he would not accept the

Democratic nomination for the presidency. The "draft-Eisenhower" movement suddenly ended. The "stop-Truman" movement halted as well. Justice Douglas announced he was not a candidate, had never been one, and had no intention of becoming one. The ADA attempted to sustain a Douglas campaign, but this attempt was a formality.[11] The "stop-Truman" movement had lost badly, and those liberals who had supported Eisenhower had come within a fraction of complete humiliation. Morris Rubin, editor of the *Progressive,* observed that "ADA, a liberal organization which purports to be, among other things, the conscience of the Democratic Party, looked pretty silly beating the drums for a man, who for all they knew, was a rock-ribbed conservative."[12] The ADA had looked even more foolish when the man for whom it drummed refused to march.

The ADA and other anti-Truman liberals recouped their losses somewhat, however, through their successful battle to include a civil rights plank in the 1948 Democratic party platform. ADA leaders themselves had early recognized the opportunity offered by the Democratic National Convention to press for the expansion of civil rights. Truman had asked for specific civil rights legislation to implement his commission's report, but by the time of the Democratic convention, he was supporting a compromise plank for the party platform. With the left wing of his party already departed to follow Wallace, Truman was reluctant to decimate party harmony and his election chances further by antagonizing the South.[13] Consequently, the ADA and other liberals were left to fight for what was known by then as the president's civil rights program.

The ADA leaders had anticipated a North-South fight over civil rights in the convention, although they had not anticipated Truman's moderate role. Their key supporter in the drive was Hubert Humphrey, who by spring 1948 had begun to round up support from prominent Democrats for Truman's civil rights program. After an unsuccessful fight within the convention's drafting committee to include the president's program in the Democratic platform, Humphrey presented the minority position to the convention and dramatically demanded the inclusion of this civil rights plank. The convention responded enthusiastically, adopted the minority resolution, and a portion of the Southern delegation bolted the convention.[14] Democratic and ADA liberals had thus won an important victory on the civil rights issue. They also had left themselves with Truman as their presidential candidate and with a party which had lost both its left and right wings—a significant portion of its membership.

| * |

Wallace and the Progressive party appeared particularly threatening to the possibility of a Democratic victory. Despite the PCA's significant losses in liberal support following its opposition to the Marshall Plan, Wallace and the Progressives threatened to siphon off much-needed liberal votes from the Democratic party. James Loeb in late 1947 told an ADA national board meeting that it would be "shortsighted to overestimate Mr. Wallace's strength in the country as a whole, but it would be equally short-sighted to underestimate his following among liberals, even among liberals who disagree with much of his thinking."[15] What was at stake was the leadership of American liberals and the direction of American foreign policy. Not only might a swing to Wallace contribute to a victory for Republicans, conservatism, and isolationism, but a Democratic defeat attributable even only in part to Wallace's candidacy might also move the national focal point of American liberalism from the Democratic to the Progressive party and signify a victory for popular-front liberalism. Consequently, the ADA and other anti-Communist liberals, encouraged by the Truman administration,[16] actively fought Wallace and the Progressive party on the national, state, and local levels.

At its February 1948 convention, the ADA issued a statement which "unreservedly condemned" Wallace's third-party candidacy and outlined the three points it would stress in its anti-Wallace campaign: that the Progressive party was Communist-dominated, that it opposed the Marshall Plan, and that third-party candidates would serve only to elect an isolationist and reactionary Congress. The "alleged 'party of protest,' " the ADA stressed again and again in the coming months, "would *silence* the voice of protest."[17] Most important of these political thrusts, however, was the frequently reiterated charge that the Progressive party was run from Moscow. This allegation, which paralleled the Democratic party's own tactics of "neutralizing Wallace" by linking him with Communism, proved to be most damaging of all to Wallace's campaign.

The question of whether the Communists dominated the Progressive party has been hotly debated since 1948 and essentially involves two related topics: the origins of the Progressive party and the degree of Communist participation in and control over it. Until recently, the most widely held view has been that the Progressive party had its origins in plans of the Communist Party USA dating back as early as 1945, and that it was controlled throughout by the Communists. According to this view, the Communists built the third-party movement, convinced Henry Wallace to accept the new party's leadership, and then manipulated both Wallace and the party. Progressive party members themselves have held quite another view: Curtis MacDougall, a Progressive candidate in 1948, has insisted that the Communists did not become active in the Progressive party until it was already underway, and that they never did control it.[18]

More recent accounts have stressed complexities and nuances and show the CPUSA as hesitant until prodded into supporting a third party by the formation of the Cominform in the autumn of 1947; these accounts indicate further that Communist support was not essential to the founding of the Progressive party, since important non-Communists had already committed themselves to such a project. Once the party was formed, its policy reflected general left-wing assumptions, and the party organization showed confusion rather than centralized Communist control. According to Joseph R. Starobin, one-time Communist and former foreign editor of the *Daily Worker*, the CPUSA was divided and confused throughout 1947 and 1948. The Communists did not use Wallace, Starobin argues; on the contrary, Wallace used them "to do the work that his own associates would not do." Starobin concludes that the Communist party did not seek to dominate the Progressive party; the Progressive party's weaknesses compelled full-scale Communist activity.[19]

The ADA had no difficulty, however, in deciding the extent of Communist influence in the new party. In April 1948 the ADA's national office published the pamphlet *Henry Wallace: The First Three Months* and distributed it widely to liberals. Two other Wallace pamphlets soon followed, stressing, as the first had done, the new party's Communist ties. Toward the end of July, Loeb surprised participants at the Progressive party's national convention by appearing to testify at platform hearings. He took the opportunity to criticize the party's opposition to the Marshall Plan and disparaged the usefulness of a third party when every liberal vote was needed to oppose conservative reaction. Above all else, however, he struck out at the party's alleged Communist ties.[20]

At the state and local level, the ADA conducted some smaller skirmishes with the Progressive party, including Hubert Humphrey's successful block of an attempt by Wallace supporters to capture the Minnesota Democratic-Farmer-Labor party. Minnesota had for years enjoyed a firm tradition of agrarian radicalism which, during the 1930s, found expression in Minnesota's Farmer-Labor party. The Farmer-Labor party reached the peak of its success under the leadership of Governor Floyd B. Olson, but Olson' death and charges of Communist infiltration helped bring about the party's decline in the late 1930s and early 1940s. In 1944, due in large part to Humphrey's attempt to strengthen the state's liberal forces, Minnesota's Farmer-Labor and Democratic parties merged under the auspices of the national Democratic party. By the late 1940s, Minnesota's Democratic-Farmer-Labor party contained anti-Communist liberals as well as popular-front leftists. The positions of the two factions on domestic issues were similar during the late 1940s; their fundamental disagreement was over foreign policy and the role of Communists within the American left. [21]

By 1948 Humphrey was the leader of the anti-Communist liberals in Minnesota and a candidate for the United States Senate on the DFL ticket. Wallace had some appeal for popular-front liberals and Communists within the DFL, and consequently Wallace forces represented a distinct threat both to the Democratic base of the DFL and to Humphrey's own political aspirations. In addition, as vice-chairman of the ADA, Humphrey shared the ADA's wholehearted opposition to the PCA and to the Progressive party. All these strands came together in early 1948 in the young Minnesota politician's leadership of the attack against state Wallace supporters. [22] What made the Democratic-Progressive party battle in Minnesota of national interest was that here a unique set of circumstances had brought the contestants together within the same party organization. Thus, all the preliminary intra-party battles could be viewed as measurable tests of strength for both parties throughout the state and even, to some extent, the nation.

Humphrey and a small group of aides, working closely with the ADA, made careful plans to assert Democratic control over the party by gaining control of local party machinery. They were totally successful. Once the precinct caucuses were in the hands of the Humphrey group, the outcome of the county and state nominating conventions was certain. The Wallace faction protested, unsuccessfully sought seating for its delegates at the state DFL convention, and finally caucused by itself in a rump convention. In a last bid for control, the Wallace convention rushed the names on its presidential slate to the Minnesota secretary of state and filed, in the name of the DFL party, well ahead of the regular convention. The state Supreme Court, however, ruled that electors from the regular convention should replace the Wallace electors on the November election ballot. At that point the Wallace faction officially broke with the DFL and filed as a third party. [23]

| * |

The creation of the Progressive party and the candidacy of Henry Wallace thus formalized the growing divisions between cold-war and popular-front liberals. It also precipitated a final crisis within the divided CIO.

Philip Murray was opposed to the Progressive party from the outset;[24] in January 1948 he presented the CIO's executive board with a resolution opposing a third party in 1948 as "politically unwise." As the ADA had done, Murray argued that a third party would "weaken the possibility of electing a progressive Congress." He neither agreed with Progressive party officials that a third party would draw a larger vote and thus contribute a greater chance to elect liberals, nor accepted official Progressive assertions that a Republican victory would give the public a taste of real reaction and thus ensure a victory for liberals in 1952. Significantly, Murray had cooled on Henry Wallace. Although the CIO president had supported Wallace in 1940 and 1944 and had known him well for many years, he now asserted that Wallace had "never in his fourteen years of public service defended the interests of organized labor" and had never really been interested in the working person.[25]

Murray and many within the CIO leadership were especially concerned about the impact of the Progressive campaign on domestic and foreign programs. While neither Murray nor any of the CIO leadership had any argument with the Progressive party's domestic program in and of itself, they were worried that a divided liberal vote would produce a conservative Congress and thus foredoom the passage of any liberal programs. They were alarmed as well by Progressive opposition to the Marshall Plan and to the administration's developing program of containment. As far as the center and growing anti-Communist right wing within the CIO were concerned, the real issue introduced by the Progressive party was the issue of Communism. An increasing majority of the CIO's leadership was convinced that the Progressive party was Communist-dominated and that Wallace was being used in an attempt to attract votes from and thus defeat the administration which had proposed the Marshall Plan. "I think some people want a Third Party in this country in 1948," stated Emil Rieve, president of the Textile Workers, "not for the purpose of electing anybody, but for the purpose of defeating someone, in order that they can show the world that anyone who has opposed them cannot be elected. . . ." Van A. Bittner, vice-president of the United Steel Workers, agreed: "I don't believe the time has come . . . when the American people will stand for some outside power, some outside nation, chasing a man out of the White House. . . ."[26]

Murray's resolution against the third party was a potentially explosive one in the already tense climate of the CIO executive board. At its previous national convention, the CIO had passed a foreign policy resolution which could be interpreted as endorsing the Marshall Plan, but which was vague enough so that the left wing could and did consider it a compromise. Now, Murray's third-party resolution pointed toward a direct CIO endorsement of the Marshall Plan. Some of the members of the left wing requested that the third party and Marshall Plan be considered as separate subjects. "The Marshall Plan is but a part of the broad program to which the resolution makes reference," Murray responded. "It is not a divided subject. . . . When we say that we oppose the Third Party we also say that we support CIO-PAC progressive policies."[27]

The proposed resolution against the third party especially unsettled the CIO's left-wing leadership, not only because the resolution opposed the Wallace third-party presidential bid but also because it pointed toward an eventual endorsement of Truman. Despite Truman's strongly worded veto of the Taft-Hartley Act, labor still carried bitter memories of the president's failure to keep the lid on prices and of his heated response to the railroad strike in 1946. In addition, Truman had not convinced organized labor that he had done all within his power to prevent the enactment of the Taft-Hartley Act over his veto. Albert Fitzgerald, left-wing leader of the United Electrical Workers, noted that in 1944 the CIO-PAC actively supported Roosevelt and was able to do so because there was such agreement among all the CIO unions at that time. In 1948, Fitzgerald contended, the situation was quite different; even without a third party there was much opposition to Truman within the labor movement. Ben Gold, head of the Fur and Leather Workers' union and an acknowledged Communist, flatly stated that his union members hated Truman and would not vote for him or any Democratic presidential candidate under any conditions. "The endorsement of Truman occurs here indirectly," added Harry Bridges, "though it is left for the future, left up in the air. . . ." Murray's proposed resolution, Bridges concluded, was a "back door move to continue the support of the Democrats as the lesser of two evils."[28]

Even more disturbing to the CIO's left wing was the resolution's claim, on behalf of the national CIO, to direct the political activity and expressions of political belief of all the CIO's affiliates and their individual leaders. This claim struck at the whole question of union autonomy, which had been raised on several occasions during the previous year and a half but which now became critical. "It is a very big question," said the Transport Workers' Mike Quill, "and I think if our Union's hands are tied here by this resolution it will be bad. It never happened in CIO before. It didn't happen when we were in the American Federation of Labor, we had that autonomy." Walter Reuther replied that the CIO had been successful where the AFL failed "because we did have a uniform political policy, because we did have a sense of discipline and direction that covered the whole group inside the CIO, and I say you are going to destroy that. . . ." Emil Rieve agreed with Reuther: "For years we have criticized the A.F. of L., we have said that they have done nothing as far as politics are concerned. . . ."[29]

Murray reminded the left wing's leadership that only a short while before it had voted to support and give allegiance to the national CIO-PAC and to its policies and programs, as an alternative to supporting either or both the ADA or PCA. The left wing remained unpersuaded: the leftists' pledge and commitment to the CIO-PAC had been made before the third party had appeared. Quill pointed out that even in John L. Lewis's speech to the CIO in 1940, when Lewis had repudiated Roosevelt, the first president of the CIO had not attempted to "tie our hands by a resolution. He said, 'Support me or repudiate me; I will not chide you.' " Murray was unmoved; the CIO executive board had made a commitment to the CIO-PAC, the CIO national convention had done the same, and Murray stressed that this commitment still existed and was binding. The CIO executive board passed Murray's anti-third-party resolution with only the left wing dissenting.[30]

The left wing interpreted Murray's resolution as an attack on Wallace and the Progressive party and an endorsement of the administration's foreign policy. Murray himself insisted that the resolution was intended to prevent a weakening of liberal political forces, which could operate only to labor's disadvantage, and was intended as well to prevent a rupture within the CIO by uniting the organization behind one policy. "The real issue," he said, is "the jeopardy in which you place your Unions. . . . A split on this Board over this political issue may very well jeopardize the perpetuity of a number of organizations affiliated with this movement." The left wing, in return, argued that a single political policy, imposed from the top, would not nurture flourishing unions. "The real guarantee of continued growth of a Union," Bridges stressed, "is its economic strength, implemented by political action." As Bridges explained it, the problem for the unions was in doing "anything that has even the appearance of ramming something down their throats. . . . Then," he concluded, the CIO "will be in trouble. . . ."[31]

The anti-third-party resolution exacerbated the split already existing within the CIO to such a degree, however, that from then on the ultimate ouster of the dissident unions was almost inevitable. As early as 1946 Murray had believed that internal strife threatened the success of the CIO, and in early 1947 he had attempted to remove the cause for strife by dissuading CIO officers from participating in conflicting liberal organizations. By 1948, however, Murray had decided to force the CIO's dissident left minority to accept the majority view on domestic politics as well as foreign affairs. In addition to obtaining official CIO opposition to the Progressive party, Murray in February 1948 formally associated the CIO with the ADA.[32]

In both 1947 and 1948, Murray gave precedence to national CIO policy over any claims for individual union autonomy. In 1947, however, his attempt to remove internal warfare by removing CIO officers from involvement with either of the warring liberal organizations had stressed abstinence from non-labor politics. There was no particular precedent for this action; the CIO had been deeply involved in liberal politics since its beginnings. Murray had simply acknowledged that the CIO could no longer "assume the hazards of becoming involved. . . ." In 1948, Murray again stressed that "there is something bigger than Wallace and bigger than Third Parties in the United States. There is this movement. That is the most important thing of all."[33] Yet it would have been difficult not to see where the anti-third-party resolution would eventually lead the CIO. Perhaps Murray had evaluated the alternatives and decided that the risk was, in all, worth taking. If a strong hand turned out to be successful in bringing dissidents into line, then so much the better. If the dissidents eventually rebelled and broke with or were forced out of the CIO, perhaps this would not be a great loss. Indeed, in the Cold War atmosphere, leftist unions could be viewed as a liability rather than an asset to an organization as vulnerable to right-wing attacks as was the CIO.

Calculations such as these may have entered Murray's consideration. As probable an influence, however, was the heightened tension and emotion surrounding the Cold War. By 1948 international affairs had long since ceased to be a topic for rational debate, even among intellectuals, and the flare-ups in the CIO reflected the emotional atmosphere created by the Cold War. No longer was it possible to banter about differing points of views on foreign affairs or on domestic topics related to the third party and its foreign policy platform. Toleration was no longer possible. Even Murray, a warm and friendly man widely beloved by CIO leadership as well as by the rank and file, was caught up in the intense personal animosities the situation bred. The relative joviality of late 1946 had disintegrated into bitterness and rancor within the CIO's leadership, and Murray, as president, was in large part responsible. His sensitivity to attacks from the left and his increasingly emotional hostility to Communism contributed greatly to the tense atmosphere at CIO executive meetings. He complained of "the character assassination to which the Communist Party is now devoting itself in attacking me. . . . I am referred to as an imperialist and a God damned Wall Street war monger. . . ." He promised that he was "not going to get particularly annoyed," but these attacks appeared to disturb him immensely.[34] "To me, the Communist Party stinks to high heaven," he fumed at one board meeting; "to me its practices are definitely treasonous and reprehensible, to me its agents are devils out of hell that will do anything to undermine a labor union or this country in the interest of the Soviets." Those members of the board who opposed the Truman administration in foreign affairs and who supported Henry Wallace had proved, to Murray, their sympathies with the Communism he so hated. "Some members of this Executive Board," he said, "by virtue of the votes which they consistently register on certain issues, indicate a very sympathetic attitude toward these Communistic activities. They follow the Line, and they live to follow the Line."[35]

The left-wing attacks of which Murray complained were unquestionably scathing. The CIO's leadership was not made up of soft-spoken individuals, and Philip Murray, usually characterized as "gentle" in manner, symbolized in his own increasingly shrill anti-Communist pronouncements the intensity and pitch to which this intra-organizational battle had risen. Despite the left wing's contribution to the acrimony of the debate, however, it is questionable whether left-wing restraint would have changed the final outcome significantly.

The attempt by Murray and such other CIO officials as Walter Reuther to throw the full weight of the CIO behind the administration thus constituted a crucial breaking point within the CIO, the first of a series of steps leading to the ouster of eleven unions in the next two years. Murray underscored the break in a significant way: he dismissed Lee Pressman as CIO general counsel after Pressman chose to run for political office on the Progressive party ticket and replaced him with Arthur J. Goldberg.[36] Goldberg, a prominent Chicago labor lawyer who had represented the Steel Workers and other CIO unions, was known to be a firm anti-Communist. He was also an able negotiator, a point which Murray particularly respected. Other powerful leaders within the CIO, such as Emil Rieve and Amalgamated Clothing Workers' Jacob Potofsky, had total confidence in him. Goldberg's status as a lawyer and not an officer of the organization may also have increased his influence with Murray: because there was little precedent for a general counsel becoming president of either a union or labor organization, Murray could give Goldberg sizable authority without fear of building up a rival.[37]

Goldberg has recalled that before accepting the position he received assurances that he would be a policy-maker in the organization.[38] These assurances may well have been given readily by Murray, whose health was poor and who also, according to one staff member who observed him closely at the time, appeared to have "sort of given up on the CIO." Murray gave increasingly more attention to his own union, the Steel Workers, and was satisfied to let Goldberg play a major role in running the CIO.[39] Nonetheless, although Goldberg was influential in the final decision to oust the left-wing unions from the CIO, in a real sense the decision to expel these unions had already been made when the break with the Wallace movement occurred and when Goldberg was asked to take Pressman's place. At this point, the leaders of the CIO center, especially Murray, had decided that they could no longer tolerate left-wing dissidence within their organization.

In late summer 1948 the CIO endorsed Truman, over the violent objections of the left. "There is no organization attached to this CIO national movement that has respected its commitments to a greater degree than yours has," Murray told Ben Gold. "But damn it, my difficulty with you boys, Ben, . . . is . . . that complete inflexibility of position." Murray stressed that were it not for foreign affairs, the CIO's leadership would not have divided over Truman. He emphatically pointed out his role as the CIO's top leader and blasted his critics: "If I should happen to disagree with a member of this Executive Board as to what I ought to do with reference to the Truman situation, then I do it from the standpoint of conviction, and when I do it from the standpoint of conviction I don't like an interloping group of irresponsible citizens to create organizations of various descriptions to invade the jurisdiction of my International Union in this political situation, condemn, castigate and vilify and refer to the leader of the union as a misleader of labor."[40] The left-center coalition within the CIO had clearly and irreversibly divided, and a new coalition had formed between the center and the anti-Communist "right." The politics of anti-Communism had triumphed in the CIO.

| * |

Truman's unexpected victory in November 1948 was interpreted as a triumph by both the new liberals of Americans for Democratic Action and the new center-right leadership of the CIO. The Wallace vote had proven insignificant and the Republicans, much to their surprise, had lost. With the Wallace-supporters on the left completely routed and the Republicans on the right at least temporarily subdued by the election of a Democratic Congress, the future seemed to belong to the adherents of the new Cold-War liberalism.

4

The Red Scare and the Politics of the Liberal Center: 1949

The victory of Harry Truman and the triumph of the new liberals brought no respite in the burgeoning Cold War; indeed, tensions increased measurably. In May 1949 the Soviet Union lifted the Berlin blockade in return for a meeting of the Council of Foreign Ministers on the question of West German unification; the meeting was held, but brought no important agreement on Germany. In August the Department of State announced through an official "White Paper" that the vast nation of China had fallen to Communist armies. September brought an even more severe shock to Americans: the Truman administration announced evidence that the Soviet Union had exploded its own atomic device.

Truman had included in his inaugural address his so-called Point Four program of technical assistance to non-Communist developing nations—a project which only slowly got underway and soon was overshadowed by the military developments of the Cold War. In April 1949 the United States abandoned its historic position against alliances and, with non-Communist nations of western Europe, signed the North Atlantic Treaty. The Senate quickly and overwhelmingly approved the treaty and in July, by a vote of 82 to 13, voted to ratify without reservation. In September Congress appropriated $1 billion for arms and equipment for the signatory nations and provided, in addition, $211 million for Greece and Turkey. Events throughout the world in 1949 had heightened the United States' concern for military security.

The dissolution of the World War II victory into Cold War had alarmed much of the nation. Similarly, the disintegration of the liberal

1948 election victory severely disappointed American liberals. The new liberals elected to the House and Senate in 1948 arrived in Congress to find conservative forces on both sides of the aisle united to block implementation of the program to which liberals believed the country had given its mandate in November. Furthermore, neither the White House nor Democratic leaders in Congress were eager to give all-out support for the program outlined in the 1948 Democratic Platform, especially the civil rights plank. Truman hoped to reunite the Democratic party and thus could not risk offending the party's conservative bloc by vigorously supporting programs offensive to it.[1]

Liberals who in 1948 believed that they had discovered in Harry Truman a homespun Roosevelt now became increasingly disappointed with his compromises, blunders, and oversights.[2] More ominous, the postwar Red Scare was mounting in intensity, and as it did, the new liberals increasingly retreated before its onslaught. As conservatives sought to brand Democratic liberals with pro-Communist sympathies, liberals responded by trying to dissociate themselves further from the old popular-front left and by stressing their own anti-Communism. The Alger Hiss case was an important index to this process. In 1948 former Communist Whittaker Chambers had charged that Hiss, once a high state department official, was guilty of espionage. Initially, most liberals rallied to Hiss's defense, picturing the case as a typical right-wing attack on the New Deal, with which Hiss had been prominently identified. His character witnesses included Supreme Court justices Felix Frankfurter and Stanley Reed, as well as Dean Acheson and Adlai Stevenson. Hiss's first trial ended with a hung jury in the summer of 1949, his second with conviction in early 1950. Though many, perhaps even most, liberals continued to believe Hiss innocent, others, especially such prominent Cold-War liberals as Arthur Schlesinger, Jr., and *New York Post* editor James Wechsler, found the evidence against him convincing.[3] Liberals who had defended Hiss were doubtless discouraged from risking themselves in the future by the response of such conservatives as Richard Nixon (and later Joe McCarthy), who were quick to hang the Hiss case around their necks.

Another trial prominent in 1949 both reflected and intensified the nation's turmoil over the Communist question. Liberals divided over the Truman administration's prosecution of eleven leaders of the Communist party who were charged with violating the Smith Act of 1940 through conspiracy to advocate the violent overthrow of the government. The Communists called the trial a political inquisition and though many liberals agreed, objecting to the political nature of the trial and to the restraints they thought it placed on the first amendment, some of the new Cold-War liberals supported the prosecution and denounced the courtroom conduct of the defense. Morris Ernst, one of the American Civil Liberties Union's general counsels, agreed with the prosecution that the dangers from Communist conspiracy were so great that the movement had to be halted. Congressman Emanuel Celler argued that "these lawyers and defendants have outrageously taken advantage of the judge's patience and humaneness," and that "punishment is long due." Senator Humphrey concluded that the verdict was a good one and that the Communist leaders had been "brought to the bar of justice. . . ."[4]

With the increasing vehemence of the Cold War and anti-Communism, long-standing liberal opposition to the House Committee on Un-American Activities began to lessen. Liberals had complained of the committee's red-baiting tactics since its founding under Congressman Martin Dies in 1938. Congressman Adolph J. Sabath of Illinois, for example, had steadily opposed HUAC since its inception. In early 1948, liberals in the House of Representatives strongly opposed further appropriations for HUAC. American Labor party members Vito Marcantonio and Leo Isacson, both of New York, were at variance with the committee for its record of red-baiting; Isacson had made HUAC one of the issues of his recent special-election campaign. John Blatnik of Minnesota opposed HUAC as "contrary to the provisions of the Constitution" and as using methods that "deliberately create the atmosphere of hysteria and emotionalism." Other congressional liberals also took issue with HUAC and argued against further appropriations: Emanuel Celler called the committee's actions "very unjust and unfair," a "disservice" to the nation, and Chester Holifield of California censured the committee's repeated practice of smears and innuendoes. Abraham J. Multer of New York complained of HUAC's "practice of pillorying persons," and other liberal Democrats spoke against the committee's methods. Republican Jacob Javits of New York also registered a complaint against HUAC's "improper methods and procedures." Thirty-seven congressmen, including most considered to be liberals, voted against the 1948 appropriation.[5]

By 1949, public opposition to HUAC from within Congress had dwindled, although twenty-nine congressmen voted to oppose HUAC's appropriations.[6] Those few who voiced their opposition focused on the committee's investigation of textbooks for Communist influence. Celler stated that such an investigation "smacks of censorship and is a blow against academic and cultural freedom." Illinois Democrat Sidney R. Yates objected to the "narrow-minded scope of [HUAC's] viewpoint" as well as to the committee's methods. But the growing Red Scare was by 1949 rapidly diminishing the degree and force of liberal protest, and liberal politicians were among the most sensitive to the direction the political wind was taking. Congressman Yates, for example, was careful to point out that his objections to HUAC did not in any way indicate that he was sympathetic to Communism. The committee had accomplished a major political coup and garnered publicity and much public support through the Chambers hearings and the entire Hiss case. The Communist issue was too dangerous, it seemed, and HUAC too strong for a liberal politician to risk a career by venturing opposition. Besides, most congressional liberals opposed HUAC's methods but had little problem with the committee's goals. They objected to indiscriminate smears of individuals for "their liberal thoughts or associations," but did not seek to define "un-American activity" or to protect an area of legitimate radical political expression. In addition, the Democratic victories in the 1948 elections meant that the Democratic party was once again responsible for the committee's actions. Liberal Democrats in Congress recognized this political fact and were somewhat wary: Congressman Holifield, for example, stressed that HUAC had changed its behavior markedly from that of "previous sessions of Congress," and he hoped that "this textbook-snooping project" would be disclaimed "by the responsible Democratic members of the committee. . . ."[7]

| * |

Following Truman's election in November 1948, Philip Murray announced to the CIO's leaders, "We have been able to beat back and hold back the forces who were obviously hell-bent upon creating division. . . ."[8] Division within the CIO, however, had never been so serious, and the right-center majority coalition now began to take action against the CIO's left-wing minority. The leadership's first move was against the CIO's industrial union councils. Unlike individual unions, the councils were creations of the national CIO, established to carry out national CIO policy in local areas and possessing no right to deviate from national CIO policy.[9] The question of autonomy did not exist with the councils and therefore they were the logical place for the leadership to begin to crack down on internal left-wing dissent.

Three unions identified with the CIO majority brought charges that the Greater New York Council had operated in ways unfavorable to their interests and opposed to the policies of the national CIO. One of the charges involved the council's opposition to a subway fare increase; another involved its failure to support a national union from which a New York local was attempting to secede. The national CIO committee evaluating these charges took special note that in the situations under question the council was "closely following the line of the Communist Party." More than coincidence was involved, the committee asserted; testimony had been given by Mike Quill—by then an ardent anti-Communist—that leading officials of the Communist party had dictated the council's actions. A difficulty with this tack, which one CIO executive pointed out, was that although the CIO could create specific guidelines governing the relationships of councils, in "some places you hit twilight zones. . . . I don't know of a single council that operates in the CIO in the U.S. that you couldn't take some infraction of rules or an interpretation of rules and say this council did this in this circumstance, especially when international unions start fighting with local unions." A particular difficulty, he stressed, was the traditional militant activism of New York labor and the misunderstandings between New York labor and labor "west of the Hudson River." "A council has a limited operation," Allan Haywood of the Steel Workers commented. "They don't have enough to do and sometimes they get in trouble. This wasn't the first time, but this brought us into real dangers."[10]

The New York council was headed by James Durkin, relatively new to the labor movement and strongly suspected of being a Communist. Among the council's officers were representatives of United Electrical Workers, the Fur and Leather Workers, and United Office Workers—unions which contained Communists and radicals of all descriptions and which had objected to the national CIO's political policies since 1947. Durkin stated that the council's actions were in the militant tradition of the CIO—in support of workers fired from their jobs and in opposition to Taft-Hartleyism. In this very real sense then, Durkin insisted, the New York council did not impede CIO policies. What was at stake, he claimed, was the CIO's independence of political action and the New York council members' opposition to endorsing Truman or being "a tail to the kite of the Democratic Party."[11]

Durkin's aggressiveness and flamboyant rhetoric did little to win support among the leadership of the CIO's majority coalition. "Was he on a soapbox?" one executive board member inquired as transcripts of the New York hearings were read. Durkin gave particular offense by accusing his opponents of participating in a conspiracy with New York business interests "to un-unionize the unions in New York" and "to destroy the CIO progressive and militant role and turn it into a company union. . . . It is a conspiracy," he exclaimed, "to dictate to the unions and to the members in the rank and file and tell them what they must do and must believe, under penalty of raiding attacks and victimization." The majority on the CIO board were unimpressed. The New York council "is no longer responsive to and representative of either the national CIO, for whom it purports to act, [or] the majority of members and local unions in the Greater New York area whom it purports to serve," concluded the report of the investigating committee. The council was "a creature of the national CIO" and was authorized to operate "only so long as it functions properly and actively in the interest of national CIO." The council had instead acted in violation of instructions from the national CIO and the international unions concerned. It had "brought discredit" upon the CIO by its "slavish adherence . . . to the line and dictates of the Communist Party. . . ." The committee therefore recommended that the Greater New York Council be disbanded. A large majority of the CIO's national executive board agreed. [12]

Meanwhile, unions identified with the anti-Communist factions within the CIO began wholesale raids on left-led unions. The United Auto Workers raided the Farm Equipment Workers and the large United Electrical Workers. United Office and Professional Workers complained of raids by the United Paperworkers. The Agricultural Workers accused the Transport Workers of similar raiding activities. The left-led Mine, Mill and Smelter Workers continued to suffer from internal unrest, as a number of locals sought to leave the organization. Murray attributed the turmoil to "the political situation of the moment" but did not acknowledge the possibility that anti-Communist unions were taking advantage of the opportunity to raid left-wing unions. Instead, he concluded that many local unions were interested in breaking with their national organizations "inasmuch as the officers of the national unions are not comporting themselves to CIO policy . . . ," and these local unions were in turn interested in linking with national unions which aligned with the majority within the CIO. Murray asserted that at no time had he given "any degree of comfort" to any of the alleged raiders, and instead told them to bring their problems back to the officers in their own national unions. [13]

The CIO leadership did become directly involved in these disputes, however, beginning with the one between the Farm Equipment Workers and the United Auto Workers. This particular quarrel had been going on for years. Indeed, in 1945, Murray could find "no moral justification" for the UAW raiding the FE, a national union "enjoying the benefit of a collective bargaining contract." By 1948 Murray and the majority of the CIO leaders viewed matters differently. The Farm Equipment Workers provided a consistent source of opposition to national CIO political policy, whereas UAW's Walter Reuther was a staunch supporter as well as a major power within the CIO's leadership. Arguing that FE was weaker than UAW in the farm equipment field, the CIO board directed it to affiliate with UAW. A committee consisting of three CIO vice-presidents, none of them sympathetic to FE, received the job of working out the merger. The members and officers of FE adamantly opposed the merger and complained that the plan was political in nature, aimed at suppressing one source of dissidence within the CIO; FE's representatives argued further that such an action was an attack on the autonomy of an international union. Murray replied, "It is not prejudice, it is not politics that prompts me repeatedly to recommend mergers of this description"; rather, he had a "sincere desire to get the ultimate in the collective bargaining strength of the people in that industry brought together." Bridges replied that he was for mergers, "but shotgun weddings are a different thing." Revoking the charter of a CIO union, he pointed out, was damaging to every other CIO union. Upon Reuther's motion, however, the CIO executive board in early 1949 recommended that the next CIO national convention revoke the Farm Workers' charter if the merger with UAW had not taken place by that time.[14]

The anti-Communist majority within the CIO leadership had clearly aligned the CIO's course with that of the liberal center. In May 1949 the executive board voted to withdraw the CIO from the four-year-old World Federation of Trade Unions because the federation, which included the Soviet labor movement, refused to endorse the Marshall Plan. "The purpose of a world organization of labor," argued CIO secretary-treasurer James Carey, "is to serve workers. It is not to serve Governments, or Politburos, or political parties, or any other group." The Marshall Plan, he stressed, was "based on the original principles of the WFTU," which were "peace and progress and well-being of workers everywhere." As a consequence of Communist and Communist-supported opposition to the Marshall Plan within the WFTU, Carey recommended—and the majority on the executive board agreed—to disaffiliate with the world organization. The Communists in the WFTU, members of the CIO majority concluded, had committed the federation to political rather than trade union action.[15] Later that year, the CIO helped found the International Confederation of Free Trade Unions, to provide labor with an alternative world organization which excluded Communists and which was anxious to "combat totalitarianism in all its forms."[16]

At the same time that the CIO withdrew from the WFTU, the CIO executive board endorsed the North Atlantic Treaty Organization as a "necessary development of American foreign policy. . . ." Representatives of the CIO had previously testified before congressional hearings on behalf of NATO. "We have every reason to believe," the CIO endorsement stated, that "the Pact will not divert money aimed for economic reconstruction to the purchase of arms. . . ." The left-wing minority had strongly disagreed. Joe Selly of the American Communications Association called NATO an "aggressive, imperialist war pact, outside the United Nations and designed to undermine the United Nations." Americans could not have both guns and butter, he said, and he preferred economic benefits for the American people. The National Maritime Union's Joe Curran, once a left-winger and by then ardently anti-Communist, replied: "Brother Selly, can you tell us how the Cominform stacks up with this? That is outside the United Nations, too." James Carey added, "As Joe Selly knows, . . . [NATO] is an effort by the one generous country in the world able to provide additional resources to enable these countries to build their own economies without fear and without aggression." The majority on the CIO executive board agreed and proceeded to pass the resolution endorsing NATO.[17]

Left-wing dissent was no longer tolerated by the CIO's anti-Communist majority, on either foreign or domestic policy. The central issue, as all concerned agreed, was a political one. Members of the left wing, one opponent summarized, "have opposed our entire political program, they have opposed us in the elections contrary to the decided politics and programs of CIO, and they have interfered with the legislative activities of CIO, both national and state. . . . [They] are in here trying to advance the cause of Sovietism rather than carrying on the battle of democracy." Murray agreed: "Plainly these differences are political. . . . Every division you have had in this board is political. Every division of major consequence affecting national policy is political. You can't beat around the bush about that. It is one of Communism and anti-Communism." Those on the CIO's left wing agreed on the political nature of the split, but blamed the majority for forcing its politics on the minority. "I am not opposed to the trades union movement using its independent strength in a political way," argued one left-wing leader, "but I am opposed to the CIO saying that unless every single affiliate of the CIO goes along with that policy they have no rights within CIO."[18]

At the 1949 spring executive board meeting, representatives of the anti-Communist majority presented a resolution requiring all members of the CIO board to "enforce the CIO constitution, . . . carry out the instructions of the CIO conventions," and carry out "the decisions of the Executive Board. . . ." Any board members unwilling to do this were asked to resign, and their unions were requested to insist upon such resignation. "This is a resolution," said Murray, "to alleviate the pains from which this organization suffers as a result of Communistic intrusion into the affairs of the national CIO. . . ." "Is it your thinking," one left-winger asked him, "that under this constitution, if I wish to enforce it, . . . our union has to endorse the Democratic Party?" "No," Murray replied; "if the national organization should adopt a policy endorsing anybody, then the national convention should take care to see to it . . . that it gives to individual affiliates the right to follow their own pursuits in that regard." When Harry Bridges questioned Murray further, Murray asked, "When you joined this organization didn't you decide to obey and respect its constitution?" "I never agreed at any time to the interpretation of the constitution now being made," Bridges replied. "Unfortunately you have indicated here again this afternoon that degree of complete irresponsibility that I have consistently attached to you," Murray told him. "[You say] to hell with the CIO's constitution, my constitution comes first . . . the most supercilious attitude imaginable."[19]

The resolution passed by a large margin and, thus armed, the anti-Communist leadership of the CIO prepared for the 1949 national CIO convention. There the committee on the constitution recommended adding a new section to prevent anyone from serving on the CIO's executive board who was a member of the Communist party or who "consistently pursues policies and activities directed toward the achievement of the program or the purposes of the Communist Party . . . rather than the objectives and policies set forth in the constitution of the CIO." Some convention delegates objected strenuously. One recalled that the chairman of the constitutional committee at the CIO's founding convention had said: "We are not writing a constitution for international unions. They have their own constitutions, and they govern insofar as their membership is concerned." "Obviously," commented one left-wing delegate, "this proposed legislation, while ostensibly directed against members of a political faith, really masks the attempt to dictate to individual international unions whom they shall choose to represent them, whom they shall choose to lead them, and what by-laws they shall or shall not adopt, under pain of punitive action." "We disagreed with you on the Board . . . on a great many . . . things," said Ben Gold, "because we have the right to disagree with the majority. . . . The majority rules only as long as it carries out the basic principles of democracy, and among those basic principles is [that] you cannot deprive the minority of its rights and its expression of opinions." "In 1933 and 1934 the minimum wage was Communistic, in the A.F. of L. books," Bridges reminded the convention; "and above all so was support of . . . industrial unionism and that rip-snorting John L. Lewis. . . ." Reuther protested against the objections by alleging, "These fellows take their instructions from the Soviet Union," and warned, "At this convention, since these brothers have not been able to make up their minds for themselves, we are going to have to make up their minds for them." The convention did so, and the constitutional amendment passed.[20]

Expulsion of the CIO's dissident left-wing unions followed shortly. The 1949 CIO convention voted to expel two international unions—the United Electrical Workers and the Farm Equipment Workers—and agreed to give the executive board power to oust any other unions whose policies and activities "are consistently directed toward the achievement of the program or the purposes of the Communist Party, any Fascist organization or any totalitarian movement, rather than the objectives and policies set forth in the constitution of the CIO." William Steinberg, a member of the executive board, promptly filed charges against ten more CIO international unions, and Murray named committees to conduct hearings.[21]

"The decision was made to have the hearings run by trade unionists, not by lawyers," recalled Thomas E. Harris, then assistant general counsel of the CIO. The CIO's anti-Communist majority evidently wanted to avoid a repeat of the recent trial of the top Communist party leaders: "The unions accused of being Communist-dominated were not permitted to have counsel in the hearings," Harris noted, "because we felt that the kind of counsel they had would result in disrupting and drawing the thing out forever. . . ." Nor was there a bill of particulars beyond the general directive given the executive board by the convention. The CIO's lawyers were also excluded from the hearings, though they interviewed the various witnesses for the prosecution and lined up the evidence, which was largely documentary. The committee members who sat in hearing reviewed the cases and made final recommendations to the board.[22]

The results were not surprising. The CIO executive board expelled nine of the ten unions brought before it, bringing the total of excluded unions to eleven.[23] "I am delighted that this board has taken these actions . . .," Murray commented. "We have cleaned our house; we have rid ourselves of these Communistic influences within the family of our trade unions and we have rendered a distinct service not only to American workers but also to our country. . . ."[24]

While the CIO leadership would not have conceded that it was losing some good labor people, it certainly was evident to those at the top that the ousted unions had a combined membership constituting a significant proportion of the CIO's total. The CIO leadership seems not to have viewed this risk as especially alarming, however, and jaunty remarks were made to the effect that, while the CIO would get along well without the left-wing unions, those unions would find the going hard by themselves. This prediction in large part proved accurate. At the 1950 annual CIO convention, Murray claimed that the organization had already regained most of its lost membership, through the return of approximately seventy percent of the expelled membership and the addition of many new members.[25]

Although the CIO leadership argued at the time that the left-wing unions were operating to the detriment of workers, even the left's harshest critics now generally concede that these unions were well run and that the arguments against them on trade union issues were, in David Saposs's words, "rather tenuous." Though some of the left-wing unions had small memberships, they could hardly be blamed for failure, since other unions in these fields had been no more successful. Unions such as the Longshoremen, the Fur and Leather Workers, and the United Electrical Workers, moreover, "were as effective organizationally . . . as any of the superlatively successful unions. . . ." During the expulsion hearings Amalgamated Clothing Workers' Jacob Potofsky told the head of one of the smaller unions, "You have done a good job, nobody is questioning what you have done organizationally. . . ."[26]

More important by far than simple bread-and-butter considerations in the CIO leadership's decision to expel the left-wing unions was its concern that these controversial organizations provided a considerable element of risk to the federation. The right-wing attacks which had pursued the labor movement from its beginnings had gained intensity and audience as the Cold War itself intensified, and the CIO, occupying the leftmost position in the American labor move-ment, was thereby most exposed to right-wing attacks. The right's campaign to link American labor with Communism took a particu-larly threatening form in legislation calculated to cut back on the rights and recognition labor had won only a few years before. The Taft-Hartley Act, with its prohibition against Communists in union offices, was angrily regarded by labor as an encroachment on its privileges made possible in part by the aroused anxieties of the Cold War. Other legislation antagonistic to labor proceeded through con-gressional hearings at a regular pace, and after 1950, the CIO found it beneficial to be able to cite its own ouster of Communism in self-defense.[27]

The real issue, of course, was not trade unionism, but politics, and in particular the divisive new anti-Communist politics of the Cold War. "I think we can all freely confess . . .," one hearings committee member said, "a bias against Communism as such, just as we are biased against murder, arson or rape; but we have approached this hearing with an open mind. . . ." What was at stake, said Potofsky, was "Communism versus our way of life, the democratic processes. . . ."[28]

Although Murray professed great concern for the threat posed by Communists to the long-range stability and success of the CIO ("What is transpiring in the United States today, . . ." he declared, "is but a repetition of the things the Communist Party has done in European countries in the trade union movement . . ."), he expressed none of these concerns during the long years of center-left alliance. It was only after the escalation of the Cold War, and after the bitter debates over American foreign policy, that Murray concluded that the pres-ence of Communists in the CIO was a danger. In the long run, it was foreign policy and the Marshall Plan in particular which became the test of loyalty, not only to the CIO but to the United States and democ-racy as well. Support of Wallace and opposition to the Marshall Plan, NATO, and Truman were the issues which "served to dramatize the growing split within the CIO" and which "irrevocably separated" the left-wing unions from the CIO's national leadership.[29] The hearings committee for Mine, Mill and Smelter Workers, for example, stressed that the union had opposed the Marshall Plan "as a means of rebuild-ing Germany, the home of Nazism, at the expense of its victim na-tions," and had in addition effectively converted its newspaper in 1948 "into a Progressive Party organ" and subordinated trade union news to "Progressive Party propaganda." The Longshoremen were held guilty of Communist domination for supporting the Chinese Communists against the Nationalists and calling the Truman plan similar to the "international gangsterism of Hitler" because it would help keep Fascist-like governments in power at the expense of democracies.[30]

The CIO hearings committees judged correlation with Communist party policy and deviation from United States foreign policy in yet another way: failure to criticize the Soviet Union. The United Public Workers, for example, proved to be " 'less blatantly and less openly' pro-Soviet than . . . other pro-Communist unions," its committee concluded; but the union was nonetheless faulted because it had "never publicly adopted any policy which in any way ran counter to the policies of the Communist party or the interests of the Soviet Union."[31] As Murray observed of all the left-wing union leaders: "I have never known . . . any of those gentlemen . . . , where the issue of Communism is a relevant question, to stand up on the floor and vote against Communism or Sovietism as such. . . . Never a word of criticism against Soviet policy has emanated from their lips."[32]

In the atmosphere of mutual hostility and condemnation prevailing within the CIO in 1949, did the left-wing unions receive a fair hearing? Arthur J. Goldberg, at that time the CIO's chief legal adviser, has strongly insisted that no civil liberties issue was at stake in any federation expulsion procedure. A federation of unions, he stressed, has the right to choose the unions with which it does or does not wish to be joined. Accordingly, a hearing was not a necessary preliminary to the ejection of a union; and Murray was within his rights in wanting, as he did, to throw out a group of unions without further delay.[33] As it was, the unions under examination were not permitted counsel, in order, CIO leaders claimed, to avoid disruptions and delays in the expulsion process. To prevent complaints, the CIO had trade unionists rather than the CIO's own legal department act as prosecutors.[34]

Setting aside the CIO's right to expel whomever it chose, for whatever reasons it chose, and in whatever manner it chose, the question of the overall fairness with which the expelled unions were treated remains pertinent, particularly as the CIO itself went to some trouble to give the appearance of impartial, objective hearings. Goldberg himself has stated that the unions in question were entitled to an objective hearing and an opportunity to present their cases,[35] but the unions complained that the hearings were a sham and that the hearings committees and the CIO leadership had decided the outcome before the defense evidence and arguments were presented.[36] One of the defendants' major contentions was that within the structure of the CIO as originally conceived, certain guarantees for individual union autonomy were provided. These guarantees, the defendants argued, had been eroded since 1946 by the national CIO, which had made every effort to impose uniformity on individual unions. These attempts, the left-wing unions stressed, had been improper in every sense and therefore any violation of them did not constitute grounds for expulsion from the federation, which had itself departed from its original function.[37]

The CIO leadership regarded the issue of autonomy as simply a smoke screen, irrelevant to the matter at hand. "Now the Communist Party and these people are going to engage themselves in the dissemination of a lot of tripe," said Murray. "They are going to use this fictitious, hypocritical slogan of theirs, conformity." "The CIO is making no effort to impose political uniformity on Mine, Mill or any other affiliate of the CIO," Jacob Potofsky commented. "This is still a free country. All of us know that there is room enough in the CIO for honest differences of opinion, and this has been made abundantly clear throughout the years." He pointed to the CIO-PAC as "one of those instrumentalities that is impartial as to parties." However, "honest differences of opinion," as a criteria setting the boundaries of discussion, did not allow for divergences on such policy matters as the Marshall Plan, Henry Wallace, or NATO. "There is no room in the CIO for an affiliate whose policies undermine the fundamental democratic objectives of the CIO," Potofsky declared. Another member of an investigating committee noted that in response to the question, "Will you or will you not carry out the policies and objectives of the CIO?" the left-wing union leaders answered, "We will carry out those policies which our union directs us to carry out." "Now that certainly is no answer to the question," he observed. "It just proves they have carried out the policies they were directed by the Communist Party to carry out . . . , and they are going to continue to carry them out. . . ."[38]

The policy the CIO's leadership insisted upon using as a gauge of dedication to the CIO was a political policy, embracing the Democratic party and the Truman administration's foreign and domestic policy. In early 1947 Murray had urged (he could not insist) that his executive board members withdraw from both the ADA and the PCA. After he had stressed that the question was one of furthering the purely trade union interests of the CIO and was not one of political parties, all of the CIO's executive leadership had pledged to support instead the activities and policies of the CIO's political arm, the CIO-PAC. The CIO had not withdrawn from politics, however, as the CIO-PAC's existence testified, and one year later Murray used this agreement as a bond of allegiance to the CIO-PAC's policies and programs—by then including opposition to Wallace and soon after including endorsement of Truman. A year later, the left-wing unions' decision to support Wallace was regarded by the CIO majority as evidence that these unions were disrupting and undermining the CIO.

Similarly, the new section added to the CIO constitution in 1949 by the anti-Communist majority acted to limit political expression. This section provided for the expulsion of unions whose "policies and activities" were "consistently directed toward the achievement of the program or the purposes of the Communist Party . . . rather than the objectives and policies set forth in the constitution of the CIO."[39] Although this section appeared to be a reasonable organizational requirement, its purpose and effect were closely linked with Cold War politics. The "objectives and policies" of the CIO could be, and in the case of the ousted unions were, political in nature, and opposition to the United States' foreign policy was regarded by the CIO's anti-Communist majority as "policies and activities directed toward the achievement of the program or purposes of the Communist Party." The issue at stake in the unions' expulsion was not devotion to trade unionism or loyalty to the CIO and its constitution but rather political solidarity in the dangerous eddies of Cold War politics.

5

A New Liberalism

The bitter debates over Cold War foreign policy, over cooperation with American Communists, over the Wallace candidacy, and over the expulsion of leftists from the CIO were accompanied by the emergence of a "new liberalism." Those liberal intellectuals who generally endorsed the foreign policies of the Truman administration, and who supported the purging of Communists from American life, sought to redefine American liberalism in response to the demands and pressures of an increasingly powerful domestic conservative movement as well as the dangers of the Cold War world. In the process they abandoned many traditional liberal tenets—the belief in progress, in man's goodness, in popular democracy, and in world peace—replacing them with a chastened and, in their view, "realistic" philosophy which stressed man's sinfulness, the seeming inevitability of conflict among nations, and the dangers of democratic rule. The new liberals identified not with the left, as had been the case in the 1930s, but with the center; they identified not with the people, but with an elite. Unlike the liberals of the thirties, who had criticized the social order, the new liberals stressed the beneficence of American political and economic institutions.

| * |

With the development and deepening of Cold War, those liberals, radicals, and former radicals who were linked by their opposition to Communism and the Soviet Union undertook a thoroughgoing reevaluation of the underlying and unifying assumptions and goals of the American left. They did so against a background of disillusionment with Stalinism and radical activism made more complex by their general disillusionment with mankind—fostered by the horrors of Nazi genocide and the compounded atrocities of World War II.

Some of the basic themes of the Cold War left's self-evaluation were early articulated by Lionel Trilling, a leading literary critic and former Trotskyist whose carefully considered views played a significant role in the development of the new, postwar liberalism. In his 1946 review of Theodore Dreiser's *The Bulwark*, Trilling wrote that prewar liberalism had failed, not from the lack of nerve which radicals had once made their standard charge against liberalism, but from a deficiency of "heart and mind"; liberalism had failed because it had shared too much in common with radicalism, in particular its focus upon utopian-oriented activism. Trilling expanded upon this theme in his highly praised novel *The Middle of the Journey*, published the following year. Here he portrayed a cast of characters ranging from naive idealists to a soured former radical in order to demonstrate his thesis that man is not fundamentally good, progress is not inevitable or even probable, and that idealistic planning for a new society is mistaken utopianism. Trilling's protagonist, however, rejects total pessimism, with its attendant social and moral paralysis; instead, he determines to affirm life, although with a keen awareness of its limitations. This, for Trilling, constituted the middle of the journey—the way of moderation, which he believed held far more promise than had utopianism.[1]

The Protestant theologian Reinhold Niebuhr had been saying much the same thing since the early 1930s. Niebuhr, a former member of the Socialist party, had early in his career rejected his initial attraction to Deweyian instrumentalism and the Social Gospel. According to Dewey, man's reason, through education and experiment, could effect beneficial social change and eventually achieve the good society; according to the spokesmen of the Social Gospel, the practical application of the Christian ethic could bring the realization of the Kingdom of God on earth. Niebuhr took issue, however, with the assumption that man could in any way perfect himself, and he proceeded to develop a Neo-Calvinist theology which stressed man's sinfulness and need for reliance upon God.[2]

Niebuhr held that man was free and self-determined but possessed of an overwhelming yearning for power which made him misuse his freedom, abuse justice, and subordinate other lives to his will. Pointing to the unpredictable but essentially negative factor of man's will, Niebuhr denied the validity of any law of historical progress. Instead, he posed a historical process which intertwined the development of both good and evil. Niebuhr condemned as "utopians" and "sentimental moralists" those who would not acknowledge man's sinfulness and the integral role of evil in the historical process; he reserved his praise for those who agreed that man's innate pride of power was a fundamental factor of human history.[3]

Niebuhr was intensely political, and his theological writings served as direct commentaries on contemporary domestic and foreign affairs. He feared individuals' unchecked drive for power and consequently feared dictatorship, where one or a few persons' power over many was total and the probability of doing evil was great. Like others on the left, Niebuhr had opposed Fascism during the 1930s and World War II; like other Socialist party members, he had also opposed the Communist party. Following World War II, Niebuhr focused his attacks on international Communism. Communists appalled him because they imagined themselves "masters of historical destiny" and thus usurped the role of God. They believed earthly perfection was obtainable and was present in their regime. The Moscow Trials had decisively confirmed Niebuhr's conviction that terrible political crimes could and would be committed in the absence of checks on power. He contended that those idealists, or "utopians," who overlooked the essential evil of any form of totalitarianism were doing a dangerous disservice to their fellow-beings. Their idealism, Niebuhr stressed, was superficial and not fundamentally concerned with justice and freedom. Instead, these idealists believed blindly in the basic goodness of all mankind and were deceived by those who, in the name of uplifting the masses, were cynically using these "sentimental moralists" for their own ends.[4]

Niebuhr assessed mankind harshly but did not regard himself as a pessimist. He stressed that he had rejected a blind optimism in order to confront the realities of life.[5] Niebuhr saw danger in idealism and called for an acknowledgment of the actualities of power, but he rejected the political "realist" label — possibly because both Hitler and Mussolini had once claimed it.[6] His critics charged that his assumptions led to complacency and passivity, but Niebuhr replied that action could and should be taken as long as it was accompanied by a deep faith and a proper acknowledgment of the tragedy of human history.[7] Fond of the metaphorical balance wheel and the middle way between extremes, Niebuhr concluded that he had chosen a moderate position between pessimism and the kind of optimism which was unrealistic and which ultimately propelled the disillusioned into pessimism and despair. He maintained that he had chosen a middle way between cynical realism, which he equated with totalitarianism, and naive idealism, which he characterized as susceptible to the "subtler types of coercion." He stressed that he had chosen a middle way between complacency and the kind of idealistic activity which ignored history's inherent tragedy and turned passive and despairing when confronted with reality.[8]

By 1949 the middle way advocated by Niebuhr and Trilling had, in the hands of liberal historian Arthur Schlesinger, Jr., become the Vital Center. In his book by that title, Schlesinger plotted freedom and totalitarianism on a circular instead of the more familiar linear political graph; Fascism and Communism thus appeared together under the common denominator of "totalitarianism" rather than at opposite linear extremes. The remainder of his circle consisted of varying realizations of freedom, and the point 180 degrees from totalitarianism represented the greatest degree of freedom. If plotted linearly, Schlesinger stressed, this point was the absolute center.[9]

According to Schlesinger's scheme, American conservatism was to the right of center and lacked both stability and political responsibility. In times of crisis, conservatism tilted toward Fascism and thus held little promise for saving free society. To the left of center, according to Schlesinger, were "doughface" liberals, those who believed in progress and human perfectibility and refused to recognize the dangers of power. These liberals were naive, unrealistic, and willing to turn to Communism to accomplish their goals. The safekeeping of free society could not be trusted to "doughface" liberals any more than to conservatives.[10]

Instead, Schlesinger pointed to the virtues of the political center, which he declared was the home of the new postwar liberalism. The political center he described possessed tough-mindedness, a firm grip on realism, a commitment to freedom, and an "unconditional rejection of totalitarianism." While these new liberals of the center understood that man was most secure in a society which protected him from want, they also realized that man was "intoxicated by power and hence most human in a society which distributes power widely." The political center, Schlesinger stressed, had no need to "invoke Marx at every turn in the road." Rather, it had returned to the historic concept of liberalism, to "a belief in the integrity of the individual, in the limited state, in due process of law, in empiricism and gradualism."[11]

Schlesinger, whose deep interest in social reform seems to have stemmed at least in part from a desire for social stability,[12] was wary of human nature and called for a wide distribution of power to check man's fundamental drive for power.[13] The Vital Center was thus the expression of a broad intellectual movement following World War II which stressed the importance of decentralization, checks and balances, and a pluralist conception of the democratic process. Pluralism as a method for understanding the political process was rooted in the liberal analysis of the early twentieth century, especially in the writings of Walter Lippman and Herbert Croly. In the late 1930s it had enjoyed a renaissance in the work of such disillusioned radicals as John Chamberlain, James Burnham, Sidney Hook, Max Eastman and others; and in the years following the close of World War II it became an enormously popular theory for liberal intellectuals seeking an alternative to Marxian class analysis. "The stability of the body politic in the United States, wrote political scientist David Truman, "does not rest on such a thin foundation as that suggested by the theories of class conflict or the dominance of occupational interests. The foundation is stronger, and . . . more complex. . . ." The pluralists did not deny conflict; they denied the Marxist stratification of classes—bourgeoisie, and proletariat—and the Marxist assumption that class interests are primary. Pluralist theory instead proposed a diversity of equally intense conflicts, which cut across any simple class stratification and provided stability through the balanced tensions of intricately dispersed group interests.[14]

In addition to providing an alternative to Marxian class analysis, pluralist theory also helped to reconcile liberals' traditional concern for individual freedom with the more recent liberal determination to improve the economic and social quality of individuals' lives. Both the traditional and the more recent liberalism were rooted in an interest in the public good; conflict arose, however, because one form of public good seemed to call for the contraction of government while the other required government's expansion. Pluralist theory helped to resolve this conflict for liberals by stressing that in actuality, power is not limited to the state but is widely distributed among interest groups throughout society. Liberals subscribing to pluralist assumptions could thus accept big government on behalf of the public good without relinquishing their long-held fear of government power in relation to individual rights.[15] Consequently, pluralist theory provided an ideological rationale for the New Deal as well as for the emerging postwar Vital Center.

Max Ascoli, an Italian liberal and journalist who had escaped from Fascist Italy, enlisted the aid of pluralist analysis to establish and defend his concept of the Vital Center. In *The Power of Freedom*, published in the same year as Schlesinger's *The Vital Center*, Ascoli rejected both Communism and Fascism as totalitarian and expressed concern about humankind's increasing dependence upon the political and economic institutions of ever more powerful states. He did not wish to return to the old laissez-faire capitalism: "A minimum of economic and political well-being for all men is a matter of inter-human and international concern. . . ." He attempted, however, to define an area of freedom between laissez-faire capitalism and the all-powerful state which would constitute a humane middle way. To accomplish this goal he enlisted the aid of a pluralistic conception of group politics on an international scale: "The more effectively the pre-political organizations operate," he wrote, "the greater the wedge that will be driven between the individual and the state. The state can never again assert that the individual belongs to it. . . ." The "oneness and massiveness of economics" which he feared would thus be counteracted by the variety in political systems in the world—the "multiplicity and elasticity of politics."[16]

The pluralist analysis also proved useful for economic theorists concerned with establishing and protecting a middle way between traditional capitalism and a totally socialized economy. The political journalist Irwin Ross had, like other new liberals, moved away from advocating total economic planning because of its "curtailment of economic freedoms and its invasion of political freedoms." Ross instead proposed a pluralist model, "freedom through diversity"—a mixed economy featuring limited, democratic, and decentralized planning to achieve the dual goal of economic well-being for all in a setting of expanding freedom. Others before Ross had written of the advantages of a mixed economy, but Ross more clearly grounded his conception on a pluralist base. The mixed economy, he wrote, would best combine "the traditional virtues of both socialism and capitalism" by "introducing into the economic realm the same principle that has long infused our political life: divided authority, a multiplicity of power blocs, and checks and balances."[17]

John Kenneth Galbraith, a leading liberal economist and important example of the postwar intellectual drawn to politics, wholeheartedly embraced the pluralist theory in its applications to the economy. Recognizing the replacement of the competitive capitalist model with concentrated centers of economic power, Galbraith rejected anti-trust measures—a typical early twentieth-century liberal solution to the big corporations—because their effectiveness was limited to an economy where monopoly was the exception rather than the rule. Galbraith stressed that since aspects of monopoly were pervasive throughout the American economy, it was unrealistic to expect that these economic giants could be forced, by law, "to act as though they had no economic power—as though each were insignificantly small."

Galbraith, however, rejected a socialized economy as an acceptable solution to concentrated economic power, and drew instead upon pluralist theory to support his belief that the American economy was an eminently workable one. Competition or government control were not the only possible restraints on private market power, he argued. Instead, the concentration of power in business corporations had been paralleled during the twentieth century by the rise of competing centers of power in the non-business sector, which provided the countervailing power necessary to check possible abuses of private interests. Labor had become organized and had grown into big labor; retailers had begun to protect their interests against the power of wholesalers. Farmers had formed organizations to protect their economic interests, and persons in professions had developed associations for the same purpose. In all, "the existence of market power creates an incentive to the organization of another position of power that neutralizes it." However, the organization of countervailing power required government assistance "in order to use [that power] against the market authority to which they had previously been subordinate." Galbraith thus subscribed to the pluralist theory that power is diversified and does not reside solely in the state; his scheme saw the state as playing an essential role, however: that of preventing any of the rival interest groups from dominating the others. The pluralist equivalent for Adam Smith's invisible hand—the substitution of group competition, or countervailing power, for market competition—would only work, according to Galbraith, with the assistance of significant governmental action on behalf of the public interest. Galbraith assured his readers, however, that this government activity was entirely normal and not to be feared: "Steps to strengthen countervailing power are not, in principle, different from steps to strengthen competition." Further, "the growth of countervailing power strengthens the capacity of the economy for autonomous self-regulations and thereby lessens the amount of over-all government control or planning that is required or sought." Government takes action, Galbraith asserted, so that future government action may be rendered unnecessary.[18]

In both politics and economics the new liberals aimed at deflecting conflict and enhancing stability. In time, they would come to see McCarthyism as a product not of conservative politics and the Cold War but of America's radical tradition. Senator Joseph R. McCarthy, they argued in a revealing phrase, was a product of the "radical right." The "people," with whom liberals had identified in the thirties, thus became in the fifties enemies of civil liberties and threats to the stability of the political system.[19]

The new liberals thus sought consensus as the desired product of the group process. The most dramatic example of consensus in postwar America appeared in the bipartisan support for the Truman administration's foreign policy during the early years of the Cold War. Consensus was also present, however, in postwar domestic politics, where despite noisy challenges from the right, both Republican and Democratic parties eventually joined in the assumption that the New Deal had come to stay.[20] Consensus was perceived as the norm, while other manifestations received little or unfavorable attention. The historian Richard Hofstadter provided historical credence for social scientists' conclusions that the McCarthy phenomenon had radical rather than conservative roots. In his contribution to *The New American Right*, as well as in *The Age of Reform*, Hofstadter portrayed the Populists and Progressives as cranks motivated by status frustrations and desire for personal economic gain, rather than by genuine interest in reform. These leftists were outside the mainstream of historical American consensus, had made little contribution to that consensus, and shared links with the more commonly despised elements on America's political right. "A large part of the Populist-Progressive tradition has turned sour, become illiberal and ill-tempered," Hofstadter wrote; consequently, he pointed out, the Populist-Progressive tradition bred a Huey Long and Father Coughlin in the 1930s and a Joe McCarthy in the 1950s.[21]

Hofstadter's thesis was widely accepted by a historical profession which previously had admired the Populists and the Progressives as progenitors of reform.[22] While historians during the 1920s and 1930s had embraced an interpretation of history which stressed the emergence of progress through conflict, historians of the 1950s stressed continuity instead of change, homogeneity and pluralism instead of dualism, and stability instead of conflict. Daniel Boorstin called attention to Americans' historically pragmatic and non-ideological response to a common challenge. From this, he pointed out, there developed a national unity unscarred by splintering doctrinairism and characterized above all else by practicality. Louis Hartz stressed the virtual unanimity and center-mindedness of the American political tradition. America had no history of true conservatism nor of true radicalism, he insisted, but only variations within a broad tradition of the center.[23] Consensus historians, in their search for stability, rejected progressive historians' assumptions that progress was a historic certainty. Consensus history was grounded on a distinct pessimism and contained an emphasis on irony, tragedy, decline, and defeat.[24]

In rejecting radicalism, pluralists rejected as well the trusted and frequently used radical weapon of appeals to the masses through revolutionary ideology. Pluralists regarded ideology as a divisive element which undermined the stability of the group process by sharpening the masses' class identity. Furthermore, they feared the emotional appeal to mob action implicit and explicit in radical ideology. Although pluralists were relieved to find ideology markedly absent from the political debates of the 1950s,[25] they remained anxious: a distrust of human nature, together with observations of revolutionary movements and the Third Reich, led them to fear the actions of masses whipped to emotional frenzy. During the 1930s progressive liberals as well as radicals had elevated "the people" to a position of special eminence and had regarded American life as a series of scenes pitting "the people" against "privilege." Pluralists during the late 1940s and 1950s, however, pinpointed the roots of the Red Scare in "the people"[26] and attempted to maintain elaborate institutional buffers between "the people" and political action, through the group process. Further, pluralist intellectuals perceived a disturbing anti-intellectualism and suspicion directed toward themselves. They probed the American lifestyle for explanations and concluded that anti-intellectualism was a theme in American life. Hofstadter noted that while McCarthyism "aroused the fear that the critical mind was at a ruinous discount in this country," anti-intellectualism had been a part of the American tradition from the beginning and had moved in cyclical patterns. David Riesman and Nathan Glazer, in developing their status-frustration theory as an explanation for McCarthyism, centered on the bigot whose frustrations were focused on eastern intellectuals. Such bigots approved of McCarthy's methods, "which [were] so obviously not sissified," but they were little interested in McCarthy's ends, "which were drawn with the foregoing constellation in mind." The political scientist Hans J. Morgenthau complained of the "loneliness to which American society relegates the intellectual in a specifically American way."[27]

Pluralists also rejected the perennial optimism and idealism embraced by the political left. They refused to mix morality and politics and buried all memories of the "visionary left," convinced that thereby they were employing a necessary tough-mindedness and attaining a firmer grip on reality. The outcome was a wide acceptance of political "realism" as a policy guide during the late 1940s and the 1950s, particularly in the field of foreign policy. The development of atomic weapons had created an excess of power at a time of increasingly dangerous confrontation between the Soviet Union and the United States. Realism, with its appreciation of power and distrust of both human nature and moralistic policy goals, seemed to many an appropriate response to the demands of the Cold War. Among others, diplomat George F. Kennan, political scientist Hans J. Morgenthau, and columnist Walter Lippmann called for an end to morally infused rhetoric and ideological crusades. In place of moral abstractions, these political realists sought a foreign policy based upon the recognition of national interest and power as the governing factors in foreign affairs.

Kennan, in his 1947 article "The Sources of Soviet Conduct," contrasted "realism" with "moralism-legalism," which he described as the dangerous belief "that it should be possible to suppress the chaotic and dangerous aspirations of governments in the international field by the acceptance of some system of legal rules and restraints." Conflict abroad was as certain as was the use of power for national ends. "To the American mind," he pointed out, "it is implausible that people should have positive aspirations, and ones that they regard as legitimate, more important to them than the peacefulness and orderliness of international life."[28] In a similar vein, Morgenthau proposed a foreign policy free from moral abstractions and guided by considerations of power. "The intoxication with moral abstractions is indeed one of the great sources of weakness and failure in American policy," he wrote in 1951.[29] Another political scientist, Robert E. Osgood, warned that idealists in foreign affairs "may underestimate the sheer military threat of organized communism in their preoccupation with its social, moral, or intellectual roots." To some degree, he argued, Americans would have to depend upon opposing force with force.[30] Though realist analysis led some critics, most notably Walter Lippmann, into sharp disagreements with the policies of the Truman administration, in general realism was placed in the service of the new foreign policy of containment.[31]

Paradoxically, political realism stressed readiness for conflict abroad, while consensus politics sought to quiet conflict at home.

Realism in foreign policy decried efforts to end armed conflict as dangerously illusionary, while consensus in domestic politics sought the end of ideology and of radical threats to the status quo. This dual response to international and domestic affairs was consistent, however, if viewed as a reaction to the pressures of the Cold War. Realism in foreign affairs meant acceptance of power politics in the active resistance to Communism's expansion abroad; consensus in domestic affairs signified maintaining the stabilizing influence of an already established system which minimized the impact of radicalism through the group process. Realism and consensus were a common response to pluralism's evaluation of human nature and its consequent call for a system of checks upon human instincts. In this sense, the domestic and foreign policy responses of realism and consensus were reflex images, shaped by an essentially pluralistic world view.

Fundamental to pluralist thought in all its postwar manifestations—realism, consensus, and the Vital Center—was a loss of optimism, a dwindling assumption of progress, and a declining conviction of the fundamental goodness of mankind. The literary and social critic Leslie Fiedler, himself a former Marxist, called it "an end to innocence."[32] Whether expressed in a disillusionment with radical politics or a Neo-Calvinist emphasis on the sinfulness of man, this "loss of innocence" described a mood which had an impact far broader than the intellectual implications of pluralist thought alone. This mood was characterized by what exponents called a tragic view of mankind's experience, an acceptance of evil, and a resignation to fate. Both liberalism and Marxism had been grounded on a faith in scientific rationalism. Science had proved to be amoral, however, and disillusioned intellectuals, shocked by the new age of atomic weaponry, branded scientists "naive."[33] Leftist intellectuals, numbed by the collapse of the modern dream, showed new respect for intuition and religion, especially of an anti-perfectionist cast, and were receptive as well to the existentialist focus on anguish as the central element of human existence. Both anguish and evil were perceived as commonplace in the human experience, and leftists accepted the banality of evil with increasing equilibrium and a sense of resignation to fate.[34]

The American left had thus undergone fundamental changes since the 1930s. Radical ranks were rapidly thinning and the American Communist party, propelled by its own internal crisis as well as by the external pressures of the Red Scare, was by the late 1940s headed for political oblivion.[35] The left-liberals, those who during the

1930s and the war years had been most receptive to the popular front, were by the end of 1948 divided and demoralized. Some defected to the political right, or joined the new liberals of the Vital Center. Still others withdrew from political activities altogether. The new liberals rejected all ties with the left and self-consciously claimed for themselves the political center. Reformism lingered on after World War II, but the thrust behind it did not reflect either the sense of urgency or the excitement of the 1930s. Radicalism dwindled away almost entirely. The decline of the old left and the emergence of a new liberalism shaped in turn the response of liberals to the growing Red Scare and to what came, after 1950, to be called McCarthyism.

6

McCarthy, National Security, and Liberal Paralysis

As the new decade opened, prospects for long-term peace and security for the United States appeared dim. The year 1950 began on an especially solemn note, as Truman in January announced that he had ordered the Atomic Energy Commission to proceed in its development of the hydrogen bomb. During the spring of 1950, newspaper headlines were dominated by the rise of Joseph R. McCarthy, whose attacks on the Truman administration soon made "McCarthyism" a household word. Then, in June, the Cold War quickly escalated into hot war on the Korean peninsula as North Korean forces crossed the thirty-eighth parallel dividing Communist North from anti-Communist South Korea. Shortly thereafter, Truman ordered two divisions of ground troops to Korea and authorized a naval blockade of the north. Five years after the end of World War II, the United States was once again at war.[1]

The American Communist party responded to news of the invasion by asserting that, contrary to official reports, South Korea had precipitated the war by invading the north, as part of a large-scale United States' plot to gain control over East Asia and establish in Korea "powerful bases from which to make war upon the new China and the Soviet Union." The remnants of the Progressive party objected to the United Nations Security Council's call to aid South Korea and opposed any United Nations action at all until Communist China received recognition and Russia returned to the council. Henry Wallace, despite his hatred of war, fully supported the Security Council's actions and United States' involvement: he told a friend, "When my country gets into war and that war is sanctioned by the United Nations, I have to support my country and the U.N." Wallace and the Progressive party split over this issue, and Wallace finally resigned from the party.[2]

As Wallace's decision indicated, the advent of a fighting war, particularly one in which the United Nations played an important role, rallied liberals in defense of Truman's actions and further weakened the old popular-front left. Members of Congress, normally jealous of congressional prerogatives, justified the presidential act which had committed the nation to war without the prior consent of Congress. Senator Paul H. Douglas, the liberal Illinois Democrat, argued forcefully that the founding fathers "did not want to tie our country's hands by requiring congressional assent for all employment of armed force," but rather intended to leave to the president the power to use force to "repel sudden attacks," even if not authorized to do so by Congress. Acknowledging the gravity of this precedent, should the United States ever be led by "a reckless and militaristic President," Douglas nevertheless insisted that presidential action of this type was "not equivalent to a declaration of war." Hubert Humphrey agreed, declaring that Congress should not delay the executive branch's actions by debate "as to whether the President can act to protect the security of this nation or to protect the security of American lives." "If the President had done any less," said Senator Estes Kefauver, "we would have forfeited the position of leadership of the United States in the free world today." Wayne Morse joined with senators on both sides of the aisle in a "clear pledge to back up the President in his statement for the defense of America's security in Asia."[3]

Support from anti-Communist liberals was never really in doubt; Morse clearly expressed the liberal relief "that we have at long last . . . made clear to the freedom-loving peoples of the world that the false, lying, vicious Communist propaganda which would make it appear that they cannot count on the United States to defend freedom in the world is really false and lying and vicious." Philip Murray enthusiastically supported the United States' actions, and the CIO executive board called for "complete and unhesitating cooperation of every individual in America." And the ADA, in line with its foreign policy statement from *Toward Total Peace*, declared that Truman had acted in accord with the tradition established by Roosevelt's Quarantine Speech.[4]

Complete accord on foreign policy had not existed even among anti-Communist liberals before Korea: at the ADA annual convention in 1949 there had still remained a small but vocal minority who "tore their souls" before accepting the Niebuhr and Schlesinger position supporting containment and NATO. The many drafts of the foreign policy statement for that convention indicated the survival of a continuing debate between supporters and opponents of the military aspects of containment. By the time of the ADA's annual convention in early 1950, however, *Commonweal* noted that despite the presence of a small group of delegates who "consistently expressed doubt about this country's present foreign policy," the ADA leadership's viewpoint—which *Commonweal* called " 'hard,' " and "sternly in accord with Acheson-Burnham-Alsop 'total diplomacy' "—had prevailed without major challenge. The Korean War quieted what little dissent remained within the ADA. The *New Republic* reported that the delegates to the 1951 convention were "surprised to find themselves in agreement, bordering unanimity, on the major crucial questions facing American liberals." By 1955, ADA leader Joseph Rauh described Reinhold Niebuhr without qualification as "the architect of the ADA foreign policy."[5]

Those liberals who assumed that the Truman administration's response in Korea would quiet red-baiting against Democratic liberals were mistaken. The war served merely to exacerbate the Red Scare by convincing Americans that world Communism did pose a threat to United States security. At home, the Red Scare was symbolized most flamboyantly by Senator Joseph R. McCarthy, the Wisconsin Republican who had risen to national prominence in early 1950 through fast footwork and a barrage of accusations against supposed Communists in the State Department. McCarthy's particularly colorful form of red-baiting, however, only barely indicated the extent to which the Red Scare had penetrated the governmental process by 1950. Conservatives had complained of the "Red" tinge of the New Deal since the time of Franklin D. Roosevelt and, from 1946 on, had intensified their efforts to link the New Deal and Fair Deal administrations with Communist conspiracy and infiltration. Truman had pungently and characteristically denounced such charges but had then, through his domestic loyalty program and his increasingly hard line in foreign policy, raised the level of public anxiety and underlined the right wing's case. By 1950, when conservative pressure for internal security legislation had reached a new peak, the White House found it impossible to contain or divert it.[6]

The internal security legislation which Truman so strongly opposed in 1950 had its roots in a 1947 bill proposed by Republican congressmen Karl E. Mundt of South Dakota and Richard M. Nixon of

California. The Mundt-Nixon bill sought to require "Communist political organizations" to register with the attorney general, while at the same time making it a crime punishable by fine and imprisonment to participate "in any manner" in any movement conspiring "to do anything" toward overthrowing the United States government on behalf of a foreign-controlled dictatorship. The registration requirement together with the punitive provision threatened the Fifth Amendment's protection against self-incrimination, and the proposed legislation in other ways appeared to threaten First Amendment guarantees of free speech as well as freedoms of the press and of assembly. Despite its constitutionally dubious provisions, the bill passed the House over the protests of only a handful of congressmen, including Vito Marcantonio and Leo Isacson, Adolph Sabath and Emanuel Celler, Chester Holifield, Jacob Javits, and John Carroll.[7]

Congress adjourned before the Mundt-Nixon bill could come to the Senate floor, but the 1948 Republican platform enthusiastically endorsed the bill and called for the election of a Republican Congress in order to pass it. In 1949, despite the Truman victory and Democratic landslide in the 1948 elections, conservative forces were once again pushing for the Mundt-Nixon legislation, and Mundt, by then a senator, introduced the bill in the Senate while Nixon proposed a companion measure in the House. Truman had opposed the legislation from the outset, but as his veto message would point out, he did so as much in the belief that such legislation would be ineffective against Communism as in protest that it would put the government "in the thought-control business." He was not adverse to proposing his own less drastic internal security measures in an attempt to sidetrack the Mundt-Nixon bill; in 1950 Senator Warren G. Magnuson, a liberal Democrat from Washington, introduced a bill containing Truman's proposals for several changes in existing laws. The administration's effort had little effect on the growing conservative demand for internal security legislation, however, and in August Senator Patrick A. McCarran, a conservative Nevada Democrat, reported out of committee an internal security bill including not only the Mundt-Nixon proposals but several additional internal security measures. A companion bill soon reported out of committee in the House passed overwhelmingly. Now Senate liberals had to confront the measure on the Senate floor.[8]

By the summer of 1950 Senate liberals were few and increasingly defensive. Senator Herbert H. Lehman, who was elected in a special off-year election to replace Robert Wagner, later noted that when he arrived in Congress there was "a strange confusion—especially among the liberals. . . . They seemed to feel somewhat isolated from the mainstream." He added, "There was an impression among them that they were aliens in an alien land and needed to accommodate themselves to the conservative majority."[9] The response of Senate liberals to the McCarran Act was a revealing example both of this need to accommodate the conservatives and of the new liberalism in action. The "only possible way of beating the McCarran bill," a small group of Senate liberals decided, was to propose a preventive detention bill in place of the registration bill. Co-sponsored by liberal Democrats Harley M. Kilgore, Paul Douglas, Hubert Humphrey, Estes Kefauver, Herbert Lehman, Frank P. Graham of North Carolina, and William Benton of Connecticut, the bill authorized the attorney general, during presidentially declared internal security emergencies, to detain persons whom he had "reason to believe" might act subversively. Lehman defended the provision as a "piece of constructive legislation," and Kefauver added his opinion that the government needed this sort of safeguard "at the present time." Humphrey argued that the detention bill was much tougher than the McCarran bill, which he called the "cream-puff special," while Douglas stressed that the detention bill would crack down on potential sabotage and espionage without endangering free speech and association. Members of the White House staff were less confident of the detention bill's potential for protecting civil liberties: one aide quietly branded the measure a "concentration camp bill" and held that it contained more dangers than did the McCarran measure. Truman decided to withhold comment until such time as the detention bill passed Congress.[10]

The detention bill did pass Congress, but in a form which its liberal sponsors had not anticipated. Senate Majority Leader Scott Lucas of Illinois, sensitive to the threat which the Communist issue posed to his reelection bid that autumn, successfully proposed that the emergency detention measure be added to the omnibus McCarran bill. Only a handful of liberal senators—including Lehman, Kefauver, and Graham—voted against the bill in its final form. Senators Humphrey, Douglas, Kilgore, and Benton, the remaining four sponsors of the original internment measure, voted with the majority to pass the McCarran Internal Security Act of 1950. Truman promptly vetoed the legislation, but the internal security issue had gotten well beyond his control, or the control of the original small band of liberal senators who had attempted to divert it. Almost immediately, the House overrode Truman's veto, 286 to 48. In the Senate, Douglas and Humphrey, with a handful of other liberals, led a filibuster to delay the vote and win supporters, but their effort finally collapsed and the Senate overrode the Truman veto by a vote of 57 to 10.[11]

The personification of the Communist issue by 1950 was clearly Joseph R. McCarthy, whose methods congressional liberals without exception strongly opposed. The Communist issue itself, however, proved to be an extraordinarily difficult one for congressional liberals, especially under the pressures of the Korean War and the McCarthy phenomenon. Liberal senators have, since that time, measured their success in dealing with "McCarthyism" by their courage in direct confrontation with Senator McCarthy himself. Wayne Morse, for example, later commented of Senator Lehman that "his record against McCarthy will stand to his everlasting credit." Lehman did show unusual willingness to confront McCarthy and to defend publicly those whom McCarthy attacked—including George Marshall, Charles Bohlen, Philip C. Jessup, John Carter Vincent, and John Paton Davies. Further, Lehman supported the challenge of a leading left-winger, Corliss Lamont, to McCarthy's Government Operations subcommittee procedures, and also made direct requests that McCarthy substantiate his charges or withdraw them. Pursuing "McCarthyism" beyond the Wisconsin senator himself, Lehman challenged Senator McCarran's investigatory Internal Security subcommittee and asked that an investigation be made on the basis of charges against it by columnist Joseph Alsop.[12]

Another liberal senator who operated with special boldness against McCarthy was the Connecticut Democrat William Benton. In 1951, immediately following the report of the Maryland Senatorial Election Investigation, which contained damaging evidence of McCarthy's interference in the 1950 Maryland senatorial election, Benton called for further investigations and proposed that McCarthy be expelled from the Senate. He submitted ten specific charges to the Subcommittee on Privileges and Elections, including statements that McCarthy had practiced unethical financial transactions and had repeatedly and calculatedly used deceit. While the subcommittee labored at its lengthy considerations, Benton waived his senatorial immunity on testimony and speeches he had made before Congress and challenged McCarthy to bring him and his accusations into court. McCarthy finally accepted Benton's challenge and sued him for libel. The suit's preliminaries dragged on for two years until, in the spring of 1954, McCarthy withdrew on the grounds that his lawyers had been unable to find anyone in the United States who would say he believed Benton's charges and that consequently it was impossible to prove that damage had been caused.[13] McCarthy clearly was the loser in this battle in the courts. By this time, however, Benton had lost his Senate seat in the 1952 elections, not so much through McCarthy's influence, as was speculated at the time, as through Eisenhower's: it was a presidential election year when it was an immense handicap simply to be a Democrat.[14]

Other Senate liberals confronted McCarthy at one time or another. Hubert Humphrey tangled with him over Owen Lattimore early in 1950, soon after McCarthy's first charges against Communists in government began to make national headlines.[15] During the first year of McCarthy's prominence, Wayne Morse joined with Maine Republican Margaret Chase Smith and five other GOP Senators to sign a Declaration of Conscience aimed at McCarthy. Morse also sent a standard reply to constituents unhappy with his anti-McCarthyism, which read in part: "I think you are overlooking the fact that guilt by association is a very dangerous policy to be following in the United States Senate. You and I and everyone else in the country can be made the victims of such a policy. Therefore, I think I am fighting for a basic American principle of justice. . . ."[16] With Senators Kefauver and Lehman, Morse co-sponsored resolutions to insure fair proceedings at congressional investigations, in an attempt to regulate and prevent the chaotic and dubious proceedings of the McCarthy committee hearings and others like it.[17] And Democratic senators Mike Monroney of Oklahoma and Tom Hennings of Missouri at certain times played important roles in the Maryland election probe and the subsequent investigation of Senator Benton's charges against McCarthy.[18]

Liberal senators thus did on various occasions directly and indirectly confront Senator McCarthy. Most did so, however, at infrequent intervals; consistent opposition often brought abandonment by liberal colleagues. Senator Benton, for example, opposed McCarthy with unusual steadiness and vigor, but found that he could rely on few other Senate liberals for support; for a long while after his initial charges against McCarthy only Senator Lehman openly praised and supported his actions.[19] More fundamentally, however, congressional liberals failed to comprehend that McCarthy was not a cause but a symbol, whose tremendously successful, gimmick-laden bid for the nation's attention was based solidly on the realities of postwar conservative politics and the nationwide fear of radicalism and nuclear disaster. Politically discrediting or restricting McCarthy, although not unimportant, was secondary to defeating the anti-New Deal conservative politics which provided him party support, and secondary as well to defusing the national alarm without which he would not have received such a willing and gullible audience. It was on this level that congressional liberals failed to come to grips with the Communist issue, for on the one hand their sensitivity to their interpretation of voter opinion helped mold their conformity to the accepted anti-Communist image, while on the other hand, their largely genuine fear of international Communism persuaded them to join in the politics of anti-Communism. Influenced thus by practical politics as well as by personal beliefs, liberals in the Senate as well as in the House voted for and in some cases even sponsored legislation whose potentially repressive features would have alarmed them in a less fearful era.

The emergency detention provision of the Internal Security Act of 1950 was one important example during the early 1950s of liberal failure to perceive fully the inherent dangers of the Communist issue. Another important example was the liberal response to the McCarran-Walter Immigration Act of 1952, which provided screening measures to keep out "subversives" and authorized the attorney general to deport immigrants, even naturalized citizens, for "Communist and Communist-front" affiliations. Senators Humphrey and Douglas did attempt to lead a floor fight against the bill and made an equally unsuccessful effort to uphold Truman's veto. Humphrey and Lehman, however, had sponsored their own alternative immigration and naturalization bill, the basic intent of which appeared to differ little from that of the McCarran-Walter legislation itself. They stressed that their legislation attempted to establish "proper review and appeals procedures" and to "eliminate as much as possible the arbitrary exercise of personal discretion or caprice. . . ." At the heart of the Humphrey-Lehman bill, however, were provisions to strengthen the United States' "legal defenses against the admission of subversive and undesirable aliens, and [to facilitate] the deportation of those already in this country."[20] The Humphrey-Lehman bill made distinctions between naturalized and native-born citizens and, based on the elusive concepts of "subversive" and "undesirable," drew possible restrictions on the freedoms of speech and association.

Within the House of Representatives, liberals also found the Communist issue a difficult one. There, too, the McCarran Internal Security Act and the McCarran-Walter Immigration Act passed with little difficulty. The House Committee on Un-American Activities, which had been a front-line disseminator of the Red Scare long before McCarthy attained national notoriety, also received decreasing opposition from House liberals during the early 1950s. In 1950, there still was some vocal opposition to the committee and some votes against further appropriations. Congressman Arthur G. Klein, a New York Democrat, objected to HUAC'S "absorption in proposed legislation which would undertake to establish in our free America a norm of political piety." Democratic Congressman Barratt O'Hara of Illinois acknowledged Democratic political leadership in the House and noted that HUAC's behavior had improved since the 80th Congress, but objected to the concept of a congressional committee being given the job of "inquisitor and prosecutor." However, Democratic Congressman Harry J. Davenport of Pennsylvania, who in 1948 had opposed continuing HUAC's existence, by 1950 lauded the committee's change of character under Democratic leadership and proclaimed its watchdog role "essential today." Only twelve voted against 1950 HUAC appropriations, including John Blatnik, Helen Gahagan Douglas, Jacob Javits, and Vito Marcantonio. Congressmen Celler and Mansfield, who had opposed HUAC appropriations only the year before, now joined the 348 who voted for appropriations. In 1951 and 1952, no liberals even asked for a roll call vote on HUAC appropriations, which were quickly and anonymously passed.[21]

| * |

General MacArthur's forces successfully pushed North Korean troops out of South Korea by early October 1950 and then moved north toward the Yalu River separating Korea from Manchuria, where they first encountered Chinese resistance. MacArthur confidently launched an offensive to drive the Chinese back beyond the Yalu and end the war before Christmas but met a devastating counterattack which split his forces and resulted in retreat and evacuation. The Chinese intervention introduced the possibility of a general war, and in December 1950, the United States began to mobilize under a declared state of national emergency.

Liberals opposed escalating the war into a full-scale conflict with China but also rejected withdrawal from Korea.[22] Senator Dennis Chavez rather emotionally proclaimed that "even if Korea turns out to be another Dunkerque, we must let the world know that we will be back in there and anywhere else in the world if necessary to protect the ideals for which free people stand." Senator Claude Pepper (who in 1950 had been defeated in a campaign alleging him soft on Communism, but who subsequently won election to the House) agreed: "I did not realize that it was part of the American tradition to pull out under fire unless we were thrown out." Pepper also stressed that the Chinese aggression was not brought on by American troops crossing the thirty-eighth parallel; rather, it was part of Moscow's aggressive campaign for "conquest of the whole of the Far East. . . ." Democratic Senator Joseph C. O'Mahoney of Wyoming agreed that the "Chinese are the puppets" to "their Red masters in the Kremlin," and Senator Chavez further underlined the concept of Soviet-controlled world Communism: "A Communist is a Communist," he stated, "whether he is a Russian, a Chinese, an American, or a Frenchman."[23]

While the Truman administration privately decided on a limited response which would accept a military stalemate at approximately the thirty-eighth parallel, MacArthur openly pushed for full-scale war in the Far East. In April 1951 Truman dismissed MacArthur from his Far Eastern commands, and in July the United States opened truce negotiations with Chinese and North Korean officials. Negotiations deadlocked, however, over the question of repatriating prisoners of war, and the Communists broke off discussions in October 1952. In the meantime, the UN forces continued defensive operations to maintain their line north of the thirty-eighth parallel, while at home Americans chafed at the disappointing and discouraging news from Korea.

The fears and frustrations of war provided a psychological climate in which the domestic Red Scare, already well rooted, began to flourish. McCarthy and other demagogic politicians appropriated the Communist issue and turned it to their own advantage. Capitalizing on Republican support and Democratic acquiescence, McCarthy came to seem almost invincible. In 1950, a subcommittee of the Senate Committee on Foreign Relations, chaired by Maryland Democrat Millard Tydings, charged that McCarthy's allegations were a "fraud," but Republicans on the committee disagreed and thus diluted the report's impact. In 1951 the Senate Subcommittee on Privileges and Elections held hearings on the 1950 Maryland election, where McCarthy had lent his staff to direct and help implement a malicious campaign against the incumbent Senator Tydings, who was defeated. The subcommittee denounced what it termed a vicious "back street" campaign and recommended that the Senate take action to prevent similar practices in the future, but was unwilling to take punitive action against McCarthy himself. The Subcommittee on Privileges and

Elections met again in 1952 to consider the charges of Senator Benton, who had proposed that the Senate expel McCarthy for unethical financial transactions and the repeated and calculated use of deceit. Contemptuous of the committee and of the investigation, McCarthy refused to attend the hearings and, according to the committee's final report, "deliberately set out to thwart the investigation." Despite some four hundred pages of damaging testimony, however, the committee submitted a report without recommendations, and no one in the Senate objected.[24]

The paralysis among political liberals was not limited to Congress alone during the early 1950s. The ADA, although a self-proclaimed liberal political lobby and the recipient of plaudits for its role in the 1948 Democratic election victory, was struck by a similar inability to deal effectively with the Red Scare. In a membership recruitment brochure from the period, the ADA prominently boasted that it had "led the fight against McCarthy and McCarthyism." The ADA clearly detested McCarthy and did contribute to the fight against him, in particular with numerous telegrams and press releases issued to protest specific examples of injustice perpetrated by McCarthy.[25] In late 1953, the ADA's vice-Chairman, Joseph Rauh, debated the McCarthy committee's chief counsel, Roy Cohn, on the radio and television program "American Forum of the Air." In the spring of 1954, the New York City ADA chapter sponsored a well-attended meeting on the topic "The People vs. McCarthy," at which persons prominent in the field of civil liberties presented the case against the Wisconsin senator.

The ADA also provided copies of the Senate Subcommittee on Privileges and Elections' report on McCarthy. The report contained detailed information on, among other matters, McCarthy's questionable financial dealings; and, as a Senate document, it was privileged and carried no risk of libel. Copies had run out quickly and the new Republican chairman of the Senate Rules committee, William E. Jenner of Indiana, refused to authorize additional printings. The ADA reprinted the report and wrote McCarthy that it would waive its immunity if he would bring a libel suit "to test out the basic truth of the subcommittee report. . . ." McCarthy never accepted the challenge, and the ADA sold over four thousand copies of the report.[26]

Despite its antipathy to McCarthy, however, the ADA proved unable to mount a sustained, organized political movement against him. During the autumn of 1950, McCarthy's first year of national notoriety, the ADA's national board appointed a committee to consider McCarthy and McCarthyism. A year later, the question arose at an executive committee meeting whether the ADA should issue a resolution on McCarthy. Those present authorized preparation of a statement "to be issued at such a time as to have greatest notice and effect." When McCarthy announced his intention of attacking General George Marshall in a Senate speech, James Loeb urged the ADA executive committee to do something, but the committee demurred and decided that it was "impossible to act until there [is] further knowledge of what McCarthy [is] to say against the Secretary of Defense." After the reprinting of the Senate report on McCarthy's financial affairs, one of the ADA's leaders asked if the ADA could pursue further this kind of activity. The executive committee again hesitated, and agreed that "activities re McCarthy should not dominate ADA's interest and activities." The committee had "no suggestions for further action at the present time."[27] The ADA thus developed no political strategy comparable to that successfully employed against McCarthy by the lobbyists of the National Committee for an Effective Congress.[28]

More significant than the ADA's unsustained political opposition to McCarthy, however, was its failure to confront the deeper dangers of the Red Scare itself. The ADA wrote reports, analyzed situations, held conferences, and generally avoided clear-cut decisions and positive action where civil liberties and the Communist issue intersected. For example, a month after the Internal Security Act of 1950 became law, the ADA's executive committee declared that the issues involved were "sufficiently complex that further study should be given, both to the law and to strategy to be used against it." The executive committee agreed to take no action until the national board meeting six weeks later. This meeting established a "watch-dog" committee "to prepare an analysis and recommendations for Board consideration" at a future date. Finally, the spring after the bill had been enacted, the ADA in its annual platform opposed the detention provisions of the McCarran Act and the act as a whole because, as the platform innocuously put it, the act contributed "nothing of value to existing laws to control subversion."[29]

The Smith Act had prohibited advocacy of the forceful overthrow of the government, and in 1951 the Supreme Court upheld the arrest and conviction of American Communist party leaders under this act. In so ruling, the Supreme Court had not distinguished between a conspiracy to overthrow the government and the teaching of Marxist-Leninist doctrine. The ADA was unable to decide whether to oppose the Smith Act and its interpretation by the Supreme Court, or simply to oppose the Justice Department's plans to use the decision as the basis for further widespread prosecutions. The ADA finally decided to demand repeal of the Smith Act and any legislation directly or indirectly outlawing any political party, but it reached this decision only after long discussion.[30]

Wiretapping was another focal point of the civil liberties debate of the 1950s. During the early 1950s, the ADA opposed the legalization of wiretapping for any purposes. In 1953, however, it urged the legalization of wiretapping, under certain safeguards, in cases involving espionage or sabotage. In 1954, it reversed itself again and once more opposed wiretapping as "an intolerable violation of civil liberties whether practiced by the federal government, by the state, or by individuals."[31]

By the early fifties the euphoria which had surrounded the 1948 triumph of the new liberalism over both the Republican right and the Wallace left had vanished, leaving new liberals demoralized and uncertain. "What liberals must do . . . is to take the offensive," the national board of the ADA asserted in 1950. Yet for all the bravado of this statement, the ADA liberals were anything but confident, either of their organization or of the future of liberalism itself. "[The] whole role of ADA [is] in question," commented the *New York Post*'s editor, James A. Wechsler, at a national board meeting in 1950. And, reporting on the ADA's 1950 annual convention, the *New Republic* observed: "Confidence that the organization will continue to flourish was high, but there was also general uncertainty as to the exact role that the ADA should play in the future. . . . More direct action, not less, was what the convention had in mind. But the agenda of the meeting was short on practical discussion." A discontented observer of the ADA's 1951 convention noted the "total lack of moving vitality" and commented that "apparently, there is a concerted effort afoot, by particular elements in the ADA, to salvage from a very boring, disquieting Cleveland convention the amorphous theme of unity." That same year, the journalist I. F. Stone, an independent radical, acidly remarked that the ADA "seems to have served principally as a way station for scared radicals moving from possible smear as fellow travelers through a simon-pure certified homogenized non-red organization like the ADA into complete political inaction."[32]

The new liberals themselves sensed the problem, though not its cause, and argued endlessly over the "future" of liberalism. The 1952 election, concluded Arthur Schlesinger, Jr., "indicated that American progressivism cannot live any longer off the brilliance and fertility of the New Deal, and that the old ideas and energies are losing their force." He stressed that "only the strength and vitality which will come from a willingness to respond directly to the imperatives of the 1950s can bring salvation and regeneration."[33] The imperatives of the 1950s, however, were a complex and highly charged set of issues, and the new liberals showed more reluctance than enthusiasm for dealing with what was perhaps the most controversial of them all—the protection of civil liberties during an era of international stress and national alarm.

7

Civil Liberties and Security

Since 1920, a distinguished de-
fender of civil liberties in the United States has been the American
Civil Liberties Union, an organization drawn largely from the political
left-of-center and dedicated to the preservation and full implementation of the Bill of Rights.[1] The ACLU and its predecessor, the National
Civil Liberties Bureau, responded strongly in many highly controversial cases, including the subversive activities cases of World War I and
the Sacco-Vanzetti trial of the 1920s, and thus appeared well prepared
to resist the pressures of the post-World War II Red Scare. By the late
1930s, however, the ACLU had become troubled over the Communist
issue, especially where it concerned the political affiliations of the
union's leadership, and this background of unresolved internal debate remained a disturbing legacy as the union entered the Cold War
years and confronted the second Red Scare of the twentieth century.

In the late 1930s, at the urging of Norman Thomas, a board
member and leader of the Socialist party, a minority within the ACLU's
board of directors began an attempt to remove Communists and
Communist sympathizers from the union's leadership. This minority
among the directors grew to a narrow majority after the Nazi-Soviet
pact in 1939 propelled both liberals and radicals away from the Communist party and popular front. The attacks of Congressman Martin
Dies, chairman of the House Committee on Un-American Activities,
who labeled the ACLU a Communist front, also contributed to pressure
to establish a strong anti-Communist image for the ACLU.[2] In early
1940 the board of directors passed a resolution declaring that supporters of totalitarian dictatorships could not serve on the ACLU's governing committees or on its staff. Shortly thereafter, the board re-

quested one of the organization's founders, Elizabeth Gurley Flynn, to resign from the board on the grounds that she was a member of the Communist party and that consequently, as an "apologizer" for totalitarianism, she could not properly participate as an officer in an organization whose sole function was to defend civil liberties. Flynn had only infrequently attended board meetings and posed no personal obstacle to the workings of the ACLU; indeed, the board had earlier reelected her to its membership in full knowledge of her party membership. Those who opposed her continued membership on the board did so from a sensitivity to the difficulties the ACLU might encounter, both in court and out, unless it was firmly and publicly anti-Communist. Those who supported Flynn's request to remain on the board argued that ousting her solely as a Communist party member sanctioned the criterion of "guilt by association." By a bare majority of ten to nine, the ACLU board of directors finally voted to expel her.[3]

Roger Baldwin, who as executive director of the ACLU from its founding until 1950 was the most influential leader within the organization, later stated that he was "satisfied with the [anti-Communist] resolution's results and the effect of Flynn's expulsion, which cleared up the troublesome question of how a civil liberties organization could tolerate in its councils an apologist for dictatorship." He himself had drafted the 1940 anti-Communist resolution, which he regarded as the means of settling a controversy that threatened to split the ACLU's board of directors. He concluded that he had acted according to what he perceived as the majority view, and that events proved his perceptions accurate.[4]

Following World War II, in the midst of the accelerating anxieties produced by the Cold War and in a reflection of the ADA's movement away from popular-front leftism and toward the new liberalism, the ACLU's board of directors attempted to further strengthen the organizations' anti-Communist credentials. In 1949, the ACLU adopted a resolution opposing "any form of the police state or the single party state, or any movement in support of them. . . ."[5] In 1951 the 1940 resolution was incorporated into the ACLU's constitution. This action diminished the prospects for reversal of the resolution by internal critics, since the constitution could only be amended by a vote of two-thirds or better of the ACLU's membership.[6] The ACLU also began to include a statement affirming its opposition to Communism in all its legal briefs where Communism was either directly or indirectly an issue.[7]

Before 1940, the ACLU had regarded Communism as a political theory and had stressed the union's role in defending the civil liberties of all Americans, including American Communists. With the 1940 resolution, the union for the first time treated Communism as a conspiracy, and critics within the organization worried that the ACLU was abandoning its long-proclaimed defense of individual rights for the theory of "guilt by association" implied in the conspiratorial view of Communism. The ACLU leaders still argued, however, that although Communism was antithetical to union aspirations, the union would nevertheless continue to defend the rights of individual party members. Through 1952 the union maintained this uneasy balance, denouncing Communism on the one hand, but maintaining on the other that individuals could be held legally responsible only for acts they committed, not for thoughts they held or organizations they joined.[8] The result of this tension was a perceptible wavering and hesitation in cases where civil liberties and the Communist issue intersected, and the ACLU's policies frequently showed signs of ambivalence and confusion.

A significant instance of a potentially effective ACLU program which suffered from the organization's internal dissension was the attempt in 1950 and 1951 to investigate and put an end to blacklisting in the entertainment industry. The ACLU was especially interested in the publications *Red Channels* and *Counter-Attack*, which listed the alleged Communist affiliations or sympathies of virtually anyone employed by radio or television. Program sponsors and executives responsible for hiring and firing knew of these listings, and as jobs became increasingly scarce for those on the "Red" lists there grew the suspicion, despite industry denials, that a direct connection existed. This suspicion appeared confirmed toward the end of the summer of 1950 when General Foods Corporation dropped Jean Muir from its NBC television program "The Aldrich Family" after receiving complaints that her name was included in *Red Channels*. Following this incident, the ACLU initiated an investigation of blacklisting and appointed Merle Miller, a board member and well-known correspondent and novelist, to head the effort. Assisting Miller were Alan Reitman, the ACLU's public relations director, and staff counsel Herbert M. Levy, in addition to a large group of union volunteers. The final report, titled *The Judges and the Judged*, took approximately five months to complete.[9]

Miller and his staff were particularly disturbed by *Red Channels'* failure to indicate its sources or the evidence upon which its charges were made. They found no evidence to show that the charges were based upon anything but hearsay. In addition, Miller believed that the information on the "Red" lists, even if correct, was relevant only if the nation's security was endangered by the accused person's activities—a matter which, Miller insisted, only the federal government could determine. Otherwise, criteria for employment should rightly include material attesting only to one's personal abilities, not to one's political beliefs.[10]

From the outset, the ACLU had intended *The Judges and the Judged* to be the basis for a widespread attack against blacklisting. The ACLU filed with the Federal Communications Commission a complaint based on the book's evidence, timed to coincide with the publicity from the book's release; the complaint charged the major networks with blacklisting. Sixty-seven publications reviewed the book, only three of these unfavorably, and the news media gave widespread coverage to the ACLU's charges to the FCC. The combination of an investigatory book and a hearing on a highly explosive subject attracted much favorable attention, and the ACLU contemplated "the beginning of a long educational program in this field."[11]

Despite its auspicious beginnings, the ACLU's drive against blacklisting began to collapse following attacks from within the union itself. The report's detractors complained of several inaccuracies (the number remained a debatable point) as well as the anonymity of its sources. Miller replied that his sources had insisted upon anonymity, but the critics held that *The Judges and the Judged* had used the same tactics as the publications it attacked. The critics' chief complaint, however, was that they doubted the existence of a threat to civil liberties in the entertainment industry.

Miller's chief critic was Merlyn S. Pitzele, labor editor of *Business Week*, who had joined the ACLU board in 1946. He had remained silent at key board meetings when the ACLU board discussed and unanimously adopted an introductory summary of *The Judges and the Judged*'s findings.[12] Pitzele made his objections to the book known in a review for the *New Leader*. He condemned what he saw as the book's lack of integrity and its resort to, in his terms, the "half-truth" and the "half-lie." He pointed out that Rabbi Benjamin Schultz, who had protested Jean Muir's radio appearance, had a right to protest, a right which the ACLU was obliged to defend. Miller had detailed the rabbi's forced resignation from his temple on grounds of irresponsibility and had shown the size of the rabbi's committee as closer to three hundred than to the two million members for whom he claimed to speak. Miller also quoted others objecting to Jean Muir's radio appearance who nevertheless believed the rabbi and his committee were irresponsible. Pitzele disagreed with Miller's approach and his evidence, and contended that the report "attacks and smears Rabbi Schultz for exercising his right of protest."[13]

Pitzele's main objection, however, was that *The Judges and the Judged* had pinpointed McCarthyism rather than Communism as the real danger in America. The Communist peril was an imminent threat, he said, whereas the peril from McCarthyism was not. "Thus far," he wrote, "what is known as McCarthyism has developed nothing which history can conceivably weigh as equal to the raids of A. Mitchell Palmer, the Sacco-Vanzetti case, and the judicial finding that a crime was committed when John T. Scopes taught Darwin's theory of evolution in the State of Tennessee." Citing Murray Kempton (one of the three unfavorable reviewers, who had commented: "The American Civil Liberties Union . . . can be excused one clinker"), Pitzele remarked: "As a member of the board of directors of the ACLU—a minority member in this case—I do not think it should be forgiven."[14]

The ACLU board immediately called a special meeting to consider Pitzele's charges and his method of airing them. After much discussion the board defeated a motion expressing regret that Pitzele "did not recognize the impropriety of his conduct" and instead adopted the more harshly worded statement that Pitzele's article contained a public attack on the ACLU "which it is grossly improper for a member of the board to make." The board adopted Pitzele's suggestion that a special committee evaluate his charges, but it refused to delay promotion efforts on *The Judges and the Judged* until after the special committee had made its report. Clearly, a majority on the board was unsympathetic to Pitzele's charges as well as to his means of expressing them.[15]

The entire issue soon disintegrated, however, into a series of posturings by both sides over who was the better anti-Communist. Before the board had officially answered Pitzele's charges, Miller jumped to his own defense. In an article in the *New Leader* he replied that he was as good an anti-Communist as Pitzele or anybody else, and that Pitzele, by implying otherwise, was practicing McCarthyism. "Pitzele does not mention that in 1947 and, for that matter, in 1948 and 1949, I was one of the most active leaders of the anti-Communist fight in the American Veterans Committee," Miller wrote. "Incidentally," he added, "Kempton also identifies me as a 'sophisticated anti-Communist.' " Pitzele replied, again in the *New Leader's* pages, that Miller "is one of those fellows who believes that the guilt of Alger Hiss is still unproven, that it's only McCarthyism America should be worried about. . . . Only last week on the radio, he said: 'If Alger Hiss is guilty. . . .' "[16]

By this time, the ACLU's special committee had submitted its report on Pitzele's charges. It concluded that there were several mistakes in *The Judges and the Judged* but that these in no way affected the correctness of Miller's conclusions. Miller and his fellow researchers had, the committee decided, made "a sincere effort to ascertain the relevant facts and to appraise them objectively," and their report deserved the ACLU's continued sponsorship.[17] The board approved the special committee's report by a large majority and unanimously voted both to correct errors in future editions and to continue the ACLU's sponsorship.[18]

Curiously, the board also renominated Pitzele (tantamount to election) for another term shortly following the special committee's report. Whether the board's motives in renominating Pitzele were a basic respect for his services to the ACLU or a reluctance to create bad publicity by ousting him, its vote to renominate him was expressly not a vote of approval for his attack: the vote to continue sponsorship of *The Judges and the Judged* came at the same meeting.[19]

The most significant aspect of the entire tangle over *The Judges and the Judged* was the distinctly defensive position which the ACLU chose to take despite its unanimous vote of confidence in the book. The board kept the special committee's report discreetly in the ACLU office. No copies went to the celebrities whose names had originally appeared in a national advertisement of endorsement. The *New Leader*, after publishing Pitzele's charges, tried to obtain a copy of the union's evaluation of those charges in order to print it, "in fairness to all sides of the dispute," but the ACLU ignored the request. Only after highly unfavorable accounts of the whole affair began to appear, first in *Commentary*, then in the *New York World-Telegram* and the *New Leader*, did the ACLU agree to air its special report to those who had reviewed the book and to all those requesting copies. The board still voted against making a general release of the report. As one of the original endorsers pointed out, "the handling of this report has been an example of public relations at its most inept, to say the least, and thereby the Union's reputation for impartiality and championship of full disclosure of facts at all times has needlessly suffered."[20]

The ACLU's attempted action through the FCC slid similarly into oblivion. In its original complaint, the union had requested that the licenses of the offending radio stations and TV networks be revoked unless they cooperated in ending their blacklisting practices. After the FCC denied this request, the ACLU requested a rehearing and an explanation. The FCC refused to clarify its earlier decision but did not rule out the ACLU's request for a rehearing. Nonetheless, the ACLU made no further attempts to obtain another hearing.[21] Under attack for being "soft on Communism," the ACLU allowed the entire effort against blacklisting to slip into a defensive, embarrassed silence.

The ACLU's uneasiness with controversial cases during the late 1940s and early 1950s was also displayed in other important instances, including the case of Harry Bridges, where the union waited four years before publicly acknowledging that a civil liberties issue was involved. Bridges, a naturalized American citizen, had been president of the powerful International Longshoremen's and Warehousemen's Union since its founding in 1937. For many years, conservatives had been demanding that Bridges be deported as a Communist. Early demands were investigated and invalidated, but in 1949 a federal grand jury indicted Bridges for perjury, charging that at his 1945 citizenship hearings he had falsely denied being or ever having been a Communist. Convicted in 1950, Bridges appealed the decision. In 1949 the ACLU board had decided to take no action on the case. In 1950, however, the ACLU's policy committee recommended that the union enter the case as a friend of the court "on the ground that the continuous hounding of Bridges amounted to a violation of due process of law." The board, however, rejected this recommendation, though it continued to appoint special committees to study the case. By late 1952 a special committee reported to the board that the ACLU should take no action in the matter. In the spring of 1953, however, the board finally decided to issue a statement that "the repeated indictment and trial of Bridges on essentially the same charge is a denial of due process."[22]

The ACLU was also reluctant to become involved with the trial and conviction of the eleven Communist party leaders tried in 1949 under the Smith Act. The union had opposed the Smith Act of 1940 as a dangerous curtailment of freedom of speech and association. For all the firmness of its position, however, the union refused to become involved actively either in the original trial or in the appeals process, justifying this refusal on the ground that action would have involved the ACLU in factual and other non-civil-liberties issues. The ACLU did petition the Circuit Court of Appeals to reverse the convictions.[23] It also wrote the attorney general to oppose the government's request to revoke bail, and it filed a friend-of-the-court brief before the Supreme Court. In 1951, moreover, after the Supreme Court upheld the convictions, the board approved the union's future participation in new cases brought under the Smith Act. All related activities had been kept well out of public view, however, and many interested in the case were not aware that the ACLU had done anything at all. Following the Supreme Court decision upholding the original convictions, Roger Baldwin, in receipt of "queries as to the Union's views, and some disquiet that they have not been given publicity," suggested to one of his correspondents that "some pressure be put on the board for action."[24]

During the postwar years, the ACLU also changed its positions on a number of issues to ones that were more strongly anti-Communist. Initially, the union had opposed the exclusion or expulsion of persons from labor unions for political opinions, "even if they are members of the Communist Party." But in late 1950 the board modified its stand by approving a change in policy that recognized the right of unions to disqualify Communists as candidates for union offices.[25] The board also changed its policy on immigration and naturalization, deciding not to challenge the government's refusal to give permanent immigrant status or citizenship to Communists.[26] In an even more dramatic reversal of policy following the outbreak of the Korean War, the ACLU, which had originated as a pacifist organization devoted to defending the rights of conscientious objectors, rescinded its opposition to military conscription.[27]

The ACLU also deemphasized direct involvement in litigation, a characteristic of the organization during the 1920s and 1930s, and focused instead on submitting friend-of-the-court briefs on behalf of defendants. The union believed that such an approach enabled it to "focus the courts' attention on vital constitutional guarantees rather than to argue the guilt or innocence of a particular individual on a fact basis." Probably more important during the Cold War years, however, was the usefulness of this indirect kind of involvement in the legal processes in lessening the possibilities for "public confusion over whether defending a person's civil liberties meant identification with his or her political philosophy." Nevertheless, some in the ACLU recognized that "as long as we confine ourselves to the amici curiae role and don't get in at the trial stage, where the basic battle is waged, we lose the initiative of demonstrating to the public that we are leading in the defense of civil liberties."[28]

The new cautiousness in the ACLU's activities may have resulted in part from a major change in executive leadership. Roger Baldwin, executive director from the union's founding until 1950, conducted the ACLU's business with great vigor and strongly exercised his leadership within the organization. Patrick Murphy Malin, who followed as executive director after Baldwin's retirement, was more cautious and less dynamic than his predecessor. He was a good administrator but, as Baldwin himself observed to a friend, Malin was "hesitant to act without his Board's approval of every move. . . ."[29]

Such approval was difficult to obtain during those years when the ACLU board was deeply divided over the Communist issue and the Red Scare was at its height. By late 1952, many on the ACLU's board of directors believed it urgent for the organization to strengthen its bulwarks more solidly against attacks from the right. Some of the board of directors pressed for a restatement of the ACLU's position on the Communist party and on such related issues as Fifth Amendment privileges, academic freedom, and employment in the United Nations. In urging the ACLU to reconsider the Communist question, these board members insisted that, in a period of so much political turbulence centering on the Communist issue, the union needed a specific and detailed statement of policy to provide guidelines for its actions. Patrick Murphy Malin agreed: "Now," he wrote, "when American civil liberties are threatened from the outside by the aggressions of Soviet Communism, and on the inside by the excrescences of our people's natural and indispensable determination to guard against acts of treasonable or revolutionary subversion, a new statement [of the ACLU's post-1940 policy on Communism] is necessary. . . ."[30]

Uppermost in the minds of these leaders was their fear of Communism's threat to western security and their belief in the necessity for establishing a firm anti-Communist image for the ACLU. "In view of the continuing though irresponsible charges and insinuations that the American Civil Liberties Union is equivocal in its attitude toward Communism, or unaware of the nature of the Communist Party in the U.S.," wrote the Reverend John Paul Jones, "the Board of Directors desires once and for all to set the record straight." Varian Fry, one of the board's more conservative members, argued, "Many feel that we have failed badly in our major duty today: to show how a secret, deadly and worldwide conspiracy against our basic freedoms can be successfully combated without sacrifice of our immediate civil liberties."[31] Led by Morris Ernst, one of the ACLU's two general counsels, by James L. Fly, a former head of the Federal Communications Commission, and by Norman Thomas, these board members were determined to place the ACLU on record as implacably anti-Communist.

Others within the board and especially within the ACLU's affiliates were equally anxious that the ACLU's traditional interest in the rights of the individual not suffer as a consequence. Osmond K. Fraenkel, an attorney long associated with the union, Arthur Garfield Hays, the ACLU's other general counsel, and Walter Gellhorn of the Columbia Law School were leaders of the major opposition group. They did not object to placing the union on record against Communism, but they feared that the movement behind such a statement might lead to a lessening of the union's concern for civil liberties. Corliss Lamont, a professor of philosophy at Columbia University and a long-time radical who frequently sided with Fraenkel in the controversy, was absolutely opposed to an ACLU policy statement on Communism. The business of a civil liberties union, he insisted, was to protect civil liberties, not to take positions against political views it found unpalatable.[32]

In the spring of 1953 the board of directors, after a series of stormy sessions, appointed a special committee to draft a single resolution for the board's consideration.[33] The special committee finally agreed to recommend a policy that largely reflected the thinking of Norman Thomas and Morris Ernst—both members of the four-man committee. The statement's first section asserted that the ACLU "does not hold that all persons who submit to the Communist Party's rigid totalitarian discipline (whether formal members or not), or even all those who are its leaders, are engaged in illegal secret conspiracy or actual subversive acts." The end of this section, however, listed a set of conditions under which a person's voluntary choice of association limited his civil liberties. By a broad definition of the individual's responsibility for his associations, the statement thus implicitly sanctioned guilt by association.[34]

Many on the board were not satisfied with the special committee's proposed policy, which came before the board in April 1953, but after much discussion, the board voted to accept the entire proposal. Moreover, in contrast to the ACLU's 1940 resolution, which had barred Communists only from leadership positions in the union and refrained from extending these conditions to the general membership,[35] the board now agreed to have membership application forms and promotional material contain the statement that the ACLU welcomed only those "whose devotion to civil liberties is not qualified by adherence to Communist, Fascist, KKK, or other totalitarian doctrine."[36]

Technically, this was not a loyalty oath; in fact, however, it moved close to being one and reflected the fears of some board members that Communists could otherwise join the ACLU and influence or control its policy.[37]

Fraenkel and others remained unreconciled to portions of the statement, and Lamont opposed the entire proposal. They took advantage of a provision in the ACLU bylaws for a referendum to the corporate membership by petition of ten members of the board of directors.[38] Enclosed with the referendum were affirmative and negative arguments, written by James L. Fly and Osmond K. Fraenkel respectively, and a statement by Ernest Angell, who was chairman of the board of directors.[39] Normally, only the affirmative and negative arguments would have accompanied the referendum; Ernest Angell had, however, requested and received permission from the board to include a statement in his capacity as chairman. In his statement Angell pleaded for the corporation's affirmative votes, warning, "If these statements are rejected, I despair of the Board being able to reach any more generally satisfactory substitute, of comprehensive nature."[40] The board then waited for the corporate membership's response.

The ACLU's corporate membership consisted of the board of directors, which was the actual governing body of the organization, an essentially figurehead national committee, and the boards of the union's twenty-three local affiliates.[41] Since the board of directors' 1940 resolution on Communism and the expulsion of Elizabeth Gurley Flynn, relations between the national board and some of the ACLU affiliates had not always been cordial. The affiliates were on the whole less anti-Communist than the board, and local groups in Boston, New Haven, Philadelphia, and northern and southern California had criticized the national body for failing to discharge its civil liberties obligations vigorously. In 1951 the board had responded to this criticism by attempting to curb the power and voice of the affiliates. Backed by Norman Thomas and his supporters, the board added a new provision to the ACLU's bylaws which stated that the board of directors would follow the dictates of the majority in any national referendum "except where it believes there are vitally important reasons for not doing so—which it shall explain to the corporation members." This new provision did not enhance the board's reputation with the affiliates nor with those like Lamont, who commented: "What these new provisions meant was that the board of directors had constituted itself . . . an inner dictatorship within the ACLU."[42]

The board was nevertheless surprised when the corporate membership voted in October 1953 to reject the Communist policy statement by a vote of 21,271 to 18,995. With the board split on its vote, the affiliates' role in this defeat was decisive. Of the twenty-three affiliates, one abstained and nineteen voted against the board's proposal. Only three voted for the proposal, and these were among the smallest affiliates.[43]

Many among the ACLU's leadership refused to accept the results of the referendum as final.[44] Following the referendum, Patrick Murphy Malin conducted an investigation of the affiliates' votes. During this procedure the Chicago affiliate, which was the largest, decided to change its original vote and concur with the board's proposed policy. The Chicago affiliate's switch reversed the outcome of the entire referendum. Lamont contested the switch on the grounds that the deadline had passed, that it would be illegal "to alter the ballot totals after the referendum had been officially concluded," and that the procedure involved in the vote change was "based chiefly on a hasty and incomplete telephone poll." Malin retorted that he was not trying to conduct a telephone ballot but was attempting to produce more ballots, as only twenty-nine percent of the Chicago affiliate's board was represented in the first vote. Following another telephone call, this time from Lamont, the Chicago group restored its original vote—thus once again reversing the outcome of the entire referendum, this time to the original decision to reject the proposed Communist policy.[45]

The board of directors itself decided, by a vote of fourteen to four (with five abstentions), to defy the referendum, holding that the proposed policy on Communism expressed "in essence the policy of the Union." Evidently hoping to avoid a clash with the affiliates, however, the board directed Malin to rework the form, although not the substance, of the policy to take into consideration the changes which the various board members and affiliates had proposed.[46] The affiliates refused to accept this solution, and when the ACLU corporation convened three months later, in February 1954, the affiliates tried to reverse the board's actions. They demanded that the Communist policy be rewritten by a special committee representing the affiliates as well as the national board of directors and the national committee. The affiliates also worked to eliminate the 1951 provision in the bylaws which had permitted the board to override a national referendum.[47] Despite Norman Thomas's suggestion that the board continue to abide by the rejected Communist policy until the special committee had met, the directors responded in part to the corporation's demands and withdrew the policy, although the contested bylaw remained.[48]

Only a month later, a televised charge by Senator McCarthy that the ACLU was a Communist front embroiled the union's board once again in debate over its policy toward Communism. Norman Thomas responded to the McCarthy attack by drafting a militant denunciation of Communism, which he urged the board to adopt in spite of its recent pledge to obtain the corporation's approval before issuing any further policy statements on Communism. Thomas, together with Morris Ernst and James Fly, threatened to resign unless the board passed and released such a statement.[49] Patrick Murphy Malin, however, was reluctant to proceed in direct opposition to the wishes of the corporate membership. In a troubled telephone conversation with John Finerty, one of the board members who opposed the proposed policy, he conjectured that the affiliates would consider it "sharp practice" for the board to anticipate the report of the special redrafting committee with a new Communist policy of its own. Finerty himself objected strongly to Thomas's proposal and wrote to Malin: "If there is any further intimation from any group that they will resign if they don't have their way . . ., I shall resign and I shall state publicly that my reason is that McCarthyism in another guise has invaded the Civil Liberties Union."[50]

Yet another attempt to obtain a strong anti-Communist policy surfaced at a subsequent board meeting. Lewis Galantiere, program director for Radio Free Europe, submitted a statement of policy to which both Norman Thomas and Ernest Angell had given their approval. The crux of this statement was that the Communist party of the United States was a conspiracy rather than a political theory and instrument: "While that movement seeks to give the appearance of being primarily a political instrument of agitation and propaganda," the statement read, "it is actually an international conspiracy to seize power—political, social, economic—wherever it can." Fraenkel tried to table the motion, but the board adopted it with an overwhelming vote of eighteen to three. Only Fraenkel, Dorothy Kenyon, and Dorothy Bromley opposed the measure. Others whom Fraenkel counted on "his side" were absent: Arthur Garfield Hays, John Finerty, Walter Gellhorn, Telford Taylor, and Elmer Rice.[51] According to the *New York World-Telegram*, the ACLU's adoption of the "strongest anti-Communist stand in its thirty-five year history" indicated a "change in its attitude on backing legal appeals of known Reds."[52] And though ACLU director Malin disputed this claim,[53] it seemed clear that the union was finding it difficult to reconcile its strong anti-Communist position with the defense of civil liberties.

The affiliates of the ACLU helped resolve the union's dilemma in favor of a more forthright defense of civil liberties. When the special committee requested by the affiliates (representing the board, the national committee, and the affiliates) met in July 1954 to redraft the original disputed Communist policy of the ACLU, it soon became evident that in this small group only Norman Thomas favored a militant statement on Communism.[54] Although no one upheld the strict civil libertarian position advocated earlier by Corliss Lamont, the committee did draft a moderate statement on the Communist party, which stressed the responsibilities of a civil liberties organization for protecting the freedom of everyone. The report began by expressing its concern over the suppression of basic liberties and safeguards and affirmed that "the abuse by wrongful un-American methods of the rightful national aim to safeguard the security of the country . . . betrays the noblest traditions of our history." The discussion of the Communist party was brief and stressed the party's dual nature rather than just its conspiratorial aspects. "It [the Communist party] is both a political agitation movement and a part of the Soviet conspiracy," the statement read. "Insofar as it is the first, its members have all the rights of members of other parties; to the extent that it is the second, its members may in some particulars be restricted by law."[55] The special committee adopted the entire report unanimously, and the board of directors also unanimously approved it. The board agreed that no further referendum to the ACLU corporation was necessary, as the Biennial Corporate Conference had not provided for one nor had there been requests for one.[56]

The ending of the long, bitter debate within the ACLU over the Communist issue coincided with the subsidence of the post-World War II Red Scare. The death of Joseph Stalin in March 1953 precipitated an immediate struggle within the upper echelons of the Soviet power structure and marked a new and somewhat more hopeful period in Soviet-American relations. The Korean War ended in July 1953 with an armistice which in essence met the limited objectives of the United States and its allies. Senator McCarthy reached the peak of his power in 1953 with investigations which included the United States Information Agency and the United States Army's Fort Monmouth Signal Corps; by January 1954 he had reached the high point of his public support, which declined rapidly thereafter. McCarthy's clash with the army erupted in the spring of 1954 into the dramatic Army-McCarthy hearings, which further contributed, through their thorough and nationwide television coverage of the man and his methods, to McCarthy's declining personal influence.[57]

The ACLU's sustained efforts in 1953 and 1954 to establish a strong anti-Communist image for itself, however, had diverted the organization's time and energy in lengthy intra-organizational debate and had unquestionably diminished the strength and consistency of its commitment to civil liberties where the Communist issue and questions of national security existed. In the highly controversial case of Julius and Ethel Rosenberg, for example, where conviction for atomic espionage had brought a death sentence, the ACLU board took the position that no civil liberties questions were involved. John Finerty, who in 1953 became associate defense counsel for the Rosenbergs, strongly disagreed with the ACLU's conclusion, and over a period of several months Osmond Fraenkel changed his mind and concurred with Finerty. Fraenkel, in studying the record of the Rosenberg trial, concluded that evidence of the Rosenbergs' Communist party membership was improperly introduced to prejudice the case rather than to establish motive and intent to injure the United States. He also questioned whether the trial was not actually a trial for treason, in view of the several occasions during the trial when the word was used. Since the crime of treason required proof by two witnesses and the crime of atomic espionage only one, Fraenkel believed that this should be a matter of great concern to the ACLU, especially as the conviction carried with it a death sentence. Despite these grave questions concerning the due process of the Rosenberg trial, the ACLU board of directors once again decided, eighteen to four, that the case involved no civil liberties issues and that therefore the union should not intervene.[58]

The ACLU was also extremely reluctant to become involved in the controversial case of Owen Lattimore. A leading Western authority on China who had been one of McCarthy's first targets, Lattimore had been investigated, subsequent to McCarthy's allegations, by a Senate subcommittee chaired by Senator Patrick McCarran. The Justice Department, at McCarran's insistence but with little substantial evidence, had Lattimore indicted for perjury on grounds that he had lied when he declared under oath that he had never been a sympathizer or promoter of Communism or Communist interests. The ACLU's board of directors cautiously discussed the case for almost two years, debating whether or not to file a brief in Lattimore's behalf and whether or not to issue a public statement. In January 1954 the board finally agreed to answer inquiries with the statement that "Certainly the case involves civil liberties" but the ACLU would offer no further statements nor take any action until court proceedings clarified the indictment. Finally, in October 1954, Lattimore's attorney, Thurman Arnold, told the ACLU's staff counsel that the union's approach to the case was "a resumption of the kind of quibbling debate which ignores the fundamental legal and constitutional issues," and he asked the union to stay out of the case. The board agreed not to intervene but, perhaps piqued by Arnold's remarks, finally decided to issue a public statement that important civil liberties issues were involved in the Lattimore case. Osmond Fraenkel was surprised that "there was practically no opposition" from the board members to such a statement.[59]

The ACLU's uncertain defense of civil liberties during the height of the Red Scare was revealed especially in the case of Corliss Lamont. During the stormy months in the autumn of 1953, while Lamont was fighting the ACLU's proposed anti-Communist policy, he also became engaged in a confrontation with Senator McCarthy himself. Lamont's books had been found in United States libraries abroad, along with the works of twenty-two other authors with suspected or acknowledged Communist ties. In late September 1953 McCarthy subpoenaed Lamont to appear before the Senate Committee on Government Operations, then conducting an investigation of the Voice of America. In his appearance before the committee, Lamont did not invoke the Fifth Amendment, "since a contempt case will not hold against an individual who uses the Fifth Amendment correctly." What Lamont sought was a court test "to halt the excesses of Congressional committees," and he saw that he could get such a test by challenging the McCarthy committee's jurisdiction. Volunteering the information that he was not and never had been a member of the Communist party and that he was not in any way employed by the United States government, Lamont cited the First Amendment and denied that the committee had any right to inquire into his personal beliefs and affairs. He refused to answer most of McCarthy's questions and challenged the committee's jurisdiction, arguing that the statutory limitations of the legislation establishing it precluded such an inquest, that the committee was "not a competent tribunal" because of the resignation of all its Democratic party members, and that any inquiry into personal beliefs and activities lay within the jurisdiction of the judicial, not the legislative, branch.[60]

The ACLU board discussed the Lamont case and agreed that the union could properly enter litigation on behalf of a board member, but it delayed actually making that commitment. One month after the

McCarthy committee's hearing a special committee of the board met and decided that the board should make no public statement on the matter until McCarthy's committee or the Senate as a whole cited Lamont for contempt. The only action the ACLU special committee recommended was that the ACLU write a letter, without publicity, to the Committee on Government Operations protesting specific violations of procedure during the hearing itself. When the union did finally comment on Lamont's hearing, it gave a summation of McCarthy's questions but not the full grounds for Lamont's refusal to respond. Lamont's attorney, Philip Wittenberg, immediately wrote the board: "To have this come as the Union's only statement is heartbreaking. Does the Union think that by ostrich-like tactics it can avoid the attacks of McCarthy . . . ?"[61]

The special ACLU committee on the Lamont case met again in December 1953, and this time it turned down Fraenkel's proposal to support Lamont.[62] Several days later, however, the ACLU board approved defending Lamont on the grounds that it was improper for the McCarthy committee to question him on his political beliefs and associations simply because he was an author of books used by the government. The board voted to issue a public statement on its position and, "if possible," file a brief supporting Lamont; it also unanimously instructed the office "to use all proper methods to prevent a citation for contempt" against Lamont. At the same time, the board voted to support Harvey O'Connor, an author who had also refused to answer the McCarthy committee's questions on First Amendment grounds. Fraenkel afterward commented that "this is the first clear-cut position taken by the Board in a long time."[63]

The union's hesitant action on the Lamont case was revealing especially because it coincided with a bitter dispute within the organization over Lamont's status as a member of the board of directors. As a result of his vigorous opposition to the anti-Communist policy in the ACLU, Lamont had become offensive to a number of board members, who were determined to prevent his renomination to the board, on which he had served for twenty-one years. Norman Thomas, Morris Ernst, James Fly, and Ernest Angell all threatened to resign if Lamont were renominated. Following Lamont's renomination by a special motion on November 2, 1953, one board member, Whitney North Seymour, actually did resign, and another, Merlyn Pitzele, declined to stand for reelection. Finally, at its November 16, 1953, meeting, the board voted to remove Lamont's name from the list of nominees by a vote of thirteen to eight. Fraenkel, who was not present at the meeting, concluded that Lamont's removal was "a shabby business which forebodes no good for the independence of the Board from right wing pressure on other issues." He recorded in his diary that he, Roger Baldwin, and several others "all agreed" that Lamont was "a useful member of the Board." Lamont, Fraenkel maintained, "had always stood for the civil liberties of all."[64]

In response, a group from the ACLU chapter in New York City offered to back Lamont for renomination by special petition, a provision in the bylaws. Lamont declined, citing the endless wrangling within the board and his sense of hopelessness in "waging a minority battle here." "I am tired of all this," he told the board. "I believe that I can be more helpful to the cause of civil liberties by giving over my energies directly to the fight against McCarthy and McCarthyism than by endlessly debating my able and eloquent opponents on this Board."[65]

| * |

Largely as a result of the ACLU's reluctance to get involved in the most controversial civil liberties cases of the postwar Red Scare, a small group of men in 1951 established the Emergency Civil Liberties Committee.[66] Its founders believed a new organization was needed "to augment the American Civil Liberties Union, but with guts enough to fight the evils of McCarthyism without fear of being sullied by the label of 'pro-Communist.' " In the interest of this goal, the ECLC intended to provide free legal counsel from the lowest to the highest courts.[67]

Non-Communist rather than anti-Communist, the ECLC sought to appeal to non-Communist liberals and radicals. The ACLU kept a watchful and, on the whole, wary eye on the new organization.[68] That Clark Foreman, the ECLC's director, had formerly been secretary of the National Citizens Political Action Committee triggered an alert among ACLU staff members, who concluded that the ECLC might be a Communist-front organization. In an information paper for ACLU members which assessed the ECLC, the ACLU staff noted the ECLC's objections to "certain positions taken by the ACLU as making too great an allowance for the claims of national security. . . ." The paper also concluded that the new organization "wants to do more than the ACLU does in 'arousing public opinion' and in 'creating pressure' " on civil liberties issues.[69] Beyond this assessment, the ACLU seemed not to have concerned itself with the ECLC or with the fact that in some quarters, the ACLU was no longer regarded as an active, fighting defender of civil liberties.

In any case, the ACLU did not need to concern itself over what a small group of leftists thought of its organization or policy. The Cold War had created a new set of guidelines, and a majority within the ACLU's leadership made every effort to adapt to them. Responding to the climate of anxiety created by the Cold War, the ACLU reconsidered its civil liberties aspirations in the light of national as well as its own security requirements. Like the ADA, the CIO, and congressional liberals, many of the ACLU's leaders during these difficult postwar years attempted to temper liberalism with Cold War "realism." In so doing, they helped redetermine the arena of permissible public debate in such a way as to exclude the left-most wing of the American political spectrum, joining the Vital Center in its redefinition of American liberalism.

8

The Demands of Cultural Freedom

The emergence of a new Cold War liberalism was reflected not only in battles over legislation, trade union membership, and civil liberties, but also in the literary and cultural wars of many of America's most gifted intellectuals. Indeed, by the early fifties Cold War liberals seemed willing to go to extraordinary lengths to enforce the conformity of the era.

The playwright Arthur Miller overstepped the narrowing bounds of permissible expression in *The Crucible*, a powerful drama in which he used the story of the Salem witch trials to convey the horrors of the postwar witch hunt. Miller elicited an especially angry review from Robert Warshow, associate editor of *Commentary*, who contended that Miller had used the Salem story to defend "the astonishing phenomenon of Communist innocence." Irving Kristol, then managing editor of *Commentary*, extolled the boundaries Miller had refused to observe. Civil liberties, Kristol claimed, were in a confused and endangered state in America because some liberals insisted on defending the civil liberties of Communists and fellow travelers. He thought it was "a calamitous error to believe that because a vulgar demagogue lashes out at both Communism and liberalism as identical, it is necessary to protect Communism in order to defend liberalism." Alan F. Westin, in a reply carried by *Commentary*, noted that Kristol possessed "a remarkably dehydrated conception of a civil liberties issue," but many, including Norman Thomas and the chairman of the ACLU board of directors, Ernest Angell, acclaimed Kristol's remarks.[1]

The line was thus drawn between those who insisted upon the need to comply with the new and narrow restraints of Cold War politics and those who refused to accept these restrictive definitions of political and intellectual freedom. In 1950 the *New Leader*, a political affairs journal appealing to extreme anti-Communist socialists and liberals, characterized the participants in this debate the "hards" and the "softs," the political sophisticates versus the political innocents. The "softs," the *New Leader* explained in an editorial, "spend their chief energies on improving democracy in the U.S.A. and can't look the Cold War in the face." The "hards," on the other hand, "are more willing to risk reaction and war . . . to fight Communism. They are as hard-boiled toward Moscow as Moscow is toward us. . . ."[2]

The editors of the *New Leader* probably thought of themselves as following a middle course between "hard" and "soft" in much the way that Schlesinger had recommended the Vital Center and Niebuhr had praised the middle way. In an unusual plea against doctrinairism, the *New Leader* closed its editorial with a warning that "a sharpening of the Hard-Soft division among liberals could prove dangerous both to liberalism and to America."[3] However, much as Niebuhr's middle way between idealism and realism proved in practice to be remarkably in step with contemporary political "realism," the *New Leader*'s own editorial position in practice epitomized its definition of "hard." The *New Leader*'s single, overriding criterion in assigning "hard" or "soft" was an individual's or group's position on Communism, both at home and abroad, and on this issue the *New Leader* was undeniably "hard." The *New Leader*, and those to whom it spoke, viewed Communism as a militant, monolithic, and dangerous foe which must at all costs be stopped before it conquered the world. The *New Leader* stressed that Communism abroad must be confronted at all points and contained, or even pushed back, by a powerful military complex and by strong economies fostered in those countries most immediately threatened. It also warned of Communist infiltration at home and called for every effort to be made to prevent Communist take-over.

While the "hards" found their political opinions well expressed in the *New Leader*, the "softs" could turn to the *Nation* for a more congenial world view. Long a prominent liberal journal, the *Nation* remained during the late forties and early fifties an advocate of the old liberalism of the New Deal and popular front. Throughout the Cold War, it had little difficulty in locating the principal danger facing the nation and the world in Fascism, rather than Communism. The Soviet Union, the *Nation* insisted, was motivated by nationalism rather than by ideology. The Cold War, it thus concluded, had resulted from American suspicion and bellicosity toward its former ally, whose national requirements for adjacent spheres of interest Americans refused to understand. At home as well as abroad, the *Nation* contended, the real threat was the totalitarian right, which posed as a friend to democracy by getting mileage out of its implacable enmity toward Communism. The Communist party USA did not worry the *Nation*, which stressed that the party had neither the capability nor the intention of overthrowing the United States government. The encroachments made upon the Bill of Rights in fighting Communism were thus wasted and tragic efforts.

The *New Leader* and the *Nation*, the "hards" and the "softs," thus held two inflexibly different pictures of world affairs. Associated with this fundamental debate, however, was a collection of symbols which bore a direct, though not always obvious, relation to the debated issues and which soon became a kind of shorthand for referring to the entire body of warring ideas. Seemingly innocuous statements implied a whole range of associated political beliefs. A key word in the collection of symbolic phrases, for example, was "hysteria." The test for political hysteria, all concerned agreed, was political reality: the hysterical were those who were responding to an unreal terror. The *Nation* and its adherents believed that the United States was in the grips of hysteria, and it defined the hysterical as those who so feared the threat of Communism that they responded by subverting basic civil liberties in their hunt for Communists. The danger, the *Nation* emphasized, was not from Communism but from those who perpetrated the hysteria. The danger from the political right, the *Nation* stressed, was real.[4] The *New Leader* and its adherents agreed that hysteria was rampant and dangerous, but it disagreed about who had become hysterical. In the *New Leader*'s view, the international and domestic Communist menace was real, and those alert to its threat were realistic. Those who thought that McCarthy commanded any real power and had committed any real damage were the ones who were hysterical. The *New Leader* emphatically did not approve of McCarthy, but it concluded that McCarthyism had not permeated American society and that McCarthy posed no real threat to American liberties. The real danger, the *New Leader* insisted, was from creeping Communism, not creeping McCarthyism.[5]

Agreeing on opposition to McCarthy, the *Nation* and the *New Leader* differed fundamentally in their assessments of his power and influence. The *Nation* presented McCarthy as a frightening individual whose personal power and pervasive influence had contaminated the mainstream of American life and thought; the *New Leader* and its contributors saw him as a regrettable aberration whose power was over-rated and whose antics helped undermine the efforts of serious anti-Communists. "Admittedly," a *New Leader* editorial stated, "McCarthy is an enemy of social progress, but by no means the enemy that Stalin is." Richard Rovere, a writer for the *New Yorker* as well as a con-tributor to the *New Leader*, wrote a thoughtful and highly critical book on McCarthy which concluded that the senator was obnoxious but that the "McCarthy hysteria" had been vastly exaggerated. Rovere observed that he had felt no personal repercussions from speaking out on McCarthy ("I owned a capacious wastebasket," he said of the pro-McCarthy hate mail he received), and thus implied that American life and civil liberties were in no special danger from the political right. James Rorty and Moshe Decter, former radicals and also *New Leader* contributors, devoted an entire book to exploring McCarthy's anti-Communist tactics and concluded that the real danger he posed was in doing nothing constructive to fight Communism but rather making matters more difficult for dedicated anti-Communists by his publicity-hunting and shotgun tactics.[6]

Another shorthand method for placing combatants in the Cold War debate was their attitude toward the quality of contemporary American life. The *Nation* deplored American life, while the *New Leader* defended it. The fundamental argument was whether or not civil liberties and essential American values had eroded during the postwar search for domestic Communists. The British philosopher Bertrand Russell touched off fireworks when he proclaimed in the *Manchester Guardian* that the United States was being swept by a reign of terror. Robert M. Hutchins, former president of the University of Chicago, created almost as much ire when he remarked on the "gen-eral atmosphere of repression" in the academic community. Sidney Hook retorted, in *Heresy, Yes—Conspiracy, No!* (from which the *New Leader* published excerpts), that shortly after Russell's evaluation of the contemporary status of American civil liberties, the ACLU and the American Jewish Committee had reported "some satisfaction with the rate of progress" of civil rights in America and "a moderate optimism for the future progress of civil rights in various fields of American life." Hook replied to Hutchins that "the facts are that no professor who was in the habit of speaking up five years ago has been silenced, many who were silent five years ago are speaking up, while those who were silent five, ten, fifteen years ago and are still silent cannot be regarded as victims of a reign of terror." Richard Rovere, in a mid-1952 article in the *New Leader*, reported that "a fraud had been perpetrated" by describing America as in the grips of McCarthyism. "The immense portion of the truth . . . is that our institutions, by and large, have stood up well." And in a representative editorial appearing in late 1951, the *New Leader* attacked talk of "thought control" in the United States. "Never has there been as much debate on the most basic issues as there is today," it stated. "Can anyone name a single phase of American life that has not, within the past year, come under the sharpest scrutiny?"[7]

The *Nation* in 1952 published a lengthy special edition on the civil liberties crisis in the United States. The *New Leader* responded with a specific challenge to each one of the *Nation*'s special edition articles. Zechariah Chaffee, a professor at Harvard Law School and a well-known civil libertarian, had written in the *Nation* that the great proliferation of ex-Communists turned accusatory witnesses constituted a grave threat to civil liberties. The *New Leader* replied that these political converts represented no threat to civil liberties and, in fact, had shown commendable wisdom in perceiving the true nature of Communism. Matthew Josephson, a leading leftist author, complained in the *Nation* that there was a clampdown in the publishing world against controversial books. The *New Leader* challenged his observations and agreed with Arthur Schlesinger, Jr., that Josephson's prime example of a victim of censorship was indeed a Communist or a Communist sympathizer and thus, by implication, outside the arena in which civil liberties were to be respected. "In the name of fighting censorship," the *New Leader* observed, "Josephson would not have us unmask any Red wolf in liberal clothing." Kirtley F. Mather, professor of geology at Harvard, had written in the *Nation* that there was an infiltration of McCarthyism into the sciences; the *New Leader* noted that he chose to defend scientists such as Linus Pauling, a Nobel Prize chemist accused by the *New Leader* of an affinity for left-wing causes. Vern Countryman, a professor at Yale Law School, had written about congressional attacks upon the National Lawyers Guild; the *New Leader* observed that, after all, the guild was pro-Communist. Arthur Eggleston, a labor reporter, had criticized the rise of McCarthyism in the unions; the *New Leader* replied that his article was merely a plea for a renewal of the popular front. Carey McWilliams, associate editor of the *Nation*, gave a vivid description of the "witch hunt" throughout American society; the *New Leader* commented that this description was "sheer baloney."[8]

The attack became increasingly bitter and personal. Thus, in assessing the *Nation*'s civil liberties issue of 1952, the *New Leader* devoted an entire article to highly partisan "biographies" of the *Nation*'s contributors. In 1954, Granville Hicks, himself an ex-Communist, devoted a column to two types of liberals whom he considered undesirable, designated the "fakes" and the "retarded." "Fake" liberals were those whose close following of Communist party line qualified them as fellow travelers, even though they chose to call themselves liberals. "Retarded" liberals were those who "blurred and distorted the issues of the present struggle," since they had pro-Soviet sympathies and did not understand that the world had changed since the war. In the 1920s and 1930s, Hicks pointed out, intellectuals had reasons for forming a loose alliance with Communists. In the 1920s, intellectuals turned to Communism from distaste for the business-dominated status quo; in the 1930s, they linked with Communists to oppose Fascism. In the 1940s, they had reason to continue their alliance because Russia was our ally in war. The world had changed since then, Hicks concluded; yet, these "retarded" liberals had not changed with it. They were "so used to standing up for dissenters that they cannot or will not understand what they are up against when they tangle with the Communists."[9]

In 1951 Clement Greenberg, former art critic for the *Nation*, directed a slashing protest against the *Nation* and its foreign editor, Julio Alvarez del Vayo. Del Vayo's articles, Greenberg charged, consistently expressed the Communist party line on foreign affairs, and del Vayo was thus using the *Nation* as a mouthpiece for Communist propaganda. "The *Nation* has the right to side with the Stalin regime when it holds itself compelled to by principle . . . ," Greenberg stated, "but not to put its pages at the regular disposal of one whose words consistently echo the interests of that regime. . . ." The *Nation* claimed that Greenberg's letter was libelous and refused to print it, and in addition warned Greenberg of libel action if he printed it elsewhere. Greenberg replied by printing his letter, plus a full account of the episode, in the *New Leader*. The *Nation* retaliated with a libel suit against the *New Leader*.[10]

Del Vayo, a Spanish Republican and sympathizer with popular-front causes, firmly believed in the necessity for reconciling both sides of the iron curtain. An adherent of democratic socialism, he feared Fascism but not Communism and repeatedly warned that the west's hostility prevented peace with Communist nations and strengthened reactionary forces in Europe. Del Vayo criticized the Truman Doctrine for bolstering reaction and opposed the Marshall Plan as "part of a deliberate move to force Europe into the free-enterprise mold."

Socialism, he believed, was "the only possible way to rebuild Europe and at the same time give political democracy a chance." He questioned the North Atlantic Treaty Organization's value and criticized the United States for branding Communist China an aggressor in the Korean War, thus jeopardizing the possibilities for a peace settlement.[11]

The Greenberg letter and subsequent libel suit served to rally the "hards" in opposition to the *Nation*'s "softness" on the Communist issue. Arthur Schlesinger, Jr., wrote the *Nation*'s editor, Freda Kirchwey, that "as an occasional contributor to the *Nation*, I would like to associate myself with the sentiments expressed by Clement Greenberg. . . ." Reinhold Niebuhr, who until this time had been a contributing editor of the *Nation*, immediately resigned. "I have long since contemplated taking this step," he wrote Freda Kirchwey. "I contemplated it precisely because I was sick of del Vayo's animadversions on foreign affairs. . . ." While the "hards" attacked the *Nation*'s stance on Communism, they also attacked the libel suit as a restriction on freedom of discussion. Norman Thomas wrote Kirchwey that he regarded the *Nation*'s suit as "an enormous mistake. . . ." It hurts the whole cause of rational discussion and puts another block of fear in the way of the business of turning on light at a time when to turn on a light is peculiarly important." Kirchwey replied to Thomas that if the issue were one of whether the *Nation* and del Vayo were pro-Communist, the *Nation* would have printed Greenberg's letter. However, Greenberg's letter constituted a charge "that del Vayo is a Russian agent and that the *Nation* is serving the interests of the Russian government. . . . It is a charge we simply cannot print and then argue about. . . . This is a serious denunciation, Norman, not an argument about policies or points of view."[12]

Both sides were quick to agree that the suit's implications went far beyond the legal issues. The *New Leader* and its supporters claimed that the suit involved "a principle of the greatest importance: the right to criticize, in a responsible manner, the politics of any person or publication whose opinions are a matter of public record." The *Nation* and its supporters replied that the charges were not within the boundaries of responsible debate, and stressed the necessity of taking them to court to "prove their danger and damage" and "give those who want to express unconventional views a far greater feeling of safety" in a period when "people whose views differ from the majority . . . are being driven to silence by fear of being branded 'Communist' and 'disloyal.' " The *New Leader* argued that the *Nation* was threatening to "set a dangerous precedent that would seriously restrict freedom of inquiry and debate." The *Nation* replied that Greenberg and the *New Leader* had not attacked opinions but had charged del Vayo and his editors with being a tool of the Soviet government.[13]

James Burnham, Sidney Hook, Norman Thomas, and William L. White soon joined to sign letters for general circulation backing the *New Leader*. The American Committee for Cultural Freedom announced that it would give financial support to the *New Leader* for its case.[14] The pre-trial maneuvering dragged on through the McCarthy years with little accomplished on either side. Finally, in 1955, both parties agreed to end the litigation without cost to either.[15] However, the attack of the "hards" on the "softs," of which the libel suit was an outgrowth, had been waged with great intensity throughout the early 1950s and had confirmed the *New Leader*'s prediction that a sharpening of the "hard-soft" division among liberals would indeed prove dangerous to American liberalism.

| * |

Foremost among those groups in the front lines of the battle against "softness" on Communism was the American Committee for Cultural Freedom (ACCF). The ACCF had been first organized in the late thirties under the auspices of a group including John Dewey and Sidney Hook. After years of inactivity it was revived by Hook and Norman Thomas following the 1949 Waldorf World Peace Conference, a popular-front endeavor which had attracted a number of prominent intellectuals.

The new ACCF was a product of the same forces and some of the same people which created the Congress for Cultural Freedom in Berlin in 1950, and the ACCF began its active career in 1951 as an affiliate of the international congress.[16] Total membership never exceeded several hundred. The first chairman of the postwar ACCF was Sidney Hook. Other officers included Norman Thomas, Diana Trilling, Daniel Bell, and Merlyn Pitzele. Irving Kristol of *Commentary* was the first executive director; he was succeeded by Sol Stein, a former political affairs analyst on Voice of America's Ideological Advisory staff. Some ACCF members were disillusioned radicals who had begun moving steadily toward the political right—James Burnham, John Dos Passos, James Farrell, and Max Eastman. Others were liberal centrists, such as Arthur Schlesinger, Jr., Elmer Rice, David Riesman, and Richard Rovere. Though divided on many issues, they were bound together by the common denominator of anti-Communism.

Nevertheless, maintaining harmony within the organization was a continuing problem.

The ACCF's goals were clear from the outset. Sidney Hook told an early executive committee meeting that the organization's function was "to expose Stalinism and Stalinist liberals wherever you may find them." Sol Stein urged the ACCF to attack "the residues of Communist influence frontally." The ACCF, he stressed, "is an active association of leaders of the American cultural community . . . devoted . . . to rallying intellectuals here and abroad in a serious and responsible opposition to Communism and all forms of totalitarianism."[17]

The main targets of the ACCF included those relatively few left-wing and popular-front groups which still stood for the old liberalism of the New Deal and the popular front. Thus, when Sol Stein learned that a Democratic congressman had agreed to speak at a National Lawyers Guild conference, Stein warned him that the guild was a Communist-front group and the congressman withdrew. It was part of his ACCF duty, Stein observed, to inform "non-Communists of Communist-dominated organizations with which they seem to get involved." Stein later commented, "The congressman will, I think, be a bit more careful in the future."[18]

During the early 1950s the ACCF focused many of its attacks on the Emergency Civil Liberties Committee, an agressive left-wing group devoted to fighting for civil liberties. The ACCF was convinced that the ECLC was Communist-dominated and dangerous,[19] and when in 1953 the ECLC proposed a conference on the Bill of Rights, the ACCF leadership became deeply worried. Many respected academic and religious figures had agreed to attend the conference. Some of these individuals, the ACCF believed, should be steered away, and therefore the ACCF privately telegraphed them a warning: "Are you aware," wired Kristol, "that this organization is a Communist front with no sincere interest in liberty in the United States or elsewhere?" Kristol contacted Reinhold Niebuhr, an ACCF member, and asked him to convince the ECLC's chairman, Dr. Paul L. Lehmann, to resign. "The general complexion of this organization can be seen from some of the people they have invited to participate," Kristol wrote Niebuhr. Some who particularly concerned him were the journalists Carey McWilliams and I.F. Stone, as well as Thomas Emerson, a professor at Yale Law School and a National Lawyers Guild member. "There are, of course, non-Communists who are also taking part," he added, "but no one who can be legitimately described as an anti-Communist."[20]

Some of the telegram's recipients responded by withdrawing from the conference, among them the noted theologian Dr. Paul Tillich and the Rabbi Ira Eisenstein, who wrote the ACCF's current chairman, Professor George S. Counts of Columbia Teachers College, that he had been "a bit hasty in accepting the invitation" and that he "should certainly have recognized some of the names of the other sponsors." Others did not resign and some took offense at the ACCF's interference. Fowler Harper of the Yale Law School replied that the telegram gravely concerned him and, in his estimation, placed the ACCF among those who react so that "whatever the Communist Party is for, they are against; whatever the Communist Party is against, they are for. . . . They are not free men," he concluded, "because they fear that some position they may take will 'associate' them with the Communist Party." Dr. Paul L. Lehmann, in replying to the ACCF, wondered if "your words conceal the kind of bitter personal feuding, which has made the liberal movements of our time and in every country the prey of whatever totalitarian power should arrive first on the scene?"[21]

Others defended the ECLC but thought it prudent to assure the ACCF of their firm anti-Communism. William L. Shirer, author of *Berlin Diary*, wrote Counts: "I need hardly point out to you that I am, and always have been a fairly vocal enemy of all tyranny. . . ." Dr. Lehmann reported he had never been "drawn either towards the Communists or toward the ex-Communists . . . ," and defended the anti-Communism of the entire ECLC. "We are opposed to Communism and other authoritarian movements," he wrote. "We are committed to civil liberties as a bulwark of American democratic strength at home and abroad." One ACCF member agreed: Roger Baldwin wrote Kristol that the telegrams were "most unfortunate" because so little proof existed that the ECLC was indeed a Communist-front organization.[22]

The ACCF's leaders, however, were not persuaded by Baldwin's argument; they would have been even less interested in a plea which disregarded the issue of Communist domination in the ECLC. The ECLC, Kristol commented, "has no intention whatsoever of protesting the destruction of civil liberties in Communist-dominated countries, or indicating its detestation of the Communist movement even while defending its rights." Replying to Fowler Harper, Kristol wrote: "We understand exactly what it is that the Communists are *really* for, as opposed to what they *say* they are for." Professor Counts agreed: "It is impossible to know whether or not someone is genuinely 'for' civil liberty without taking into account his posture toward Communist totalitarianism."[23]

The ECLC had, upon its inception, declared that its sole concern lay in domestic affairs and that it did not intend to debate on foreign policy. "Ours is not an international organization," it had stated, "and does not propose to be drawn into controversies dealing with American policy and international affairs. . . ." During its altercation with the ACCF, however, the ECLC conceded that it had better go on record on the Communist issue and released a statement which rejected a "double standard" of political conduct: "We will not judge our country by one standard, and other countries by a less rigorous democratic standard. . . . We condemn without reservation antidemocracy, anti-Semitism, and political persecution wherever they occur. We condemn these practices in the Soviet Union."[24]

The ECLC also brought the ACCF's telegrams to the attention of the press and challenged the ACCF for evidence that it was indeed Communist dominated. Kristol replied that since the ECLC, not the ACCF, had made the matter public, the consequences rested with the ECLC. He told questioners that he had no ready facts at hand but was in the process of collecting them. Kristol explained that he had not put together a "formal dossier on the ECLC" before the telegrams were sent because the telegrams were personal in nature. "We simply wanted various people, whom we felt had no place [in the ECLC] to discuss the matter with us." The ECLC's press agent was, Kristol pointed out, a very able man—"otherwise, he would not have been doing publicity for Corliss Lamont for the past few years"—and had self-inflicted the smear in public "for purposes of publicity."[25]

Kristol was shortly forced to retract his characterization of the ECLC as a "Communist front" and instead resorted to branding it a "popular front." A popular-front organization was hardly a lesser danger, however, so far as the ACCF was concerned, and a year later, when the ECLC planned a conference on academic freedom in honor of Albert Einstein's seventy-fifth birthday, the ACCF again felt compelled to act. Einstein had previously incurred ACCF disapproval by advising intellectuals not to testify before congressional committees inquiring into their political beliefs. The ACCF called his advice "ill-considered and irresponsible" and urged a policy of "clean hands" and "speaking out" as "the only choice possible for non-Communists who seek to preserve the climate of political freedom."[26] Nevertheless, the ACCF did not want Einstein's illustrious reputation to enhance the ECLC's own public image, and consequently it did everything possible to dissuade him from participating in the conference.

J. Robert Oppenheimer, a key figure in the development of the atomic bomb and, at that moment, suspended chairman of the Atomic Energy Commission's General Advisory Committee, offered his services to the ACCF, in which his membership was then pending. When he heard of the ECLC's proposed project he immediately contacted Einstein, who told him that "he did not go to such things" but had agreed to answer a set of questions in writing, which he had already sent. Oppenheimer then contacted the ACCF to report that Einstein appeared unwilling to withdraw from the role he had agreed to play: "He might be willing to say that it wasn't his idea of a birthday celebration, but he can't retract the letter. I do not know what we can do unless we can get someone to choke them [the ECLC] off and stop it."[27]

Sol Stein, the ACCF's new executive director, urged Oppenheimer to talk once more with Einstein. American Jewish leaders, he reported, feared Einstein's actions might link Judaism and Communism more firmly in the public mind. In addition, Stein noted, any support which Einstein gave the ECLC would "help to spread the notion one hears so often nowadays about physical scientists being political babes-in-the-woods"—a particularly unsubtle appeal to Oppenheimer's personal interests. Stein himself wrote Einstein, "These Communist sympathizers want very much to give the impression that scientists, Jews, and members of other minority groups do not feel concerned about Communism or do not believe that the role of the United States now is to defend freedom." He asked if Einstein would put in writing his view of the harm that Communists had done to America. Einstein agreed and in reply to the question, "What do you think about the nature of Communism and what are the best methods of combating its influences?" he wrote:

> I do not know what one should understand of the 'nature of Communism'; but I know well that the Communist Party has made use of such methods which have essentially contributed to the creation of the present atmosphere of general mistrust. Democracy has an effective means to make ineffective damaging influences of any kind; mainly, by enlightenment, by free and objective discussion of all problems. This means is always effective in the long run, and it is the only means which democracy has at its disposal.[28]

There is no record of Stein's response to Einstein's remarks nor any indication of what the ACCF's leadership thought about them. On behalf of the ACCF, however, Norman Thomas continued to press

Einstein to withdraw from the upcoming ECLC conference. The members of the ECLC "work under a double standard which I am sure you do not accept," he wrote. Einstein replied: "I see with a great deal of disquiet the far-reaching analogy between Germany of 1932 and the U.S.A. of 1954." He credited the ECLC for upholding civil liberties "with a decisiveness and in a sense which is close to my convictions." He loathed the Russian Communist state's arbitrary rule but believed it was the problem "of the Russian people to make changes there." As for the Communist conspiracy in America, "in my eyes, [it] is principally a slogan used in order to put those who have no judgment and who are cowards into a condition which makes them entirely defenseless. Again, I must think back to Germany of 1932. . . ." Thomas replied, "I need hardly tell you I despise McCarthyism. I still believe, however, that it is an ugly skin disease on the face of liberty rather than a cancer."[29]

The ACCF readied itself for the ECLC conference by preparing a press release planned to demonstrate unquestionably that the ECLC was a Communist front. Among the ACCF's evidence was a 1952 ECLC meeting called to protest attacks on and suspensions of teachers who refused to reveal their political affiliations. Another item was the ECLC's opposition to the conviction of American Communist party leaders under the Smith Act. The ACCF also noted that at a luncheon given by the ECLC in honor of a member of the National Lawyers Guild, the honored individual attacked the attorney general for listing the guild as a Communist front. Finally, the ACCF pointed to the background of such ECLC leaders as Corliss Lamont, to whom the ECLC had awarded a citation as a "courageous and uncompromising supporter of the Bill of Rights for all." "This is not to say that any one of these circumstances is in itself evidence of Communist views," the ACCF observed. However, taken all together, "these facts are revealing." The ACCF itself had no question about the ECLC's true function. It was convinced that Communists controlled the ECLC and were "(a) trying to monopolize the American anti-McCarthy fight in order (b) to eliminate decent anti-totalitarian and anti-Communist organizations and people from this internationally popular battle."[30]

Oppenheimer, whose own loyalty hearings were about to be held before a special Atomic Energy Commission panel, publicly disavowed any involvement in the ECLC's conference. Sol Stein released a statement that the ACCF was not in general opposed to meetings on academic freedom or civil liberties but that it was nonetheless opposed to this particular one. "Because we are devoted to those freedoms," he stated, "we are opposed to any *exploitation* of them by persons who are at this late date still sympathetic to the cause of the Soviet Union."[31]

Although the ECLC held its conference as planned, attacks by the ACCF continued.[32] Norman Thomas wrote to the *New York Times*: "The Emergency Civil Liberties Committee believes in civil rights in an extreme sense for Communists and fellow-travelers in America but defends or at least condones the complete denial of those rights behind the iron curtain." Upon Einstein's request, Thomas withdraw the letter before publication (in it he had quoted from Einstein's correspondence to him). However, Thomas's letter found its way into the *New Leader* and brought an angry response from the ECLC, which argued that it, too, was on the record as opposed to all authoritarian regimes and practices and as believing in civil liberties for all. In its defense, the ECLC attempted to answer its critics and even threatened a law suit against the *New York Post* for biased coverage of the ECLC-ACCF fracas. Neither Oppenheimer nor the ACCF, however, responded to the ECLC's attempts to clear its name, and the ECLC found its correspondence, questions, and pleas ignored.[33]

| * |

The ACCF's combativeness was wide ranging and extended even to its own parent organization, the Congress for Cultural Freedom in Paris, taking issue with the congress's particular style of defending cultural freedom. ACCF leaders noted with dismay that the congress was de-emphasizing its belligerence toward Communism and devoting the greater part of its energies toward promoting cultural activities. The ACCF office complained to its executive committee that the congress's activities "were becoming decreasingly directed toward the goal for which the Congress was created, namely: active opposition to totalitarianism with special awareness that Communism is the greatest present threat to cultural freedom." Sponsorship of international meetings of composers, performers, and music critics did not serve the interests of cultural freedom well "when such meetings did not materially contribute to the struggle with Communist totalitarianism." "The Congress seemed to be holding arts festivals in Rome while Europe burned," the ACCF office complained. In addition, the ACCF was disappointed with the "inadequate role" played by the congress's magazines, particularly its England-based journal, *Encounter*. *Encounter*'s "apparent unwillingness to offend what it presumes are English sensibilities with explicit anti-Communism" had

channeled its interests to "primarily literary material. . . ." Neither
Europe nor Asia was as hostile to a "forthright anti-Communist program" as the international congress assumed.[34]

In part, the ACCF's quarrel with its parent organization stemmed
from the old debate among leftist intellectuals over the proper relationship between politics and culture. The majority of the ACCF
agreed—in practice if not in spoken policy—that culture should directly serve the purposes and interests of politics, in this case the politics of democratic capitalism.[35] The Congress for Cultural Freedom
dissatisfied its affiliate by increasingly stressing the importance of cultural events on their own merit, apart from politics. The international
congress, however, had by no means forgotten politics. Having taken
note of European and Asian intellectuals' unreceptivity to hard-line
anti-Communism, it had merely accommodated its message to its
audience and now peddled a more sophisticated and palatable anti-
Communism. This subtle bid for the allegiance of the world's intellectuals was financed, in part, by the United States Central Intelligence
Agency, which had channeled funds to the international congress
and *Encounter* since their founding. Aware that hard-line tactics were
winning few converts from radical politics abroad, the CIA had
evolved a new strategy to support and infiltrate liberal organizations
and "take on the Russians by penetrating a battery of international
fronts."[36]

Whether the ACCF knew of the international congress's CIA backing is not certain. It is clear, however, that the ACCF knew the congress
received financing from the Farfield Foundation, which was, in turn,
a probable conduit for CIA funds to the congress.[37] In 1954 the congress cut off the ACCF's monthly stipend of $500 in favor of funding
"critical areas where possibilities for local fund-raising [were]
nonexistent." Pressured by a serious need for funds, the ACCF in early
1955 asked the international congress to request financial assistance
on its behalf from the Farfield Foundation. The foundation quickly responded with a grant of $10,000. Despite such largess, when the
ACCF's disagreements with the international congress led the ACCF to
declare "independent affiliation," the ACCF's executive committee
made a private stipulation that, although desperate for funds, the
American committee would accept no further money from the Farfield Foundation.[38]

Basic differences had made the ACCF's relationship with the congress increasingly unworkable. "I have no desire to tell them what
they should do," chairman James Farrell told the executive committee

in late 1955, "and I am perfectly willing to let them pick their editors and run their magazines and congress the way they wish." Neither he nor others of the ACCF leadership, however, wanted the ACCF in any way "responsible for the policies and acts of the International Congress in Paris. . . ." Finally the ACCF declared "independent affiliation" with the Congress, a loose arrangement which offered the ACCF the opportunity to pursue more closely its concept of the interests and requirements of cultural freedom.[39] Ironically, the ACCF had sundered its ties with the CIA-financed Congress for Cultural Freedom because the international congress was insufficiently anti-Communist.

| * |

The ACCF had welded together a new kind of united front with its Cold War coalition of former radicals and anti-Communist liberals. As James Burnham observed, however, even though all ACCF members were "against totalitarian society," this single tenet provided a "very thin ideological basis."[40] Even during the peak of the Cold War the feat of balancing liberals on the one hand and radicals turned conservative on the other was extremely difficult. At a spring conference in 1952, several members clashed on the nature and intensity of the Communist and the McCarthy threat. Elmer Rice, for example, charged that the current Communist-hunt and its threat to individual self-expression constituted the greatest threat to cultural freedom in America; while Max Eastman, on the other hand, made a strong defense of Joe McCarthy and requested those present to give the Wisconsin sensator their support in his fight against Communism. Eastman also charged "'fuzzy-minded' liberals 'in the name of cultural freedom' with helping the enemy to destroy all freedoms throughout the world." Richard Rovere and novelist Mary McCarthy took a middle course by stressing the dangers of both Communism and McCarthyism but singling out McCarthyism as distinctly the lesser of the two evils.[41]

Relatively few in the ACCF supported Eastman's outright pro-McCarthyism, but, as Rovere noted to Schlesinger, a number believed in "the importance of accommodating men like Eastman." Rovere did not particularly appreciate Rice's interpretation of current events but, as he told Norman Thomas, "I'll admit frankly that if, God forbid, I had to choose between Rice and Eastman, I'd choose Rice. He's not very wide-awake, but I think he cares about freedom, and I don't believe Eastman cares about anything but working off old grudges."

Rovere, himself a former radical, "reluctantly" concluded that "the leadership of the ex-Communists has on the whole been a bad thing in this country: "If you examine the extreme and irrational positions on this [McCarthyism] and related questions, you will find that in nearly every case they originate with people who have at one time or another been deep in the Communist movement. . . . I am coming fervently to hope that the influence of these aggrieved and unhappy people will soon be shaken off."[42]

In the attempt to hold the anti-Communist coalition together, however, liberals in the ACCF were for the moment willing to accept right-wing fanaticism from former radicals. In 1953 James Burnham created a stir by writing the preface to *The Secret War for the A-Bomb*, whose author, Medford Evans, proposed that fissionable material had been and continued to be smuggled out of America to Russia, which otherwise would have been unable to produce its own nuclear weapons. Evans blamed prominent American scientists for this treasonous activity. Burnham called the book "old-fashioned American writing for Americans" and highly recommended it. Eugene Rabinowitch, editor of the *Bulletin of the Atomic Scientists* and member of the ACCF's executive committee, strenuously objected to Burnham's endorsement. Other ACCF leaders, among them Norman Thomas, agreed that Burnham had become "organizationally a dubious asset to the Committee. . . ." However, the *Partisan Review* had already asked Burnham to resign from its advisory board and, as Daniel Bell wrote Hook, "It would be fanning the flames for us now to step in and ask Burnham to go; it would only polarize the situation." In the name of organizational harmony, the executive committee thus proposed its own dictum for tolerance: reminding Rabinowitch of the Congress for Cultural Freedom's Berlin Manifesto, it concluded that "within the confines of [that] Manifesto there can, and must be, room for all shades of opinion."[43] So long as opinion was not leftist, the ACCF would tolerate it.

The ACCF existed on the extreme promontory of anti-Communism, however, and by 1954, as the Cold War tensions somewhat subsided, the organization found its financial and membership support receding. With the creation of the Ford Foundation's Fund for the Republic in the early 1950s, the ACCF briefly thought it had found a financial backer. The fund was initially interested in financing the ACCF to write a definitive history of American Communism, a study of the abuses of congressional procedure, and a third study of the existing threats to freedom from both the extreme right and the extreme left. When Robert M. Hutchins became chairman of the fund, however, relations between the fund and the ACCF cooled, and despite continued efforts by the ACCF to win the fund's support, its requests were repeatedly turned down.[44]

The ACCF began to court other sources of funds, including the Robert Marshall Civil Liberties Trust, of which Roger Baldwin, an ACCF member, was a trustee. The ACCF in 1954 submitted to him a list of its activities, prompting Baldwin to remark that "anti-Communism in itself is an inadequate and negative policy, which only partially contributes to cultural freedom." By this time, the ACCF's financial plight made it willing to devote some of its attention to opposing McCarthyism in the hopes of attracting new backers. Stein wrote Sidney Hook that the ACCF would have to disprove its "softness" on McCarthy to "the 'open-minded' segment of American liberalism. . . . I am not talking about 'Trotskyites, fellow-travelers and an assorted variety of idiots,' " he explained, "but sensible people who thrive on the Archibald MacLeish variety of libertarianism." Winning approval from these would be "unpleasant but . . . necessary if we are to get a more sympathetic following in the academic community." On this premise, Stein replied to Baldwin, "You will be happy to know that we have under way now what will be in effect a Human Rights Commission . . . which will take a special interest in combating the unjust blacklist in the entertainment field and [in helping] persons deprived of employment because of past associations."[45]

The ACCF's most important anti-McCarthyism project was its sponsorship of James Rorty and Moshe Decter's *McCarthy and the Communists*, published in 1954. The book, which sold well, gave a detailed documentation of McCarthy's activities and concluded that his methods were evil precisely because they imitated the very totalitarianism he pretended to root out. The danger McCarthy posed to the nation, Rorty and Decter concluded, was in undermining the efforts of respectable and serious anti-Communists. The book pleased many, but not those liberals the ACCF was now attempting to court. Rorty and Decter had, in effect, proposed that McCarthy's chief danger was in giving less flamboyant anti-Communists a black eye. Followers of the *New Leader* would appreciate this viewpoint, but few others would. Arthur Schlesinger, Jr., and the ADA took offense at Rorty and Decter's conclusions, chiefly because of the book's interpretation of Yalta and its plaudits to McCarthy for having uncovered lax security procedures in the State Department. Much to the distress of the ACCF's leadership, the book also created consternation among the right wing of its membership. James Burnham submitted his resignation and accused the ACCF of becoming "a narrow partisan clique." George S. Schuyler, a conservative Black journalist, resigned and stated that "the anti-McCarthy drive which the ACCF so enthusiastically joined is indeed an intellectual mob action: i.e., a lynching."[46]

Stein and the ACCF leadership stated their belief that "whatever power the committee has derives to a great extent from the large part of the political spectrum represented in it . . . ," although they appeared to have little personal respect for members of the organization's right or left wings and continued to court them only for the purpose of keeping the membership rolls as impressively full of intellectuals as possible. "Burnham . . . is Schlesinger's mirror image," Stein told the current ACCF chairman. "Both, I think, belong in the intellectual community and could, I feel, be talked back into it." Stein attempted to coax Schuyler back into the organization and, after failing, persuaded Whittaker Chambers to join. Delicate diplomacy was involved, since Chambers was at first reluctant to join an organization in which J. Robert Oppenheimer was also a member. Chambers finally agreed to join after receiving assurances that Oppenheimer had proved his staunch anti-Communism by his activity against the ECLC.[47]

It became increasingly difficult, however, to hold together a coalition based on the negative common denominator of anti-Communism. With pressures from the Cold War as well as from McCarthy somewhat abated by the mid-1950s, members with fundamentally different beliefs were unable to work together. Harold C. Urey, the Nobel Prize chemist, taxed the ACCF leadership's patience by defending the Rosenbergs and Morton Sobell. "In my opinion [the ACCF] does not have the slightest understanding of what cultural freedom is," he retorted after Stein warned that he was only helping the Communists. David Riesman wrote Stein that he objected to the ACCF's "preoccupation with parochial and intellectually dead if politically live themes." He observed that "good and thoughtful people do not want to spend their time daily discussing American Communists, but only semi-intellectuals with nothing better to do"; such disinclination ought to serve as a clear signal that "this issue is not one that a group devoted to cultural freedom should examine."[48]

Discontent from the ACCF's liberals came to a head when the ACCF executive committee decided to reply to an article in the *New Republic* attacking the proceedings of the McCarran Committee in its investigations of Owen Lattimore. The ACCF's reply, published by the *New Republic*, stated, "Lattimore was indeed a willing instrument of the Soviet conspiracy against the free world"; that he helped "in however small a measure that conspiracy to victory in Asia and yet is vindicated in the pages of the *New Republic* is surely a commentary on the 'political lag' among some elements of American liberalism." Riesman, portraying Lattimore as a "shattered man" who hardly needed the ACCF's condemnation, chastised the executive committee for "mouse-hunting" and resigned. "The meetings," he later explained, "have a polemical, even fanatical quality . . . which cannot be justified by the importance of the issues involved." Rovere, Schlesinger, and Herbert J. Muller also were disturbed by the Lattimore incident and joined with Riesman in writing the *New Republic* to disclaim any part in or approval of the ACCF's reply.[49]

Such public dissent angered the ACCF leaders, who were by then prepared to wash their hands of members whose anti-Communism seemed to be flagging. Norman Thomas wrote Rovere that while he had the right to send any letter he wanted to the *New Republic*, if this one should be published "there will be a flood of letters from the other side, letters which are not likely to do much good for Lattimore, if you are interested in that side of it." Stein attempted to discredit the dissenters, who, he argued, were on the organizational fringes of the ACCF and did not represent its views: Muller and Schlesinger, although both vice-chairmen, occupied honorary positions and Riesman, Muller, and Schlesinger "have attended a total of one meeting in the last few years between them." Schlesinger, in turn, accused the committee of abandoning its original objectives and of descending into petty vindictiveness, as if "refighting in the fifties the old, dead battles of the thirties and forties."[50]

Some, like Urey, now concluded that the ACCF had never understood the meaning of cultural freedom. Others, like Schlesinger, believed the world had changed but the ACCF had not changed with it. Schlesinger agreed that when the ACCF was first organized it had "important jobs to do in the way of exposing illusions about Communism and of identifying Communist activity in the United States. . . ." But, he concluded, the time when Communism could be considered the overriding enemy of cultural freedom within the United States, "in my judgment, has largely passed."[51]

Even some of the right wing in the ACCF had begun to view the world differently by the mid-1950s. James Farrell, whose anti-Communism had previously known no bounds, remarked in 1956 that the ACCF had not been able "to work and contribute sufficiently in the necessary and continuing struggles for the further achievement of liberal aims here. . . . We are not in the main current of American life," he told the ACCF's new director. Farrell, at the time of these observations, was chairman of the ACCF, and his criticisms displeased the executive committee, which announced his resignation with the comment that "Mr. Farrell's usefulness to the American Committee for Cultural Freedom unfortunately [has come] to an end." Other former radicals were also mellowing on the Communist issue. When, at the ACCF's 1955 forum, Diana Trilling warned that Communists were "regaining all the strength they had [in America] in the thirties and more," Granville Hicks retorted that she was "seeing things." Other speakers in the program agreed with him, causing Lionel Trilling to conclude: "It looks as if the ACCF sponsored what turned out to be an anti-anti-Communist meeting."[52]

Increasingly, ACCF leaders became frustrated and isolated. When Michael Josselson, chairman of the parent Congress for Cultural Freedom, wrote the ACCF in the autumn of 1954 that Senator McCarthy was losing ground and that, consequently, "there is no immediate threat to intellectual freedom in America," ACCF executive director Sol Stein was appalled. There is "a refusal to understand that the gravest danger to civil liberties in the free world . . . continues to come from Communism," he wrote to a sympathetic Sidney Hook in 1955. "Things were easier when the conflict was more dramatic as at the time of the outbreak of the Korean War when the Congress for Cultural Freedom was founded," he reminisced. "Since then, the conflict has grown less and less dramatic, which is in some measure an indication of the success of Soviet propaganda and diplomacy. . . ."[53] By late 1956, only the ACCF's stalwarts remained active, and in early 1957, after a losing battle for continued interest and financial support, the ACCF surrendered to the changing times and agreed to end its active role as an organization.

Throughout its history the ACCF had equated anti-Communism with cultural freedom. Consequently, the organization declined when it became evident, as the Red Scare declined, how very little the ACCF had to offer American intellectuals. In the name of defending freedom, it had attempted to curtail the individual's freedom of choice in thought, speech, and association. The ACCF was only one form of pressure, although a highly significant one, which anti-Communist intellectuals exercised upon their colleagues during the Cold War years. Those who complied with the prescribed brand of anti-

Communism sought security from Communism's global spread, while at the same time they hoped through their anti-Communist activities to protect themselves from right-wing attacks. Those remaining liberals and radicals who refused to capitulate to the anti-Communist credo found themselves the immediate targets of attack from both the right wing and the anti-Communist left alike. As a result, the intellectual community during the postwar years suffered from endless conflict, great personal hostilities, and a general willingness on the part of too many creative thinkers to exchange their individualism—and that of others—for a single and narrow mode of thought and action. That this exchange was made in the name of fighting totalitarianism was just another of the many ironies of the postwar years.

9

The Vital Center and
the Politics of
Anti-Communism: 1954

In the Congress of the United States, the death of Stalin and the end of the Korean War had little immediate, perceptible impact on the political fortunes of the Communist issue. McCarthy in 1953 was at the peak of his political career, and investigations of Communists in government proliferated throughout both houses of Congress. Throughout the nation the Red Scare had not yet noticeably subsided, and in Congress, liberals continued to operate on the assumption that their careers depended upon the care with which they dealt with this still-explosive issue.

In the House of Representatives, liberal congressmen still were reluctant to oppose publicly the House Committee on Un-American Activities. In 1953, Congressman Holifield stated that he had "no complaint to make of the procedures of the committee in the last two or three years," and no other liberals rose to comment or object. The HUAC appropriations passed in 1953 with 113 members not voting and only two, Emanuel Celler and Minnesota Farmer-Labor-Democrat Roy W. Wier, in opposition.[1]

By early 1954, however, there were indications that the public mood had begun to shift, and some liberal politicians cautiously began to respond. Congressman Jacob Javits in February 1954 stated that he had voted for the 1953 HUAC appropriation because he and others understood that his vote did not mean he had to accept everything the committee did. "Now," he said, "there is a great stir in the country about this type of investigation," and he cited the protests of several "highly respectable" conservative organizations. When such organizations "oppose the methods of investigation by committees in this field," he concluded, "the Congress must listen," and he advised that the "prestige of the whole Congress is at stake." Nevertheless, Javits did not oppose the 1954 HUAC appropriation, and only one congressman, Roy Wier, voted against it.[2]

In the Senate, liberal Democrats remained relatively silent on matters where Senator McCarthy was directly involved, insisting that he was a Republican problem and refusing to do anything which might rally Senate Republicans around him. They avoided occasions when they might be accused of partisanship on the McCarthy issue and ran little risk of personal political reprisals, arguing that, "to take the curse of partisanship off the matter," a Republican would have to take the first important steps in opposing McCarthy. This event finally occurred toward the close of the Army-McCarthy hearings in June 1954, when Republican Senator Ralph E. Flanders of Vermont, a moderate, introduced a resolution calling for removing McCarthy from his committee chairmanships on the basis of the earlier findings of the Senate Subcommittee on Privileges and Elections.[3]

Senator Lehman quickly supported Flanders's resolution and also asked the Senate to remove McCarthy from his committee chairmanships. Arkansas Democrat J. William Fulbright rallied support for Flanders's resolution with the aid of liberal Democrats Tom Hennings, Mike Monroney, Herbert Lehman, and John J. Sparkman of Alabama, and liberal Republican John Sherman Cooper of Kentucky. The Flanders resolution, however, did not prove popular with most Republicans or Democrats: Republicans refused to oppose McCarthy, and Democrats feared retaliation by a future Republican minority. Flanders retreated and agreed to refer his resolution to the Senate Rules Committee, and then changed his tactics, announcing in July 1954 that he would call on the Senate to censure McCarthy. The *New York Times* reported that neither Democrats nor Republicans relished censuring a fellow-member of the Senate. The censure measure did prove more popular with Democrats than Flanders's first resolution, however; censure involved a moral judgment and did not directly touch on the delicate question of McCarthy's political power, which most Democrats were still reluctant to challenge.[4]

The debate on the motion to censure began on the last day of July, and the *Nation* commented that, "to nearly everyone's surprise, the arguments for some action on McCarthy grew stronger as the three-day debate progressed. . . ." Ultimately the Senate voted to refer the motion to a select committee, which was to submit recommendations before the Senate adjourned. Since the McCarthy problem had been before select committees before, with little success, many considered this vote merely another example of the Senate's reluctance to deal with McCarthy. Others drew hope from the solid characteristics of the select committee's appointees: headed by Utah Republican Arthur V. Watkins, these were conservatives of the South and West, where McCarthyism had made few inroads and was not an especially explosive political issue. In September this group of "drab, neutral men" unanimously recommended that the Senate censure Senator McCarthy and charged him with contempt of the Subcommittee on Privileges and Elections as well as abuse of Brigadier General Ralph W. Zwicker, a special target of McCarthy's during the Army-McCarthy hearings. The committee declared itself unable to consider thirty-three categories of charges which, it held, were political and moral rather than strictly legal issues. Nevertheless, liberals responded to the Watkins report with surprised praise.[5]

| * |

Despite Senate liberals' increased willingness by summer of 1954 to confront McCarthy in a sustained and meaningful way, they demonstrated that they still were unable to understand or to confront the essential issues of the Red Scare itself. In a highly significant episode which occurred shortly after the Senate debate on Flanders's censure resolution, liberals in both houses of Congress rallied to support a liberal-sponsored measure to outlaw the Communist party in the United States—legislation in which McCarthy himself played no active role. Senator Hubert Humphrey introduced the Communist Control bill on the morning of August 12, 1954. Co-sponsoring the measure with him was an ideologically mixed group of senators, most of whom were considered liberal Democrats.[6] The measure declared the American Communist party "the agency of a hostile foreign power," an "instrumentality of a conspiracy to overthrow the Government of the United States," and "a clear, present, and continuing danger to the security of the United States." Having thus proscribed the Communist party by name, the bill provided penalties for membership under the Internal Security Act of 1950: fines of up to $10,000 or imprisonment for five years, or both.[7]

The measure was from the outset an unusual piece of legislation. Technically proposed as a substitute amendment for legislation already under consideration in the Senate, the bill had bypassed the usual process of committee hearings and deliberations and gone directly to the Senate floor. The *New York Times* reported that the entire proposal was drafted between midnight and 1:00 A.M. on the morning on which it was presented to the Senate. Advance notice was sent to the Government Printing Office and the measure was rush-printed in time to circulate to the senators when they convened at 10:00 A.M.[8] As a result, apart from a brief floor debate, the Communist Control Act of 1954 has no recorded legislative history. Its history must be written from other sources.

The speed with which Humphrey and his co-sponsors introduced this legislation raises a question of motives, since the concept of outlawing the Communist party was hardly a new one in 1954. Harold Stassen, in his 1948 bid for the Republican presidential nomination, had advocated outlawing the Communist party in the United States, while his successful rival for the nomination, Thomas E. Dewey, had opposed such outlawing. Republican Senator Margaret Chase Smith of Maine and Democratic Senator Mike Mansfield of Montana had introduced bills to outlaw the Communist party in the United States months before the Humphrey proposal was submitted. Members of the House had introduced numerous bills on the subject, and the House judiciary subcommittee had held hearings on outlawing the party. Several legal scholars and political scientists had argued for the necessity of outlawing the Communist party, and some former radicals were especially enthusiastic about the proposal. Max Eastman, in a widely read article in *Reader's Digest*, had insisted that "a government which fails to suppress a conspiracy to overthrow it is not democratic but weak." Several states—Indiana, Massachusetts, Pennsylvania, and Texas—had passed legislation outlawing the Communist party by name in 1953 and 1954.[9]

One possible motive for the sudden appearance of the Communist control measure was the desire of Senate liberals to derail the bill for which they were proposing their substitute: an amendment to the Internal Security Act of 1950 aimed at combating Communism in the labor unions.[10] Liberals and union leaders viewed this legislation as an attempt by conservatives to weaken the entire labor movement. John M. Butler, the Republican from Maryland who was linked with McCarthy in a successful 1950 campaign to defeat Senator Millard Tydings, had sponsored this worrisome piece of legislation, and both Republicans and conservative Democrats in the Senate gave it their support. The Butler bill proposed to give the Subversive Activities Control Board, on petition by the attorney general, the power to determine whether an organization was in fact "Communist-infiltrated." An organization in which Communist influence was found would then lose its standing as a labor organization under terms of the National Labor Relations Act and thus lose governmental protection for organizing and collective bargaining. As Senator Herbert Lehman pointed out, although the terms of the Butler bill did not apply only to unions, the consequences applied effectively only to unions and thus placed a "powerful weapon to cripple labor" in the hands of an attorney general unfriendly to labor.[11]

Organized labor unanimously opposed the Butler bill. The CIO in committee hearings attempted to convince both House and Senate that the 1949 and 1950 purge of left-wing unions from the CIO had eliminated the threat of subversion from within its ranks.[12] Organized labor also lobbied to remind liberal politicians of shared interests. Thomas E. Harris, an assistant general counsel for the CIO, frequently handled the subject of anti-Communist legislation and was given the job of lobbying against the Butler bill. He later recalled meeting for dinner with Senator Humphrey and Max M. Kampelman, then Humphrey's legislative assistant, to discuss the matter. This meeting produced an agreement by all three that Humphrey should introduce a substitute provision for outlawing the Communist party.[13] Harris and Kampelman drafted the amendment with, as Kampelman later recalled, "a little help from [Senator] Wayne Morse."[14]

"In the atmosphere of the time," Harris later declared, "it seemed impossible to derail [the Butler bill] without coming up with some substitute that would enable the Senators on our side to say that they had struck a really effective blow against Communism." Under the circumstances, then, it did not much matter what the Communist control bill said; and Harris has concluded that it "never was anything but mumbo-jumbo. If you read it, you can't figure what the hell it was about."[15] Liberals had, of course, tried this tactic only a short time before, with the Internal Security Act of 1950, and had ended by contributing to the passage of both the original bill and the substitute. The Communist control bill followed a similar route. A Texas Democrat, Senator Price M. Daniel, proposed to join the Butler and Humphrey bills into one piece of legislation "to accomplish both purposes which have been discussed: outlaw the Communist Party . . . and at the same time adopt the provisions concerning Communist-infiltrated organizations. . . ." Humphrey accepted this arrangement and the Senate voted its approval, with only Lehman, still opposed to the Butler bill, voting in opposition.[16] No senator opposed passage of the entire Butler-Humphrey package.[17] "All we did was tack that bill of nonsense onto the other nonsense," Harris concluded of the Communist control bill episode. "Why we should have made that same mistake four years later, I cannot tell you."[18]

Butler definitely suspected that the Humphrey bill had been intended to destroy his own legislation. Before the two bills were joined, he commented that the Humphrey amendment "is merely another way to keep the [Butler] bill from coming to a vote."[19] If knocking out the Butler bill was the purpose of the Communist Control Act, however, the question remains why Humphrey accepted so quickly Daniel's amendment to attach the Butler bill to his own. In addition, Humphrey accepted a severability clause, which provided that the Butler portion of the bill would remain intact should the Humphrey portion prove unconstitutional—a further defense against possible sabotage to the Butler bill. According to this arrangement, the Humphrey amendment afforded no threat whatever to the anti-labor Butler bill. Harris thought that Humphrey "felt that the tide was running so strongly against him that he could do nothing about it."[20] Humprey told his fellow senators that he "readily" agreed to join his bill with Butler's, but this concession followed floor debate and strong opposition to the amendment from Butler, Michigan's Homer E. Ferguson, and other Republican senators. Majority leader William F. Knowland of California indicated that he would support the Humphrey bill only if it were joined to the Butler bill.[21] Nevertheless, Humphrey's quick capitulation made his commitment to fight the Butler bill appear less than wholehearted. Humphrey evidently had additional objectives in mind when he proposed his amendment—objectives which were not impaired by linking the Butler bill with his own.

Kampelman, Humphrey's former legislative assistant, later stated that Humphrey and he were interested in using the amendment to oppose the Butler bill, and the Humphrey bill came in a rush during the closing days of Congress for that reason. The Butler bill, however, only influenced the occasion and the strategy. Despite the suddenness of Humphrey's decision to introduce the bill, the idea was something that Kampelman and the senator had discussed for several years. Humphrey, according to Kampelman, had far deeper motives than merely opposing a bill which threatened labor.[22]

Immediately after its introduction to the Senate, Humphrey's amendment had drawn opposition not only from supporters of the Butler bill but also from many Republicans and conservative Democrats who feared that such legislation threatened the effectiveness of the Smith Act and, in particular, the Internal Security Act of 1950, which required "Communist-action" and "Communist-front" organizations to register with the attorney general. Since the Humphrey amendment provided penalties under the Internal Security Act for Communist party membership, members of groups that under the Internal Security Act were required to register with the attorney general might avoid doing so by pleading their Fifth Amendment privilege against self-incrimination. Furthermore, many believed that Humphrey's proposal would drive the Communist party underground. The Republican administration—Attorney General Herbert Brownell, Jr., and the Federal Bureau of Investigation's J. Edgar Hoover in particular—objected to the idea of outlawing the Communist party and had done so even before the Humphrey bill.[23] The Internal Security Act's registration section was then in its last stages of its court tests, and administration spokesmen stated they did not want to endanger a potentially effective weapon against Communism. Senators such as Patrick McCarran and Homer Ferguson, who had pushed the Internal Security Act through the Senate, agreed with the administration.[24]

According to Kampelman's recollection, those in the administration and Congress who feared that the proposed Communist Control Act might undermine the Internal Security Act and other anti-subversive legislation, were completely correct; the Humphrey bill's drafters had that intent. Humphrey's bill, Kampelman stated, "was intended to change the whole pattern [of internal security legislation] and replace it with a new philosophy." This new philosophy, which already had gained some acceptance among members of the academic and legal communities as well as among politicians,[25] was "designed to protect innocent people from being attacked ruthlessly and recklessly." By making membership in the Communist party a criminal act, the decision whether or not a particular individual was a party member would then be a matter for court determination, with all the protections provided in the Bill of Rights: the right to counsel, the right to face one's accuser and to know the evidence against one, and the right to defend oneself against the accusation—none of which were guaranteed or usually provided under the government security program. In addition, according to Kampelman, such legislation protected the non-Communist liberal or radical from being unfairly labeled as a Communist, since such slurs would be subject to libel and slander action.[26]

Shortly after the Humphrey bill's passage in the Senate, powerful conservatives sought to weaken it. McCarran called the Humphrey amendment "a monstrosity" and said he had voted for the bill in its final form only because he supported the Butler bill.[27] Ferguson, chairman of the Republican Policy Committee, worked with administration and House leaders to draft a substitute House amendment, one which would remove those provisions that they feared threatened the anti-Communist laws already on the books.[28] The Republican measure, as presented to the House on August 16, proposed to strip the Communist party of its rights, privileges, and immunities, but did not impose any specific penalties for membership in the party. It also contained a provision to protect the Internal Security Act of 1950. The House passed this Republican version, in conjunction with the Butler bill, after forty minutes of debate, with only two members opposing. Democrat Abraham J. Multer of New York and Republican Usher L. Burdick of North Dakota both voted against the bill on civil liberties grounds.[29]

Humphrey, displeased by the House version, proposed to change the House bill by making membership in the Communist party a crime subject to penalties and by incorporating a new section listing fourteen criteria for determining Communist party membership. These criteria had originally been part of a bill proposed by Congressman Martin Dies, former chairman of the House Committee on Un-American Activities. They subjected to prosecution those who had "conferred with officers or other members of the [proscribed] organization in behalf of any plan or enterprise" or had "prepared documents, pamphlets, leaflets, books, or any other type of publication in behalf of the objectives and purposes of the organization." The Senate accepted Humphrey's amendment by a close vote[30] and then re-passed the Humphrey-Butler bill, as amended, by an overwhelming vote, with only Estes Kefauver in opposition.[31] Within two hours, the House of Representatives voted, 208 to 100, to accept the Senate version.[32] The bill then went into a House-Senate conference.

The conferees were strongly in favor of removing Humphrey's penalty provisions for Communist party membership.[33] Six of the ten opposed the penalty provisions, and the majority included McCarran. J.G. Sourwine, then counsel to the Senate Judiciary Committee and present at the House-Senate conference on the bill, later stated that McCarran dominated the conference, strongly opposing a bill with penalty provisions. Butler and Congressman Chauncey W. Reed, chairman of the House Judiciary Committee, stood by the Eisenhower administration's position and held out for a bill without penalty provisions.[34] Congressman Francis E. Walter, who had worked closely with McCarran in legislative efforts to exclude left-wing aliens, evidently concluded that strong support for a tough-sounding anti-Communist bill would bolster his anti-Communist image. Congressman Emanuel Celler had voted for the bill with penalty provisions to prove he was no "bleeding heart," but did not seem anxious to bring this sort of bill out of conference.[35] McCarran had conferred in advance with Walter, Butler, and Reed and circulated drafts of the bill as he thought it should come out of conference. It would have been difficult and even foolhardy for any of the conferees to have attempted to outmaneuver someone as influential as McCarran in his bailiwick, internal security, and the bill which emerged was what McCarran had demanded: it lacked penalty provisions for membership in the Communist party and instead deprived the party of the rights, privileges, and immunities of a legal body. The bill also deprived party members of certain citizenship rights, possibly including the right to run for elective office. After three hours of debate, the Senate approved the conference committee's bill unanimously, and shortly after, the House approved by a vote of 265 to 2.[36]

Kampelman later commented that the final form of the Communist Control Act was unfortunate and defeated its basic original purpose of protecting the civil liberties of the non-Communist left. The fact that the act contained no penalties for Communist party membership, he concluded, made it an ineffective, meaningless piece of legislation: "The way it was introduced, it was a good provision. The way it got out, it was nothing."[37] Clearly, the legislative strategy had not worked as Humphrey had anticipated. Nevertheless, the senator made no attempt to oppose the final outcome. Commenting to his Senate colleagues on the Communist Control bill's final form, he said: "Maybe we did not strike as strong a blow as Hubert Humphrey would have liked to strike in the bill, but we have not injured the laws which are now on the books. . . . We have closed all the doors. These rats will not get out of the trap."[38]

Humphrey has continued to defend the Communist Control Act and his role in it on civil liberties grounds.[39] In 1959, however, he did acknowledge the political benefits of the act and stated that its passage had saved the political careers of several liberal senators who might otherwise have been defeated in the 1954 elections.[40] In addition to Humphrey, those among the Communist Control Act's cosponsors who were seeking reelection in 1954 were Paul Douglas, James Murray, Clinton Anderson, Robert Kerr, and Bernet Maybank. Edwin Johnson was a candidate for governor of Colorado. Of these, Douglas, opposed by a strong supporter of Joe McCarthy, faced the toughest campaign fight. Murray was challenged by some red-baiting in his campaign, as was Humphrey. All three won reelection.[41] Certainly, none of the politicians supporting the Communist Control Act had missed the obvious point that it offered them a means to build their reputations as true anti-Communist Americans—reputations that had suffered considerably from the anti-liberal, as well as anti-radical, fervor of the McCarthy years. "I am tired of reading headlines about being 'soft' toward Communism," Humphrey said in introducing his bill. "What is sought to be done by the amendment is to remove any doubt in the Senate as to where we stand on the issue of Communism," Morse added. "I think the time has arrived for all of us to stand up and be counted," Mike Mansfield stressed.[42]

Supporters were also well aware that the Communist Control Act afforded them an unmatched opportunity to embarrass the Republican party. With the administration opposed to outlawing the Communist party, Democrats took delight in the distinct possibility that the Communist Control Act's passage might force a veto from Eisenhower—a tremendous Democratic coup coming just before the congressional elections. Following the House passage of the bill minus its penalty provisions, Morse said: "Let the public understand who is trying to save the Communists in this country from prosecution, individual by individual, for the conspiracy to which they belong. It now appears that the White House thinks the Senator from Minnesota is a little too harsh on the Communists." Humphrey agreed that the House bill was "a little 'soft' on Communism the way it is now."[43] Viewed in this light, the Communist Control Act can be seen as a partisan measure, not simply a liberal one—which explains the backing it received from the Senate minority leader, Lyndon B. Johnson, and from conservative members of the Democratic party.[44] Nevertheless, the opportunity to capture the Communist issue from the Republican party was of particular value to Democratic liberals, who from the outset had been among the bill's most ardent supporters.

Humphrey, according to Kampelman, was not vulnerable in his 1954 bid for reelection in Minnesota. Humphrey's Republican opponent, a moderate, did not resort to a smear campaign; a third-party candidate, however, did accuse Humphrey of "softness on Communism" and used this approach as the basis of his campaign. In 1952, furthermore, Eisenhower had won Minnesota's electoral votes, the first time a Republican had done so in many years. Humphrey actually won reelection by a substantial margin in 1954. But, "you never know you're going to win," Kampelman later commented, "and you never know what issues are going to be used against you."[45]

Despite its obvious political benefits, the Communist Control Act does not appear to have been offered completely in the spirit of political expediency. Humphrey, Kampelman, and many of the liberal senators co-sponsoring the bill were genuinely interested in taking stern measures to halt any possible growth of internal Communism. Humphrey had a record of great hostility to Communism and to those he believed Communist, dating from his mayorship of Minneapolis and then his successful fight against the Henry Wallace Progressives in 1948 for control of Minnesota's Democratic-Farmer-Labor party. Evidently, Humphrey felt keenly the injustice of Republican attacks on him for "softness" on Communism. "Let the record be clear," he emphasized when introducing his bill. "This Senator has been fighting the Communist movement ever since he entered public life, and before." "I did not wait until I got to the Senate to start my crusade," he said on another occasion. In response to Homer Ferguson's sarcastic "welcome to the fold," Humphrey responded: "I do not want to be merely in the fold. I have been in the main arena."[46] Nevertheless, by the 1960s a Humphrey biographer reported his saying that the Communist Control Act was "not one of the things I'm proudest of."[47]

Other congressional liberals were not proud of the Communist Control Act but hesitated to say so openly. In the House, only representatives Abraham Multer and Usher Burdick openly opposed the measure on civil liberties grounds.[48] Emanuel Celler spoke against the bill as a "hodgepodge" which "bristles with constitutional questions." However, he told the House that he had "no use for commies or for their party," and he concluded that much as he disliked some portions of the bill, he favored others. Subsequently, Celler voted for the stern version of the Communist Control Act with the penalties provision and represented this point of view when attending the House-Senate conference.[49]

In the Senate, although Kefauver's was the only opposing vote on the re-passage of the Humphrey bill with penalty provisions, he had earlier allowed his negative vote against the Humphrey amendment to the House bill to be withdrawn and paired with the vote of an absent Democrat, thus making possible the narrow Senate acceptance of this tougher version of the bill.[50] Kefauver defended his opposition to the bill on grounds both that it might weaken the operation of the Smith and Internal Security Acts and that it might proscribe "a person's feelings, beliefs, and opinions. . . ." Clearly he did not believe he could afford to oppose the Communist Control Act solely on civil liberties grounds. He told the Senate that he had voted in favor of the final bill as it came out of conference because he believed the bill no longer threatened to prosecute a person merely because of his beliefs. He also told the Senate that "a grievous wrong" inflicted on the Democrats by the Republicans "does not justify our inflicting an even greater wrong upon the protections given our people by the Bill of Rights." He felt compelled to justify his vote, however, by revealing that a "top official of the FBI" had complimented him on it.[51]

John Sherman Cooper, a Kentucky Republican, was more openly opposed to the Humphrey bill on civil liberties grounds. Cooper was "not too greatly moved by the argument of 'stand up and be counted,'" and he protested that the Humphrey bill as originally presented to the Senate was probably unconstitutional since it proscribed mere membership in the Communist party without overt acts of violence. Consequently, he proposed an amendment of his own which would require the commission of an overt act by Communist party members before such members could be prosecuted. After Humphrey and the Senate approved his amendment, Cooper was satisfied with the bill and voted for it.[52]

Congressional civil liberties opposition to the Humphrey bill was limited. Most liberals, both in the Senate and in the House, did not make even a token opposition to it but instead ardently supported it.[53] A few of these, Senator Lehman in particular, later expressed regret for their action. Humphrey has recalled that Lehman voted for the bill "with some reluctance," and Kampelman agreed that Lehman was "very anguished about it," going along with the measure at first and then later being sorry he had done so.[54]

Most of the criticism given the Communist Control Act on fundamental civil liberties grounds came from the diverse and dwindling non-congressional American left. I.F. Stone declared that it "would undermine the Constitution, . . . widen the witch hunt and the terror, and serve the purposes of the extremists." Michael Harrington labeled it "an abject capitulation by liberalism to illiberalism." The Emergency Civil Liberties Committee, then under broadside attack as a Communist front from the American Committee for Cultural Freedom, somewhat cautiously denounced the act for undermining "our self-esteem at home and our prestige abroad," adding that, while such legislation could be justified in times of "extraordinary internal danger to national security," that danger did not exist. The remnants of the Progressive party called it a bill "conceived in hate and passed in hysteria by a cowardly Congress." Even Norman Thomas denounced it as "a low grade partisan maneuver."[55]

A few liberals condemned the act outright as a threat to civil liberties. Adlai Stevenson broke with congressional Democrats on the issue, commenting that he did not believe "we need to do anything even suggesting punishment for what people might think." The *Nation* accused Democratic liberals of a "neurotic, election-year anxiety to escape the charge of being 'soft on Communism' even at the expense of sacrificing constitutional rights." The *New York Post* called the act "a monstrosity" and a "wretched repudiation of democratic principles." The ACLU, which had testified earlier in the year against House bills intending to outlaw the Communist party, declared the Communist Control Act made "a mockery . . . of our most basic Constitutional guarantees."[56]

Most liberals, however, hedged their opposition to the act and did not stress the civil liberties question raised by the legislation. The *New Republic* rather blithely noted that the Democrats were "harvesting political hay" and seemed to relish the Republicans' dilemma. Newspapers generally supporting Democratic positions, including those with a liberal bent, shared the viewpoint of the *New York Times*, which strongly objected to the haste and irrationality with which the act had been passed and noted that such legislation "may do violence to the liberties of loyal Americans." The *New York Times* reminded its readers, however, "We think there is much to be said for removing the Communist party from the ballot and depriving it of legal rights. . . ."[57]

The ADA opposed the Communist Control Act and thereby split with Humphrey, who was one of the ADA's leaders. The ADA's opposition to the act came slowly, however, and its leadership clearly was reluctant to take an opposition stand. The ADA platform of 1952 had opposed outlawing the Communist party, but such a statement had been omitted from the platforms of 1953 and 1954. When the question of the Communist Control Act arose, the ADA's executive committee decided not to commit itself on a matter on which the annual convention had not acted, and it referred the entire problem to the national board for consideration at its meeting in January 1955. The organization then telegraphed a plea to Eisenhower to veto the bill, but not on account of the bill's provision to outlaw the Communist party. Arthur M. Schlesinger, Jr., then ADA's national co-chairman, stated that his organization opposed the Butler portion of the bill; "ADA does not take a position on the question of outlawing the Communist party," he said. The ADA finally committed itself to a position on the issue only after it had relegated the topic to a special study committee and the act itself had passed into relative oblivion.[58]

Probably the most revealing gauge of the response to the Communist Control Act was the White House mail room before Eisenhower signed the bill. The White House reported that mail and telegrams on the bill were "relatively light." While many of the telegrams were from New Yorkers opposing the bill, only about a hundred telegrams, in total, were received on the subject.[59] Most Americans, including most liberals, either did not voice their objections, or had no objections to voice.

The Communist Control Act never became a major weapon in America's legislative arsenal against Communism. In New Jersey it was used to prevent Communist party members from appearing on the state ballot.[60] The courts determined that the act neither amended nor repealed the Smith Act[61] and was neither a bill of attainder nor an ex post facto law.[62] The courts have also found that under the Communist Control Act, the Communist party is not entitled to recognition as an employer under New York State's unemployment compensation system.[63] Other than these instances, the Communist Control Act of 1954 has never been used and, although never held unconstitutional, it has had little practical significance.

In political terms, the Communist Control Act revealed that, despite the beginnings of Senate action against McCarthy, congressional liberals in August 1954 were still deeply afraid of the influence of anti-Communist politics. It was not just McCarthy they feared, but the politics he symbolized, and the Communist Control Act was a clear illustration of how deeply those attitudes at the root of McCarthyism had penetrated American society during the decade following World War II, affecting even those who attempted to fight the Red Scare and McCarthy himself.

In particular, the defense which Humphrey and others offered, that the Communist Control Act was fundamentally a civil libertarian measure, indicates a failure to comprehend the basic dangers of the Red Scare—the threat to the freedom of speech and assembly of an unpopular minority. According to the act's provisions, guilt by association would be replaced with guilt by membership. The technique of guilt by association had been slipshod and had caught anti-Communists as well as Communists in its net. Anti-Communist liberals wanted to limit the catch to bona fide members of the Communist party. In short, the measure sought to protect liberals and non-Communists by excluding Communists from participation in the political process.

No violent action on the part of individual Communist party members was to be necessary to establish guilt, according to the act's provisions. As further amended by Humphrey's fourteen criteria for determining party membership, the Communist Control Act (before the House-Senate conference deleted its penalty provisions for party membership) subjected to prosecution even those who had published anything in support of Communist party objectives, a criteria that, in its broadest sense, could include legitimate responses to a multitude of domestic and foreign policies. Here the Communist Control Act offered its most blatant threat to civil liberties, by establishing the legal means to regulate and limit political expression to what was considered acceptable and safe to the current majority.

| * |

The year of 1954 and in a broader sense the entire post-World War II era had presented American liberals and the entire left with immensely difficult and demanding problems, chief among which was the conflict between national security demands and civil liberties during a time of great international stress and danger. In this atmosphere of anxiety and frustration, the censure resolution against McCarthy emerged as a kind of symbolic breakthrough—symbolic in the sense that McCarthy had himself been symbolic. On December 2, 1954, almost five years after McCarthy's spectacular rise to national notoriety, the Senate voted, sixty-seven to twenty-two, to condemn him. The charge concerning General Zwicker was dropped, leaving only charges of contempt and abuse of the Senate. Technically speaking, the censure involved no direct action against McCarthy and dealt with very limited charges. "The smug old body condemns browbeating Senators but not private citizens," the New Republic columnist T. R. B. had commented. "We have condemned the individual, but we have not yet repudiated the 'ism,' " said Senator Lehman.[64]

Nevertheless, for all its actual limitations, the censure was the expression of great expectations that the sordidness and fear of an era had come to a close, and this one event quickly assumed the status of a major dividing line. "What has changed is not Mr. McCarthy but his opponents," wrote James Reston in the New York Times the day after the Senate action. "During most of the [McCarthy] period there has been a kind of political paralysis among the anti-McCarthy faction, and it was never entirely clear who was for him and who was against him. This doubt has now been removed." Senator Hennings agreed: despite the fact that the resolution did not attack McCarthy directly, he commented, "we are gradually coming out of the wilderness and . . . the majority of people are beginning to realize that intolerance and conformity are in no sense acceptable elements in a democratic political economy."[65]

Despite hopes to the contrary, however, an era had not come abruptly to a close. The Cold War continued, although with somewhat diminished intensity, and the fears which bred the Red Scare correspondingly decreased, although they did not disappear. There was relief that the scourge of McCarthyism had been exorcised, but liberals for the most part had little cause for self-congratulation. Their own role in McCarthy's downfall had been minimal and more than counterbalanced by their ardent support for the Communist Control Act. In 1954 the new liberalism of the Vital Center was, as it would remain throughout the rest of the decade, weak and ineffective. The attack of the McCarthyite right and the inner civil war on the left had combined to produce a decade in which the left was in virtual eclipse.

Conclusion

During the brief period from 1947 through 1954—which may have seemed like an eternity to some—the Cold War pressure points spread rapidly from eastern Europe and the Mediterranean to China and Korea. War erupted and the threat of nuclear disaster became an accepted, if not acceptable, commonplace. In response to the dangers and accompanying anxieties produced by a world in flux, Americans at mid-century gave their allegiance to a form of patriotism which was in itself dangerous and unstable, and which provided the fuel for the postwar Red Scare.

The Red Scare itself was not, however, the simple occurrence it at first appeared. Although it has become synonymous with the name of Joe McCarthy, McCarthy neither created the Red Scare nor set its bounds. He did personally exemplify the traits of the Red Scare so remarkably that his name quickly became a shorthand description for its more frightening and turbulent aspects, but the Red Scare was, nevertheless, a far more pervasive and subtle mood than the McCarthy image allowed for; it permeated and fundamentally reshaped the attitudes and activities of all portions of the political spectrum, especially the American left.

The Cold War had sparked a struggle within the left which revolved around the issue of United States foreign policy toward Russia and the question of cooperation with Communists at home. This struggle reached its peak with the Wallace candidacy in 1948 and resulted in defeat, not only for Wallace and the Progressive party, but for the popular front and the old left as well. The new liberalism which emerged in its place, although still humanitarian in its thrust, was "realistic" rather than idealistic, more cautious and conservative, and fundamentally elitist. Above all, postwar liberals identified with the political center and clearly delineated their differences with traditional leftist politics as well as with the remnant of the American political left. Responding to the dangers of the Cold War world, these liberals excluded domestic Communists and popular-front leftists from the arena of permissible public debate and, as a result, lost sight of vital civil liberties and limited the free marketplace for ideas.

The old left was thus the victim of escalating international tensions and the domestic politics of anti-Communism. By mid-century, in the place of the united left, there had emerged a new liberal center which stressed its ties to the New Deal but which expressed a yearning for stability and security that was distinctly a product of the new nuclear age. Above all, the politics of the old left had been the politics of risk, based on rejection of the status quo and faith in the future. The prosperity as well as the tensions of postwar America, however, discouraged risk and placed the highest premium on safety and stability. Reformism lingered on, but without the impatience of the 1930s, and radicalism almost entirely dwindled away.

One of the major ironies of the period was the unexpected role which liberals played, first in constructing a new liberalism which rejected the American left, and then in accepting some of the basic assumptions and tactics of the Red Scare itself. For years, American leftists had fought to defend fundamental civil liberties and then, in response to grave international danger as well as attacks from the political right, the majority of liberals at mid-century became reluctant to defend the rights of the least popular left-wing minority. The liberal failure to defend these liberties was, given the great fears and pressures of the Cold War, explainable and even understandable. Nevertheless, liberal failure in this important instance marked a loss not only for the American left, but for the nation as a whole.

Notes

Chapter One

1. See John Lewis Gaddis, *The United States and the Origins of the Cold War, 1941–1947* (New York, 1972), pp. 224–30, 242, 244–46, 282–315. For more critical appraisals of this period see Thomas G. Paterson, *Soviet-American Confrontation: Postwar Reconstruction and the Origins of the Cold War* (Baltimore, 1973), Walter LaFeber, *America, Russia, and the Cold War, 1945–1966* (New York, 1967), and Joyce Kolko and Gabriel Kolko, *The Limits of Power: The World and United States Foreign Policy, 1945–1954* (New York, 1972). See also *Public Papers of the Presidents of the United States*, Harry S. Truman (Washington, D.C., 1946), pp. 145, 147–48.
2. See Alonzo L. Hamby, *Beyond the New Deal: Harry S. Truman and American Liberalism* (New York, 1973), chaps. 3 and 5.
3. See ibid., especially chap. 3.
4. See Norman D. Markowitz, *The Rise and Fall of the People's Century: Henry A. Wallace and American Liberalism, 1941–1948* (New York, 1973), chaps. 1–3, and Hamby, *Beyond the New Deal*, chaps. 1, 2, and 5.
5. See Markowitz, *Rise and Fall of the People's Century*, pp. 220–21.
6. See Hamby, *Beyond the New Deal*, chaps. 4 and 6.
7. Norman Markowitz, "A View from the Left: From the Popular Front to Cold War Liberalism," in *The Specter: Original Essays on the Cold War and the Origins of McCarthyism*, ed. Robert Griffith and Athan Theoharis (New York, 1974), pp. 102–3, 106–7.
8. See Clifton Brock, *Americans for Democratic Action: Its Role in National Politics* (Washington, D.C., 1962), pp. 46–51.
9. *New York Times*, January 6, 1947; circular from James Loeb, Jr., May 8, 1947, box 65, Administrative File, Americans for Democratic Action Papers, State Historical Society of Wisconsin, Madison, Wis. (hereafter cited as ADA Papers).
10. *New York Times*, January 5, 1947, March 31, 1947, and April 16, 1947; National Office to ADA chapters, April 28, 1947, p. 2, box 65, Administrative File, ADA Papers.
11. *New York Times*, January 5 and 6, 1947, and March 31, 1947.

12. The ADA's "General Purposes," adopted at its 1950 convention, significantly defined liberalism as including a "high sense of individual responsibility for oneself and one's neighbor" and a "deep belief in the dignity of man," in addition to an "awareness of human frailty" ("General Purposes," *ADA World,* April 1950, p. 2).

13. *New York Times,* January 5, 1947; Freda Kirchwey, "Mugwumps in Action," *Nation,* January 18, 1947, p. 62; Helen Fuller, "The Liberals—Split as Usual," *New Republic,* January 13, 1947, p. 27.

14. Robert Bendiner, "Revolt of the Middle," *Nation,* January 18, 1947, p. 66; James Loeb, Jr., "Letter of the Week," *New Republic,* January 27, 1947, p. 46. Also see Robert Bendiner to James Loeb, January 8, 1947, box 64, Administrative File, ADA Papers.

15. The *New Republic,* after a brief spurt in circulation in the late 1940s due to the attraction of Henry Wallace as editor, declined from 52,022 in 1950 to 30,661 in 1954, with a low point of 24,156 in 1953. The *Nation*'s circulation was steadier but also declining — from 45,331 in 1947, to 39,439 in 1950, to 31,900 in 1954 (*N. W. Ayer and Son's Directory of Newspapers and Periodicals,* 1947–1954).

16. Freda Kirchwey, "Mugwumps in Action," *Nation,* January 18, 1947, p. 62; Robert Bendiner, "Revolt of the Middle," *Nation,* January 18, 1947, p. 65. Kirchwey never reconciled herself to the anti-Communism of the ADA but, after the formation of the PCA-based Progressive party in late 1947, strongly opposed the Wallace candidacy and its invitation to a Republican victory: "It is all very well for Communists to entertain the hope that after the deluge their turn will come, but why should Henry Wallace invite either consequence?" she asked (Kirchwey, "P.C.A.'s Quixotic Politics," *Nation,* December 27, 1947, p. 693).

17. James Loeb to Michael Straight, June 3, 1947; Straight to Loeb, June 5, 1947, pp. 1–2—both in box 70, Administrative File, ADA Papers.

18. Loeb, "Letter of the Week;" Daniel Mebane to Loeb, November 18, 1947; Loeb to Bruce Bliven, October 7, 1947—both in box 70, Administrative File, ADA Papers. Also see Straight to Loeb, October 10, 1947, box 70, Administrative File, ADA Papers.

19. The standard histories of Communists and the CIO are Max Kampelman, *The Communist Party vs. the C.I.O.* (New York, 1957), and David Saposs, *Communism in American Unions* (New York, 1959), pt. III. Also see Philip Taft's history of the labor movement, *Organized Labor in American History* (New York, 1964). Histories which challenge the standard accounts include Frank Emspak, "The Break-Up of the Congress of Industrial Organizations, 1945–1950" (Ph.D. diss., University of Wisconsin, 1972), and David M. Oshinsky, "Labor's Cold War: The CIO and the Communists," in *The Specter,* ed. Griffith and Theoharis, pp. 118–51.

20. On Catholic sources of anti-Communism in the CIO, see Oshinsky, "Labor's Cold War," pp. 135, 138, 139, 143–44; Donald F. Crosby, S. J., "The Politics of Religion: American Catholics and the Anti-Communist Impulse," in *The Specter,* ed. Griffith and Theoharis, p. 35; and Kampelman, *Communist Party vs. the C.I.O.,* pp. 135–36, 152–53, as well as p. 37 on Murray's Catholicism.

21. Kampelman, *Communist Party vs. the C.I.O.,* p. 35; Saposs, *Communism in American Unions,* p. 151.

22. On Murray's unifying role see Kampelman, *Communist Party vs. the C.I.O.*, p. 37, and Len DeCaux, *Labor Radical: From the Wobblies to CIO, A Personal History* (Boston, 1970), pp. 373, 378. On Bridges, see CIO international executive board meeting, March 10–12, 1945, pp. 456–64, in CIO International Executive Board Proceedings, James Carey Papers (CIO Office of the Secretary-Treasurer Papers), Wayne State University Archives of Labor History and Urban Affairs, Detroit, Mich. (hereafter cited as CIO Proceedings). The CIO's special defense fund eventually raised $54,450.38 in Bridges's behalf (CIO Proceedings, March 1946, p. 148).

23. James R. Prickett, "Some Aspects of the Communist Controversy in the CIO," *Science and Society* 33 (Summer-Fall 1969): 299–321; Kampelman, *Communist Party vs. the C.I.O.*, p. 59; Saposs, *Communism in American Unions*, p. 154; Taft, *Organized Labor in American History*, p. 529.

24. Oshinsky, "Labor's Cold War," p. 121; Taft, *Organized Labor in American History*, chaps. 38 and 39, and p. 524.

25. CIO Proceedings, November 1–2, 1945, pp. 231–34, 249, 265–69, and March 15–16, 1946, pp. 94–95.

26. Oshinsky, "Labor's Cold War," pp. 125–26; Kampelman, *Communist Party vs. the C.I.O.*, pp. 36, 39 (Carey quoted on p. 39); Saposs, *Communism in American Unions*, pp. 145–47, 149.

27. Murray quoted in Kampelman, *Communist Party vs. the C.I.O.*, pp. 38, 40.

28. CIO Proceedings, November 13–23, 1946, pp. 90–93, 111; Kampelman, *Communist Party vs. the C.I.O.*, p. 54. Kampelman defines the CIO industrial union councils as "organizations of various CIO locals in the same area, usually a state or large city, which join together to sponsor legislation and other forms of mutual aid and obtain a CIO charter for that purpose" (*Communist Party vs. the C.I.O.*, pp. 54–55).

29. John Brophy to Philip M. Connelly, November 26, 1946, box 32, Philip Murray Papers, Archives, Catholic University, Washington, D.C.; Kampelman, *Communist Party vs. the C.I.O.*, pp. 56–57.

30. CIO Proceedings, November 13–23, 1946, pp. 112, 113, 117–20, 128.

31. Ibid., pp. 119, 129–30, 132–33, 137–38.

32. Ibid., pp. 205, 210–13, 218–19.

33. Prickett, "Some Aspects of the Communist Controversy in the CIO," pp. 303–15; Kampelman, *Communist Party vs. the C.I.O.*, p. 49.

34. DeCaux, *Labor Radical*, pp. 239–41, 299, 315–18, 333, 381.

35. CIO Proceedings, November 13–23, 1946, pp. 216–17.

36. *New York Times*, February 28, 1947.

37. CIO Proceedings, November 13–23, 1946, p. 126.

38. Ibid., March 13–15, 1947, pp. 329–30, 337, 374.

39. Ibid., pp. 340–42.

40. Ibid., pp. 330–31, 372, 388. Neither the ADA nor the PCA was pleased with this outcome, and the *New York Times* reported that ADA officials suspected Murray of yielding to Communist pressures to weaken the ADA (February 28, 1947).

41. CIO Proceedings, May 16–17, 1947, pp. 73, 88–90, 98–99, 122–24, 133, 166–67, 174.

42. Ibid., pp. 81–86.

43. Ibid., pp. 122, 133, 167, 180, 233–34; ibid., October 10, 1947, pp. 193, 195.

44. Ibid., May 16–17, 1947, pp. 93–94.

45. Ibid., p. 85; Kampelman, *Communist Party vs. the C.I.O.*, p. 184.
46. CIO Proceedings, May 16–17, pp. 216, 220–21.

Chapter Two

1. See John Lewis Gaddis, *The United States and the Origins of the Cold War, 1941–1947* (New York, 1972), pp. 348–51; *Public Papers of the Presidents,* Harry S. Truman (Washington, D. C., 1947), p. 179. Also see Joseph M. Jones, *The Fifteen Weeks* (New York, 1955); Dean Acheson, *Present at the Creation: My Years in the State Department* (New York, 1969), chaps. 22–25; and Richard M. Freeland, *The Truman Doctrine and the Origins of McCarthyism: Foreign Policy, Domestic Politics and Internal Security, 1946–1948* (New York, 1972), pp. 70–114.
2. David A. Shannon, *The Decline of American Communism: A History of the Communist Party of the United States since 1945* (New York, 1959), p. 29.
3. Curtis D. MacDougall, *Gideon's Army,* 3 vols. (New York, 1965), 1:128–35; Norman D. Markowitz, *The Rise and Fall of the People's Century: Henry A. Wallace and American Liberalism, 1941–1948* (New York, 1973), pp. 225, 234–42.
4. See Walter Lippmann, *The Cold War: A Study in U.S. Foreign Policy* (New York, 1947), pp. 44–45, and Hans J. Morgenthau, *In Defense of the National Interest: A Critical Examination of American Foreign Policy* (New York, 1951), pp. 115–21. Also see Barton J. Bernstein, "Walter Lippmann and the Early Cold War," in *Cold War Critics: Alternatives to American Foreign Policy in the Truman Years,* ed. Thomas G. Paterson (Chicago, 1971), pp. 18–53, and Lloyd C. Gardner, *Architects of Illusion: Men and Ideas in American Foreign Policy, 1941–1949* (Chicago, 1970), chap. 10.
5. *New York Times,* June 25, 1947.
6. Clifton Brock, *Americans for Democratic Action: Its Role in National Politics* (Washington, D.C., 1962), p. 52.
7. *New York Times,* March 31, 1947.
8. Leon Henderson to Executive Committee, November 22, 1947; Joseph Rauh to Executive Committee, November 21, 1947; James Loeb, Jr., to Executive Committee, November 22, 1947—all in box 34, Administrative File, ADA Papers.
9. National Board minutes, May 24, 1947 [p. 12], box 65, Administrative File, ADA Papers.
10. *Congressional Record,* 80th Cong., 1st sess., March 31, 1947, 93, pt. 3:2866–68, 2873, April 10, 1947, 93, pt. 3: 3280–81, 3285, and April 15, 1947, 93, pt. 3:3387. Also see William C. Pratt, "Senator Glen H. Taylor: Questioning American Unilateralism," in *Cold War Critics,* ed. Paterson, pp. 147–52, and Thomas G. Paterson, "The Dissent of Senator Claude Pepper," in *Cold War Critics,* ed. Paterson, pp. 128–31. Senator Edwin C. Johnson, a conservative Colorado Democrat, also strongly opposed the Greek-Turkey aid proposal, and stressed that it would be difficult to support freedom in Greece while that nation was still under the rule of its "venal" and "hated" monarchy. He viewed military aid to Turkey as a threat to Russia, from the Soviet Union's point of view, and thus as dangerous military aggression. The military aspects of the aid bill particularly worried him, since the legislation included no limitations except on the amount of money that might be spent, and such a limit would be easy to exceed. "This is only the first installment," he pre-

dicted. "No man knows what will follow" (*Congressional Record*, 80th Cong., 1st sess., April 16, 1947, 93, pt. 3: 3496–3500, 3504, and April 22, 1947, 93, pt. 3:3791–92).

11. Ibid., pp. 3491–93, 3495.

12. Ibid., 80th Cong., 1st sess., May 7, 1947, 93, pt. 4:4723, 4706–7, 4715, 4733, May 9, 1947, 93, pt. 4:4956, May 8, 1947, 93, pt. 4:4909, 4815, and May 9, 1947, 93, pt. 4:4934. Senator Taylor agreed with Congressman Sabath that Middle East oil was at the root of the administration's request. See Pratt, "Senator Glen H. Taylor," in *Cold War Critics*, ed. Paterson, p. 151.

13. *Congressional Record*, 80th Cong., 1st sess., April 22, 1947, 93, pt. 3:3763, 3781, May 7, 1947, 93, pt. 4:4741, May 8, 1947, 93, pt. 4:4792, May 7, 1947, 93, pt. 4:4695, and April 1, 1947, 93, pt. 10:Appendix, p. A1422.

14. Ibid., 80th Cong., 1st sess., April 16, 1947, 93, pt. 3:3498, April 11, 1947, 93, pt. 3:3328, May 9, 1947, 93, pt. 4:4967–68, April 1, 1947, 93, pt. 3:4643–44, and May 8, 1947, 93, pt. 4:4810, 4815.

15. Ibid., 80th Cong., 1st sess., April 22, 1947, 93, pt. 3:3793, and May 9, 1947, 93, pt. 4:4975.

16. See MacDougall, *Gideon's Army*, 1:130–31; Eleanor Bontecou, *The Federal Loyalty-Security Program* (Ithaca, N.Y., 1953); Alan Harper, *The Politics of Loyalty: The White House and the Communist Issue, 1946–1952* (Westport, Conn., 1970); Athan Theoharis, "The Escalation of the Loyalty Program," in *Politics and Policies of the Truman Administration*, ed. Barton Bernstein (Chicago, 1970); and Athan Theoharis, "The Threat to Civil Liberties," in *Cold War Critics*, ed. Paterson.

17. *New York Times*, March 31, April 12, and May 14, 1947; MacDougall, *Gideon's Army*, 1:130–31; Arthur M. Schlesinger, Jr., "What is Loyalty?" *New York Times Magazine*, November 2, 1947, p. 49.

18. *Congressional Record*, 80th Cong., 1st sess., April 15, 1947, 93, pt. 3:3388, and July 15, 1947, 93, pt. 7:8945–46, 8975, 8948–49; *New York Times*, July 16, 1947.

19. *Congressional Record*, 80th Cong., 1st sess., July 15, 1947, 93, pt. 7:8950, 8947, 8942–43.

20. Ibid., p. 8950. See Freeland, *Truman Doctrine and the Origins of McCarthyism*, p. 202.

21. See Freeland, *Truman Doctrine and the Origins of McCarthyism*, pp. 151–200; Acheson, *Present at the Creation*, chap. 26.

22. Shannon, *Decline of American Communism*, pp. 29–31; Markowitz, *Rise and Fall of the People's Century*, pp. 246–49; MacDougall, *Gideon's Army*, 1:170, 185.

23. Murray quoted in David M. Oshinsky, "Labor's Cold War: The CIO and the Communists," in *The Specter: Original Essays on the Cold War and the Origins of McCarthyism*, ed. Robert Griffith and Athan Theoharis (New York, 1974), pp. 132–34. On organized labor and Cold War foreign policy also see Philip Taft, *Organized Labor in American History* (New York, 1964), pp. 599–604, and Ronald Radosh, *American Labor and United States Foreign Policy* (New York, 1969), pp. 435–52.

24. *Congressional Record*, 80th Cong., 1st sess., November 28, 1947, 93, pt. 9:10970–71, and December 11, 1947, 93, pt. 9:11304, and 80th Cong., 2d sess., March 9, 1948, 94, pt. 2:2385–87.

25. Ibid., 80th Cong., 1st sess., November 28, 1947, 93, pt. 9:10972, 80th Cong., 2d sess., March 13, 1948, 94, pt. 2:2725, 2728, 80th Cong., 1st sess., July 25, 1947, 93,

pt. 12:Appendix, pp. A3860–61, November 26, 1947, 93, pt. 9:10910, and November 24, 1947, 93, pt. 13:Appendix, p. A4293, and 80th Cong., 2d sess., March 12, 1948, 94, pt. 2:2651, 2684, March 29, 1948, 94, pt. 3:3620, March 22, 1948, 94, pt. 3:3243, March 24, 1948, 94, pt. 3:3447, March 30, 1948, 94, pt. 3:3760, and March 31, 1948, 94, pt. 3:3858, 3869–70. Also see Paterson, "The Dissent of Senator Claude Pepper," in *Cold War Critics,* ed. Paterson, pp. 131–32. In the final legislation, aid to China was separated from the European Recovery Program and specific mention of military aid to China was deleted (Freeland, *Truman Doctrine and the Origins of McCarthyism,* p. 289).

26. Minutes of Joint Meeting of the Executive and National Political Committees, July 16, 1947, pp. 1–2, box 34; "Abridged Proceedings of National Board Meeting of Americans for Democratic Action," September 21, 1947, 2:66–75, box 65; "A Liberal Foreign Policy for the United States," foreign policy draft, October 24, 1947, pp. 21, 28–30, box 65—all in Administrative File, ADA Papers.

27. "Liberal Foreign Policy," pp. 21, 25–26, 28–30; Americans for Democratic Action, *Toward Total Peace: A Liberal Foreign Policy for the United States* (Washington, D.C., 1948), pp. 23–24.

28. Markowitz, *Rise and Fall of the People's Century,* pp. 246–49; James Loeb, "Report to the National Board Meeting of December 13–14, 1947," pp. 1–2, box 65, Administrative File, ADA Papers.

Chapter Three

1. See Alonzo L. Hamby, *Beyond the New Deal: Harry S. Truman and American Liberalism* (New York, 1973), chap. 7, especially pp. 184–85.

2. In 1946, Truman appointed a commission to study the problems of blacks in America and to arrive at recommendations for their aid. The commission submitted its report the following year and went beyond what most observers had anticipated. It recommended a renewed Fair Employment Practices Commission, federal anti-poll-tax and anti-lynch legislation, and desegregation in the armed forces. See William C. Berman, *The Politics of Civil Rights in the Truman Administration* (Columbus, Ohio, 1970), pp. 41–78.

3. See Hamby, *Beyond the New Deal,* chap. 9.

4. Norman D. Markowitz, *The Rise and Fall of the People's Century: Henry A. Wallace and American Liberalism, 1941–1948* (New York, 1973), pp. 266–76; Hamby, *Beyond the New Deal,* pp. 230–31, 246.

5. Some liberals did suspect Eisenhower's conservatism and from the start refused to back him (interview with Arthur J. Goldberg, June 20, 1973, Washington, D.C.). On the other hand, Arthur Schlesinger suspected that Eisenhower was being manipulated by popular-front liberals who opposed the Third Party "as a dangerous piece of political adventurism" and who hoped to "manipulate [Eisenhower] as they manipulated Wilkie into the ONE WORLD mood" (Arthur [Schlesinger] to Joe [Rauh], May 1, 1948, box 34, Administrative File, ADA Papers).

6. National Board minutes, April 10–11, 1948, p. 2, box 66; "Statement on Political Policy," April 11, 1947, box 66; "Address of General Dwight D. Eisenhower before the Eighth Constitutional Convention, CIO, November 20, 1946," mimeographed,

p. 1, box 34; Address by General Dwight D. Eisenhower, June 12, 1945 [London], p. 2, box 34; James Loeb to Mrs. Laura Z. Hobson, April 24, 1948, box 34; Evelyn Dubrow to Richard Huber, April 3, 1948, box 34—all in Administrative File, ADA Papers; Eisenhower quoted in Francis Trevelyan Miller, *Eisenhower: Man and Soldier* (Philadelphia, 1944), p. 199. After the election the ADA completely repudiated Eisenhower's liberalism, implying that he had changed his views since 1948. See statement for release to press in Executive Committee minutes, December 10, 1949, box 35, Administrative File, ADA Papers.

7. *New York Times,* January 24, 1948; "Memorandum Re the Availability of General Eisenhower," April 27, 1948, p. 1, box 66, Administrative File, ADA Papers.

8. *New York Times,* March 28 and April 13, 1948. Max M. Kampelman, in *The Communist Party vs. the C.I.O.: A Study in Power Politics* (New York, 1957), has written that "it was as a result of CIO interest and persuasion that the ADA, prior to the national convention of the Democratic Party, worked to obtain the nomination for General Eisenhower" (p. 104). Arthur J. Goldberg, then general counsel for the CIO, has dissociated himself from all CIO interest on Eisenhower's behalf and has indicated that he helped avert any official CIO endorsement (interview with Goldberg, June 20, 1973).

9. Henry Wallace, "Farewell and Hail!" *New Republic,* July 19, 1948, pp. 14–18; Curtis D. MacDougall, *Gideon's Army,* 3 vols. (New York, 1965), 1:242; Michael Straight, "Who Is Wrecking the Marshall Plan?" *New Republic,* January 12, 1948, pp. 9–11; "There Are Great Fears," *New Republic,* March 22, 1948, pp. 6–7; "Truman Should Quit," *New Republic,* April 5, 1948, cover; "If Not Truman, Who?" *New Republic,* May 17, 1948, p. 27.

10. *New York Times,* April 17 and June 14, 1948, "Political Action Report to Executive Committee," June 3, 1948, pp. 1–2; Chester Bowles to Ted [Dudley], June 18, 1948; John L. Lawkins to James Loeb, April 29, 1948—all in box 34, Administrative File, ADA Papers.

11. *New York Times,* July 6, 7, and 10, 1948; National Board minutes, July 10–11, 1948, box 66; John P. Tucker to Herbert L. Will, July 22, 1948, box 34—both in Administrative File, ADA Papers.

12. Morris H. Rubin, "State of the Union," *Progressive,* August 1948, p. 29.

13. Andrew Biemiller to National Board, September 20, 1947, box 66, Administrative Files, ADA Papers; Berman, *Politics of Civil Rights in the Truman Administration,* chap. 3.

14. James Loeb to Executive Committee, March 16, 1948, pp. 1–2, box 34, Administrative File; Executive Committee minutes, May 1, 1948, box 34, Administrative File; Hubert H. Humphrey to Jacob M. Arvey, May 7, 1948, box 1, Political File—all in ADA Papers; *New York Times,* July 11, 12, and 15, 1948.

15. James Loeb, "Report to the National Board Meeting of September 20, 1947," p. 23, box 65, Administrative File, ADA Papers.

16. See Markowitz, *Rise and Fall of the People's Century,* p. 257.

17. "Political Policy" (as approved by the February 22, 1948, ADA convention), box 2, Convention File, ADA Papers.

18. See David A. Shannon, *The Decline of American Communism: A History of the Communist Party of the United States since 1945* (New York, 1959), chaps. 4 and 5, espe-

cially pp. 113–14, 131, 177, 181–82; MacDougall, *Gideon's Army*, 3:274–75, and chap. 13.

19. Markowitz, *Rise and Fall of the People's Century*, pp. 254–55 and chap. 8, especially pp. 284–87; Joseph R. Starobin, *American Communism in Crisis, 1943–1957* (Cambridge, Mass., 1972), pp. 155, 170–73, 177, 183–86.

20. James Loeb to Executive Committee, March 16, 1948, p. 1; Executive Committee minutes, March 18, 1948—both in box 34, Administrative File, ADA Papers; Americans for Democratic Action, *Henry Wallace: The First Three Months* (Washington, D.C., 1948); idem, *Henry A. Wallace: Bat Boy for Reaction* (Washington, D.C., 1948); idem, *Henry A. Wallace: The Last Seven Months of His Campaign* (Washington, D.C., 1948); *New York Times*, July 23, 1948; Brock, *Americans for Democratic Action*, pp. 76–78; MacDougall, *Gideon's Army*, 2:549–50; Markowitz, *Rise and Fall of the People's Century*, pp. 278, 286.

21. Winthrop Griffith, *Humphrey: A Candid Biography* (New York, 1965), pp. 93–94, 110–12, 144, 146.

22. Ibid., pp. 93–96, 110–12; Genevieve Steefel to Elinor [S. Gimbel], Minnesota Progressive Party Papers, Library of Congress.

23. *New York Times*, February 20, 1948, April 17, 1948, June 13 and 14, 1948, and September 3, 1948; Griffith, *Humphrey*, pp. 147–49.

24. Murray had on several occasions in 1947 opposed the idea of forming a third party and had persuaded a majority at the CIO's annual convention in October 1947 to oppose a third party officially in 1948, should one be formed (see Markowitz, *Rise and Fall of the People's Century*, p. 253).

25. CIO Proceedings, January 22–23, 1948, pp. 23–25, 221, 223. Others on the CIO executive board were also critical of Wallace both as a supporter of labor and as a practical politician. Henry Wallace was not, said Reuther, "God's gift to the working class people of the world . . ."; Wallace "never delivered when he had the power and status to deliver" to the labor movement. "We of Amalgamated," said Jacob Potofsky, "think that he is a high class person, a man of religion, a man of integrity, but a damn poor politician, always was, and . . . he is not practical in representing labor." Joe Curran of the National Maritime Union referred to him as an "intellectual flyweight" and a "cloudbuster" (ibid., pp. 47, 69, 162–63).

26. Ibid., pp. 135–36, 177. Labor's major reason for discontent with Wallace was clearly disgruntlement with his associates and with his failure to consult CIO leaders, rather than any failure to perform for labor. "Unfortunately," said Reuther, "Wallace is being used. . . . Why didn't [he] go to the people who were closest to Roosevelt when he was in power? He didn't talk to Philip Murray or anybody close to him. . . ." "Wallace was our man," said Potofsky. "We have built him up. . . . Henry Wallace should have consulted labor, certainly CIO, on a matter of such vital importance as a Third Party" (ibid., pp. 47, 69).

27. Ibid., pp. 26–27.

28. Not only left-wingers in the CIO opposed Truman; Walter Reuther, a leader of the developing anti-Communist wing in the CIO, was a strong critic. Reuther, however, supported Murray's proposal (ibid., pp. 78–79, 96, 118, 126).

29. Ibid., pp. 43, 65, 134. Significantly, Murray had opposed a third-party movement on an earlier occasion, when in 1942 a faction of the American Labor Party in New

York, led by David Dubinsky, attempted to expand the ALP as a challenger to the Democratic party. In that instance Murray and Sidney Hillman were already allied with the Communists in support of Roosevelt and the war effort; Dubinsky's faction was made up of Socialists, Trotskyites, and other radicals opposed to the war, to the New York Democratic machine, and to the all-out support given by the CIO to the Democratic party and its policies—epitomized by the CIO's ready agreement to a "no-strike" pledge for the war's duration. Opposition to the Democratic party and CIO policies, as well as support for a third-party movement, appeared within the CIO itself, especially among such leaders as the Textile Workers' Emil Rieve. In response, Murray and Hillman in 1943 guided the CIO into creating the CIO's Political Action Committee, with the intent both of steering CIO members from third-party activities and of supporting Roosevelt's 1944 reelection bid. See Nelson N. Lichtenstein, "Industrial Unionism under the No-Strike Pledge: A Study of the CIO during the Second World War" (Ph.D. diss., University of California, Berkeley, 1974), pp. 531–47.

30. CIO Proceedings, January 22–23, 1948, pp. 43, 86, 107.

31. Ibid., pp. 114, 127, 129, 220, 227.

32. Kampelman, *Communist Party vs. the C.I.O.*, pp. 103–4.

33. CIO Proceedings, March 13–15, 1947, p. 384, and January 22–23, 1948, p. 240.

34. Ibid., January 22–23, 1948, pp. 19–21. "You laughingly make reference and chidingly make reference to the fact that the Communist Party attacks me in the *Daily Worker*," he told a mid-1948 CIO executive board. "That makes no difference to me either; that makes no difference . . . because down within the innermost recesses of my own soul I believe they are wrong . . ." (ibid., August 30–31 and September 1, 1948, p. 221).

35. Ibid., May 17–19, 1949, pp. 811, 813. Murray hated the FBI as much as the Communist party and linked the two together. As Murray saw it, an FBI agent who was allegedly a member of the party and was in fact a labor spy, attempting to destroy the CIO from within, was worse than a Communist party member. Murray suspected Joe Selly, president of the American Communications Association, of being such a spy: "I don't know how many FBI agents are in this room when I am making this statement right now, who are allegedly members of the Communist Party . . .," he told one executive board meeting. "There is no doubt in my mind but that some of these agents of the FBI who are members of the Communist Party are laying around the headquarters of a good many of the International Unions, providing information to the companies and to their agencies designed to destroy and undermine the labor movement in the United States of America" (ibid., pp. 811–12). Thomas E. Harris, then assistant general counsel for the CIO, recalled Murray's suspicion of Selly: "Selly was always well dressed and seemed prosperous, and he had a scruffy little union that didn't amount to a row of pins. I remember Murray used to always wonder where he got the money" (interview with Harris, June 14, 1973, Washington, D.C.).

36. Earlier, in 1947, Len DeCaux had resigned his position as *CIO News* editor at Murray's urging. See Kampelman, *Communist Party vs. the C.I.O.*, p. 107, and DeCaux's own account in *Labor Radical: From the Wobblies to CIO, a Personal History* (Boston, 1970), p. 470.

37. Interview with Harris, June 14, 1973.
38. Interview with Goldberg, June 20, 1973.
39. Interview with Harris, June 14, 1973.
40. CIO Proceedings, August 30–31 and September 1, 1948, pp. 109–14, 217, 220, 226–27, 239.

Chapter Four

1. See Alonzo L. Hamby, *Beyond the New Deal: Harry S. Truman and American Liberalism* (New York, 1973), chaps. 14 and 15.
2. Ibid., chap. 15.
3. Ibid., pp. 379–86.
4. David A. Shannon, *The Decline of American Communism: A History of the Communist Party of the United States since 1945* (New York, 1959), pp. 196–200; Hamby, *Beyond the New Deal*, p. 387. Celler's and Humphrey's remarks appear in the *Congressional Record*, 81st Cong., 1st sess., May 11, 1949, Appendix, p. A2872, and 81st Cong., 2d sess., Sept. 8, 1950, p. 14432.
5. *Congressional Record*, 80th Cong., 1st sess., March 24, 1947, 93, pt. 2:2462, and 80th Cong., 2d sess., March 9, 1948, 94, pt. 2:2405–9, 2412–14. Among those voting for the 1948 HUAC appropriation were Democrats John F. Kennedy (Mass.), Mike Monroney (Okla.), and Lyndon B. Johnson (Texas). Tennessee Democrat Estes Kefauver did not vote (ibid., 80th Cong., 2d sess., March 9, 1948, 94, pt. 2:2414). In 1945, the House had voted 208 to 108 (with 40 not voting), to establish HUAC as a permanent committee (ibid., 79th Cong., 1st sess., January 3, 1945, 91, pt. 1:15). In 1946, 240 congressmen voted in favor of further HUAC appropriations; 81 voted to oppose, and 108 did not vote (ibid., 79th Cong., 2d sess., May 17, 1946, 92, pt. 4:5224). In 1947, 324 congressmen voted in favor of HUAC appropriations, among them Democrats Kefauver, Monroney, Kennedy, Henry M. Jackson (Wash.), and Mike Mansfield (Mont.); 106 congressmen did not vote, among them Blatnik, Celler, Holifield, Javits, and Lyndon B. Johnson. Helen Gahagan Douglas (Calif.) registered the only opposing vote (ibid., 80th Cong., 1st sess., March 24, 1947, 93, pt. 2:2463).
6. Among those voting for the 1949 HUAC appropriation were Kennedy, Usher Burdick (R., N.D.), and Andrew J. Biemiller (D., Wis.), formerly the ADA's legislative director (ibid., 81st Cong., 1st sess., Feb. 9, 1949, 95, pt. 1:1045).
7. Ibid., 81st Cong., 1st sess., June 21, 1949, 95, pt. 14:Appendix, pp. A3917, A3916, 80th Cong., 2d sess., March 9, 1948, 94, pt. 2:2405–9, 2412–14, especially p. 2413, and 81st Cong., 1st sess., June 21, 1949, 95, pt. 6:8065.
8. CIO Proceedings, November 17, 20, and 27, 1948, p. 11.
9. See change in CIO rules governing CIO industrial union councils, 1946, chap. 1 above.
10. CIO Proceedings, November 17, 20, and 27, 1948, pp. 153–74, 251, 254, 260.
11. Ibid., pp. 182–83, 275.
12. Ibid., pp. 172–75, 294.
13. Ibid., August 30–31 and September 1, 1948, pp. 252, 256.
14. Ibid., March 10–12, 1945, p. 262, November 27, 1948, p. 358, and May 1949, pp. 471–72, 474, 483, 490, 521–22, 537, 540, 544–45, 563, 567, 579.

15. Ibid., May 1949, pp. 411, 414, 417, 480.

16. Ibid., February 14, 1950, pp. 105–9. On organized labor and Cold War foreign policy also see Philip Taft, *Organized Labor in American History* (New York, 1964), pp. 599–604, and Ronald Radosh, *American Labor and United States Foreign Policy* (New York, 1969), pp. 435–52.

17. CIO Proceedings, May 1949, pp. 748, 750, 755–56, 760–61, 769.

18. Ibid., May 17–19, 1949, pp. 775–76, 798.

19. Ibid., pp. 770, 801, 803–4, 823–24.

20. Ibid., p. 828; CIO, *Proceedings of the Eleventh Constitutional Convention of the Congress of Industrial Organizations, 1949* (Cleveland, Ohio, 1949), pp. 240–41, 245, 257, 267–69, 281.

21. CIO, *Eleventh Constitutional Convention*, pp. 288, 327, 347–48. The ten additional unions were: American Communications Association; Food, Tobacco, Agricultural and Allied Workers Union of America; International Fishermen and Allied Workers of America; International Fur and Leather Workers Union; International Longshoremen's and Warehousemen's Union; International Union of Mine, Mill and Smelter Workers; National Union of Marine Cooks, and Stewards; United Furniture Workers of America; United Office and Professional Workers of America; United Public Workers of America. Charges against the United Furniture Workers were dropped after a change of leadership brought the union strongly into the anti-Communist camp (Max Kampelman, *The Communist Party vs. the C.I.O.* [New York, 1957], pp. 160–61).

22. Interview with Thomas E. Harris, June 14, 1973, Washington, D.C.

23. Charges against United Furniture Workers were dropped; see note 21 above.

24. CIO Proceedings, August 29, 1950, p. 74.

25. Saposs, *Communism in American Unions*, pp. 211–12. The CIO may have been able to regain much of the membership lost in the ousters, but at mid-century its strength as an organization was debatable. The American Federation of Labor during the late 1940s and early 1950s had a much larger membership than did the CIO, both before and after the expulsion of the CIO's left-wing unions. The CIO officially merged with the AFL in 1955, less than twenty years after the CIO's leaders had themselves been expelled from the AFL and had founded their rival federation. The CIO may never have been as strong an organization as it appeared: Nelson N. Lichtenstein contends that even during its early years, the years of greatest momentum, the CIO was a "tentative, incomplete, even shaky structure, the bulk of whose membership was concentrated into a few relatively large industrial unions." After the war, the labor movement as a whole was unable to increase the proportion of organized workers among the nation's work force (Lichtenstein, "Industrial Unionism under the No-Strike Pledge: A Study of the CIO during the Second World War" [Ph.D. diss., University of California, Berkeley, 1974], pp. 2–4, 716).

26. David Saposs, *Communism in American Unions* (New York, 1959), pp. 183–85; CIO Proceedings, February 14–16, 1950, p. 436. Monsignor Charles O. Rice, former head of the Association of Catholic Trade Unionists' Pittsburgh branch, has commented: "I have changed my original opinion regarding these unions. There was Communist control, but they were doing a good job as bread and butter trade

unions. . . . I regret that they . . . were destroyed since they were a force for keeping the Labor Movement on its toes" (Rt. Rev. Msgr. Charles O. Rice to author, November 13, 1974). Max Kampelman has indicated that the very economic success of some of these left-wing unions may have explained their members' acceptance of Communist leadership, since union members have shown little concern about who controls the union as long as wages go up and working conditions improve (*Communist Party vs. the C.I.O.*, pp. 253–54).

27. The CIO did defend itself by citing its expulsion of Communist-dominated unions in testifying against the anti-labor Butler bill in 1954 (see chap. 9 below).
28. CIO Proceedings, February 14–16, 1950, pp. 253–54, and August 29, 1950, p. 22.
29. CIO Proceedings, June 15, 1950, pp. 152–54; Kampelman, *Communist Party vs. the C.I.O.*, p. 207. See ibid., pp. 182, 185–98, 206–7, for examples of unions' positions on foreign policy used by the CIO hearings as tests of loyalty. The "so-called left-wing unions," Murray observed in 1949, "create disruption in our local unions, they create disruption within our national unions, they are responsible for secession and raiding and all the difficulties that this organization has had to contend with in the course of the past four years . . ." (CIO Proceedings, May 17–19, 1949, p. 806). With the departure of the expelled unions, there was little further debate within the CIO on foreign and domestic policy. The infighting continued, however, and on a large scale. One board member commented, "Now that we've kicked out the Communists, we can start fighting among ourselves" (quoted by Thomas E. Harris in June 14, 1973 interview). The great rivalry between the two powerful unions, UAW and Steel Workers, continued, acerbated by Walter Reuther's succession to the CIO presidency after Murray's death in 1952. "Relations between unions were not any better than when we had the Communists to fight," Harris has recalled (ibid.).
30. Quoted in Kampelman, *Communist Party vs. the C.I.O.*, pp. 182, 206. In their own defense, the left-wing unions correlated pre-1947 national CIO policy with their own. Mine, Mill and Smelter Workers, for example, charged that "the CIO was just as 'guilty' as it was of following the Communist Party line from 1939 to 1947" (cited in ibid., p. 186).
31. Quoted in ibid., pp. 169–70.
32. CIO Proceedings, May 1949, pp. 800–801.
33. Interview with Arthur J. Goldberg, June 20, 1973, Washington, D.C.
34. Interview with Harris, June 14, 1973.
35. Interview with Goldberg, June 20, 1973.
36. For example, see CIO Proceedings, February 14–16, 1950, pp. 294–99, 325, 397–98.
37. For example, see ibid., pp. 245, 306, 400–401, 415–16, 419.
38. Ibid., pp. 225–26, 267, 571.
39. CIO, *Eleventh Constitutional Convention*, p. 288.

Chapter Five

1. Lionel Trilling, "Dreiser and the Liberal Mind," *Nation,* April 20, 1946, pp. 466–72; Lionel Trilling, *The Middle of the Journey* (New York, 1947), pp. 81–83, 94–96, 104, 138–40, 156–57, 302.

2. See Arthur M. Schlesinger, Jr., "Reinhold Niebuhr's Role in Political Thought," in *Reinhold Niebuhr: His Religious, Social, and Political Thought,* ed. Charles W. Kegley and Robert W. Bretall (New York, 1956), pp. 127–34; William Lee Miller, "The Rise of Neo-Orthodoxy," in *Paths of American Thought,* ed. Arthur M. Schlesinger, Jr., and Morton White (Boston, 1963), pp. 332–35; John Dewey, *Liberalism and Social Action* (New York, 1935); and Reinhold Niebuhr, *Moral Man and Immoral Society: A Study in Ethics and Politics* (New York, 1932). Also see Gordon Harland, *The Thought of Reinhold Niebuhr* (New York, 1960); June Bingham, *Courage to Change: An Introduction to the Life and Thought of Reinhold Niebuhr* (New York, 1961); and Palmer W. Wright, "The 'New Liberalism' of the Fifties: Reinhold Niebuhr, David Riesman, Lionel Trilling, and the American Intellectual" (Ph.D. diss., University of Michigan, 1966).

3. Reinhold Niebuhr, *The Nature and Destiny of Man: A Christian Interpretation,* 2 vols. (New York, 1943), 1:7, 190–91; Reinhold Niebuhr, *Faith and History: A Comparison of Christian and Modern Views of History* (New York, 1949), pp. 3, 6.

4. Schlesinger, "Reinhold Niebuhr's Role in Political Thought," pp. 138–40; Reinhold Niebuhr, *The Irony of American History* (New York, 1952), pp. 65, 67, 80; idem, *Christian Realism and Political Problems* (New York, 1953), pp. 33–42; idem, *The Children of Light and the Children of Darkness: A Vindication of Democracy and a Critique of Its Traditional Defense* (New York, 1944), pp. 9–12.

5. Reinhold Niebuhr, *Christianity and Power Politics* (New York, 1940), pp. 186–202.

6. Despite Niebuhr's aversion to "legalism-moralism" in foreign policy and his prominent role in postwar "realist" political thought, he equated completely consistent political "realism" with totalitarianism. "Any political philosophy," he wrote, "which assumes that natural impulses, that is, greed, the will-to-power and other forms of self-assertion, can never be completely controlled or sublimated by reason, is under the necessity of countenancing . . . perpetual conflict and perennial tyranny. . . ." Interestingly, Niebuhr considered himself a political moralist, but he insisted upon an "adequate political morality," one which did justice to the insights of both moralists and political "realists" by recognizing injustice and coercion but limiting it to "rationally acceptable social end[s]" (*Moral Man and Immoral Society,* pp. 231–34).

7. Niebuhr, *Nature and Destiny of Man,* 2:284; idem, *Faith and History,* pp. 159–60. Critics who find passivity inherent in Niebuhr's theology include Mack B. Stokes, "Passivity in the Thought of Reinhold Niebuhr," *New Christian Advocate,* June 1957, p. 16. Also see Holton P. Odegarde, *Sin and Science: Reinhold Niebuhr As Political Theologian* (Yellow Springs, Ohio, 1956), p. 190, and Harland, *Thought of Reinhold Niebuhr,* pp. 129–60.

8. Niebuhr, *Christianity and Power Politics,* pp. 186–202; idem, *Moral Man and Immoral*

Society, pp. 231–34; idem, *Nature and Destiny of Man*, 2:284; idem, *Faith and History*, pp. 159–60.

9. Arthur M. Schlesinger, Jr., *The Vital Center: The Politics of Freedom* (Boston, 1949), pp. 141–45.

10. Ibid., pp. 14, 25, 36–43, 50.

11. Ibid., pp. 150, 156, 161.

12. Schlesinger's observation that man is "most secure in a society which will protect him from want" indicates an interest in reform for its stabilizing influence (ibid., p. 156).

13. Schlesinger wrote that man is, by nature, "intoxicated by power and hence most human in a society which distributes power widely" (ibid., p. 156).

14. Richard H. Pells, *Radical Visions and American Dreams: Cultural and Social Thought in the Depression Years* (New York, 1973), pp. 354–56; Theodore J. Lowi, *The End of Liberalism: Ideology, Policy, and the Crisis of Public Authority* (New York, 1969), pp. 42–45; David B. Truman, *The Governmental Process: Political Interests and Public Opinion* (New York, 1951), pp. 165, 167, and passim. See also Robert A. Dahl and Charles E. Lindblom, *Politics, Economics, and Welfare: Planning and Politico-Economic Systems Resolved into Basic Social Processes* (New York, 1953), especially chap. 17.

15. See Lowi, *End of Liberalism*, pp. 42, 44, 46.

16. Max Ascoli, *The Power of Freedom* (New York, 1949), pp. 105, 134, 137, 143–44, 152, 115, 170.

17. Irwin Ross, *Strategy for Liberals: The Politics of the Mixed Economy* (New York, 1949), pp. 7–9, 44, 50.

18. John Kenneth Galbraith, *American Capitalism: The Concept of Countervailing Power* (Boston, 1952), pp. 57–58, 118–19, 121–24, 131, 133, 142, 155; Lowi, *The End of Liberalism*, pp. 29, 79–80. See also Alonzo L. Hamby, *Beyond the New Deal: Harry S. Truman and American Liberalism* (New York, 1973), chap. 13.

19. The social scientists represented in Daniel Bell's *The New American Right* (ed. Bell [New York, 1955]; revised as *The Radical Right* [New York, 1963]) were in particular interested in explaining the rise and the power of Senator Joseph McCarthy. They found their explanation by referring to America's agrarian radical tradition. Comparing the new McCarthy movement with the old Populist movement, they found similar emotional and moralistic appeals to the people for a radical change of society and its institutions. Thus Bell and his fellow contributors concluded that the McCarthy movement was a manifestation of the radical right which had developed out of the radical American left, and they implicitly used this link to condemn both movements. They pointed out that McCarthy and his followers had no respect for the democratic process or for the offices and officers the process created. McCarthy's methods, they stressed, were anti-constitutional and fundamentally totalitarian.

The contributors to *The New American Right* looked beyond immediate sources of McCarthyism's origins, such as the anxieties and frustrations of the Cold War, and sought an explanation which would be valid for the earlier protest movements as well. The common denominator, they discovered, was a thread of deep-seated anxiety over status running through the histories of both the radical right and the radical left (Richard Hofstadter, "The Pseudo-Conservative Revolt," in *The New American Right*, ed. Bell; Seymour M. Lipset, "The Sources of the 'Radical Right' "in ibid., p. 214; David Riesman and Nathan Glazer, "The Intellectuals and the Discontented Classes," in ibid., pp. 70–71; Talcott Parsons, "Social Strains in America," in ibid., p. 127).

20. See Eric F. Goldman, *The Crucial Decade: America, 1945–1955* (New York, 1956).

21. Richard Hofstadter, *The Age of Reform: From Bryan to F.D.R.* (New York, 1955), pp. 20–21, 81. See also idem, "The Pseudo-Conservative Revolt," in *New American Right*, ed. Bell.

22. See especially John D. Hicks, *The Populist Revolt: A History of the Farmers' Alliance and the People's Party* (Minneapolis, 1931), and Charles A. Beard and Mary R. Beard, *The Rise of American Civilization*, 2 vols. (New York, 1927).

23. Daniel Boorstin, *The Genius of American Politics* (Chicago, 1953); Louis Hartz, *The Liberal Tradition in America: Interpretations of American Political Thought Since the Revolution* (New York, 1955). See also Richard Hofstadter, *The Progressive Historians: Turner, Beard, Parrington* (New York, 1968).

24. John Higham has commented on consensus histories: "Many of our best historians acquired a positive relish for the burdens, the losses, and the intractable dilemmas of history"; indeed, "instead of looking backward from the crest of a historical movement to observe its rise, as progressives usually did, the newer historians often looked forward from the crest to watch its decline" (Higham, with Leonard Krieger and Felix Gilbert, *History* [Englewood Cliffs, N.J., 1965], p. 227).

25. Daniel Bell, writing in 1960, concluded that the "end of ideology" was a milestone of the 1950s. He observed with some concern, however, the New Left's readiness to embrace ideological rhetoric: "If the end of ideology has any meaning," he wrote, "it is to ask for the end of rhetoric, and rhetoricians, of 'revolution' . . ." (*The End of Ideology: On the Exhaustion of Political Ideas in the Fifties* [New York, 1960], pp. 406–7).

26. Note Trilling's anti-proletarian slant in *The Middle of the Journey*. Trilling portrayed the novel's single proletarian character, a laborer by the name of Duck Caldwell, as unpleasant, menacing, and finally dangerous. The "utopian" radicals in the novel are impervious to Caldwell's flaws.

27. Richard Hofstadter, *Anti-Intellectualism in American Life* (New York, 1964), pp. 3, 6, 22–23, 394; Riesman and Glazer, "The Intellectuals and the Discontented Classes," pp. 70–71; Hans J. Morgenthau, *The Purpose of American Politics* (New York, 1960), p. 68. See also William E. Bohn, "The Drive Against the Intellectuals," *New Leader*, July 26, 1954, p. 6.

28. George F. Kennan, *American Diplomacy: 1900–1950* (Chicago, 1951), pp. 82–83, 87. See Lloyd C. Gardner, *Architects of Illusion: Men and Ideas in American Foreign Policy, 1941–1949* (Chicago, 1970), chap. 10.

29. Morgenthau argued, however, that a policy based on the national interest was not devoid of morality: "The choice is not between moral principles and the national interest, . . . but between one set of moral principles derived from political reality" (*In Defense of the National Interest: A Critical Examination of American Foreign Policy* [New York, 1951], pp. 4, 13, 33).

30. Robert E. Osgood, *Ideals and Self-Interest in America's Foreign Relations* (Chicago, 1953), pp. 439–41.

31. Walter Lippmann, *The Cold War: A Study in U.S. Foreign Policy* (New York, 1947), pp. 44–45.

32. Leslie A. Fiedler, *An End to Innocence: Essays on Culture and Politics* (Boston, 1955).

33. Note the frequent references during this period to scientists as "naive" and as "dupes" of the Communist party. Observations of this sort were common among the anti-Communist left as well as the political right. The anti-Communist left's response to Albert Einstein and J. Robert Oppenheimer's efforts to compensate for "political naiveté" are particularly noteworthy (see chap. 8 below).

34. See Pells, *Radical Visions and American Dreams*, p. 358; R. Alan Lawson, *The Failure of Independent Liberalism, 1930–1941* (New York, 1971), pp. 179, 260.

35. See Joseph R. Starobin, *American Communism in Crisis, 1943–1957* (Cambridge, Mass., 1972), especially chaps. 7–10.

Chapter Six

1. See Glenn D. Paige, *The Korean Decision: June 24–30, 1950* (New York, 1968), pp. 79–263, and David Rees, *Korea: The Limited War* (New York, 1964), pp. 3–35.

2. David A. Shannon, *The Decline of American Communism: A History of the Communist Party of the United States since 1945* (New York, 1959), p. 206; Wallace quoted in Norman D. Markowitz, *The Rise and Fall of the People's Century: Henry A. Wallace and American Liberalism, 1941–1948* (New York, 1973), p. 311.

3. *Congressional Record*, 81st Cong., 2d sess., July 5, 1950, 96, pt. 7:9647–48, June 29, 1950, 96, pt. 7:9462, and June 27, 1950, 96, pt. 7:9331, 9233. See Alonzo L. Hamby, *Beyond the New Deal: Harry S. Truman and American Liberalism* (New York, 1973), pp. 403–4.

4. *Congressional Record*, 81st Cong., 2d sess., June 27, 1950, 96, pt. 7:9231; Philip Taft, *Organized Labor in American History* (New York, 1964), p. 636; Hamby, *Beyond the New Deal*, p. 403.

5. "If Not ADA, Then Who?" *New Republic*, April 18, 1949, p. 8. Foreign policy statement draft from Arthur M. Schlesinger, Jr., March 3, 1949, accompanied by letter to James Loeb, p. 4; foreign policy statement draft from Schlesinger, March 30, 1949, accompanied by letter to Loeb, p. 4; "Foreign Policy" (as adopted by the 1949 ADA convention), original mimeograph with typewritten inserts, p. 3—all in box 3, Convention File, ADA Papers; William Pfaff, "Report on ADA," *Commonweal*, May 5, 1950, p. 90; "ADA Convention," *New Republic*, March 5, 1951, p. 6; Joseph L. Rauh, Jr., to Morris Rubin, July 9, 1955, box 75, Administrative File, ADA Papers.

6. See William R. Tanner and Robert Griffith, "Legislative Politics and 'McCarthyism': The Internal Security Act of 1950," in *The Specter: Original Essays on the Cold War and the Origins of McCarthyism*, ed. Robert Griffith and Athan Theoharis (New York, 1974), p. 182; and Athan Theoharis, *Seeds of Repression: Harry S. Truman and the Origins of McCarthyism* (Chicago, 1971), pp. 29–33, 101–22, 142–46 and passim.

7. This discussion of the Internal Security Act is based on Tanner and Griffith, "Legislative Politics and 'McCarthyism,' " pp. 174–89.

8. *Public Papers of the Presidents*, Harry S. Truman (Washington, D.C., 1950), pp. 574–75; Tanner and Griffith, "Legislative Politics and 'McCarthyism,' " pp. 177–83.

9. Herbert H. Lehman, *Liberalism: A Personal Journey* (New York, 1958), p. 21.

10. Tanner and Griffith, "Legislative Politics and 'McCarthyism,' " pp. 183–84, Herbert H. Lehman to Ernest Angell, September 20, 1950; Estes Kefauver to Angell, September 21, 1950—both in vol. 22, 1950, American Civil Liberties Union Archives, Princeton University Library, Princeton, N.J. (hereafter cited as ACLU Papers).

11. Democrats Theodore F. Green (R.I.), Edward L. Leahy (R.I.), James E. Murray (Mont.), and Glen H. Taylor (Idaho) were the remaining senators voting against the bill in its final form (*Congressional Record*, 81st Cong., 2d sess., September 12, 1950, 96, pt. 11:14628). Those senators who voted to sustain the president's veto were Humphrey, Douglas, Lehman, Kilgore, Graham, Green, Kefauver, Leahy, Murray, and New Mexico Democrat Dennis Chavez. William Langer, a North Dakota Republican, would have voted to support the veto but was taken to the hospital before the vote (*Congressional Record*, 81st Cong., 2d sess., September 23, 1950, 96, pt. 11:15726).

12. Interview with Wayne Morse, July 23, 1957, pp. 74–75, Herbert H. Lehman Oral History Project, The Oral History Collection, Columbia University, New York; Allan Nevins, *Herbert H. Lehman and His Era* (New York, 1963), pp. 336–39, 345–46.

13. *Congressional Record*, 82d Cong., 1st sess., August 6, 1951, 97, pt. 7:9498–9500, August 20, 1951, 97, pt. 8:10319, 10332–37, and September 18, 1951, 97, pt. 9:11857, and 82d Cong., 2d sess., March 18, 1952, 98, pt. 2:2441–45, and April 10, 1952, 98, pt. 3:3935–54; U.S., Congress, Senate, Committee on Rules and Administration, Subcommittee on Privileges and Elections, *Investigation of Senator Joseph R. McCarthy, Hearings* on S. Res. 187, 82d Cong., 1st and 2d sess., 1952, pp. 7–53; idem, *Investigations of Senators Joseph R. McCarthy and William Benton*, Committee Print, 82d Cong., 2d sess., 1952, p. 105; Sidney Hyman, *The Lives of William Benton* (Chicago, 1969), pp. 454–65, 467–68, 484–85.

14. See Robert Griffith, *The Politics of Fear: Joseph R. McCarthy and the Senate* (Lexington, Ky., 1970), pp. 194–95; Richard M. Fried, *Men Against McCarthy* (New York, 1976), pp. 248–49. See also Hyman, *Lives of William Benton*, p. 458.

15. *Congressional Record*, 81st Cong., 2d sess., March 30, 1950, 96, pt. 4:4375–93. Humphrey infrequently participated in debates with or concerning McCarthy after that encounter. See Fried, *Men Against McCarthy*, pp. 79, 207.

16. *New York Times*, June 2, 1950; Morse quoted in A. Robert Smith, *Tiger in the Senate: The Biography of Wayne Morse* (Garden City, N.Y., 1962), pp. 261–64.

17. *Congressional Record*, 83d Cong., 1st sess., April 1, 1953, 99, pt. 2:2605; Smith, *Tiger in the Senate*, pp. 276–80.

18. See Fried, *Men Against McCarthy*, pp. 141–42, 149, 206–7, 211–14.

19. Herbert H. Lehman to William Benton, March 12, 1954, Herbert H. Lehman Papers, Columbia University, New York. Fried concludes that Benton offered "what sustained opposition McCarthy was to encounter" in the Senate (*Men Against McCarthy*, p. 218).

20. Herbert H. Lehman to Arthur Garfield Hays, April 23, 1952; "Joint Statement by Sponsors of New Immigration and Naturalization Bill," March 12, 1952—both in vol. 25, 1952, ACLU Papers.

21. *Congressional Record,* 81st Cong., 2d sess., March 23, 1950, 96, pt. 3:3942–44, 82d Cong., 1st sess., February 8, 1951, 97, pt. 1:1160, and 82d Cong., 2d sess., March 20, 1952, 98, pt. 2:2646.

22. Hamby, *Beyond the New Deal,* pp. 423–24.

23. *Congressional Record,* 81st Cong., 2d sess., December 4, 1950, 96, pt. 12:16045, December 22, 1950, 96, pt. 12:16998, and November 28, 1950, 96, pt. 12:15941.

24. See Griffith, *Politics of Fear,* pp. 65–106, 152–87. Benton was defeated in the 1952 elections and thus was not present to comment when the Subcommittee on Privileges and Elections' report was submitted in January 1953.

25. "Will You Join With Us?" ADA brochure, n.d. For examples of specific ADA protests against McCarthy, see "Civil Liberties Inquiry Again Asked by ADA," *ADA World,* December 1950, p. 1; "ADA Demands Senator McCarthy Make Public Secret Hearings of James A. Wechsler, Editor of *New York Post,*" ADA press release, April 26, 1953; ADA press release, n.d. [April 2, 1954?], ADA Papers; "ADA First to Hit Choice of Sears," *ADA World,* April 1954, p. 1; "Guarantee of Freedom, United Action Urged in Indo-China Crisis," *ADA World,* May 1954, p. 1.

26. "Rauh Debates McCarthy Aide on Radio, TV," *ADA World,* December 1953, p. 1; "Case Against McCarthy Heard by Two Thousand," *ADA World,* June 1954, p. 2. Executive Committee minutes, April 1, 1953; ADA press releases, [April 25], 1953, and [July] 1953; Executive Committee minutes, July 22, 1953, p. 1—all in box 35, Administrative File, ADA Papers; *New York Times,* July 16, 1953.

27. National Board minutes, September 23–24, 1950, p. 2, box 66; Executive Committee minutes, August 15, 1951, p. 2, June 12, 1951, p. 3, and August 6, 1953, p. 1, box 35—all in Administrative File, ADA Papers.

28. Robert R. Nathan, executive committee chairman of ADA, was, however, a member of the National Committee for an Effective Congress. On the NCEC and McCarthy, see Griffith, *Politics of Fear,* pp. 224–37, 240–42, 275–91, 301–3.

29. Executive Committee minutes, October 23, 1950, p. 2, box 34; National Board minutes, December 8–9, 1950, p. 3, box 66—both in Administrative File, ADA Papers; "ADA Platform, 1951," *ADA World,* March 1951, p. 4-A.

30. Furthermore, with the appearance of the Communist Control Act of 1954, the ADA was no longer certain it wished to oppose such legislation. See chap. 9 below. Executive Committee minutes, June 26 and July 25, 1951, both in box 35; National Board minutes, October 6–7 and December 15–16, 1951, both in box 66—all in Administrative File, ADA Papers; "Policy Statement, 1952 Platform," *ADA World,* June 1952, p. 1-A; "The Shape of Things," *Nation,* January 5, 1952, pp. 1–2.

31. "Domestic Policy, 1950 Platform," *ADA World,* April 1950, p. 4-A; "ADA Platform, 1951," *ADA World,* March 1951, p. 4-A; "Policy Statement, 1952 Platform," *ADA World,* June 1952, p. 1-A; Executive Committee minutes, June 22, 1953, box 35, Administrative File, ADA Papers; "Platform, 1954," *ADA World,* May 1954, p. 3.

32. National Board minutes, June 18, 1950, p. 6; National Board minutes (stenographic notes), September 24, 1950, p. 2—both in box 66, Administrative File, ADA Papers; "The ADA Convention," *New Republic,* April 17, 1950, p. 15; "Correspondence," *New Republic,* April 9, 1951, p. 4; I. F. Stone, "The Implications of Redbaiting," *Monthly Review* 3 (September 1951): 161–62.

33. Arthur M. Schlesinger, Jr., "Stevenson and the American Liberal Dilemma," *Twentieth Century*, January 1953, p. 29. See also Doris Grumbach, "The Lost Liberals," *Commonweal*, March 28, 1952, pp. 609–10; "The State of Liberalism," *Commonweal*, May 23, 1952, p. 163; Joseph C. Harsch, "Are Liberals Obsolete?" *Reporter*, September 30, 1952, pp. 13–16; Robert Bendiner, "The Liberals' Political Road Back," *Commentary*, 15 (May 1953): 431–37; Eric F. Goldman, "The American Liberal: After the Fair Deal, What?" *Reporter*, June 23, 1953, pp. 25–28; Joseph S. Clark, Jr., "Can the Liberals Rally?" *Atlantic Monthly* 192 (July 1953): 27–31.

Chapter Seven

1. The National Civil Liberties Bureau, the predecessor of the American Civil Liberties Union, was founded in 1917. The ACLU itself was established in 1920. For the history of the ACLU's founding and early years, see Donald Johnson, *The Challenge to American Freedoms: World War I and the Rise of the American Civil Liberties Union* (Lexington, Ky., 1963), pp. 145–203.

2. In 1939, Dies labeled the ACLU a Communist front and announced his intentions of calling the organization before his committee. Later, and quite unexpectedly, Dies announced a reprieve for the union, saying that it was not Communist and therefore did not require investigation. Some time after this event, Dies wrote a long-time ACLU board member that he had proposed to the ACLU's two general counsels "that if we worked together, we could destroy the Communist apparatus and influence within a few months, and that the liberals would share in the credit." As Dies told the story, the ACLU attorneys had not agreed to his plan. Corliss Lamont, the ACLU board member to whom Dies had written, continued to suspect, however, that an understanding had been reached between Dies and the ACLU's general counsels: the ACLU did in fact drop its original plan to challenge the constitutionality of HUAC's procedures on the basis of the First Amendment (Corliss Lamont, *Freedom Is As Freedom Does: Civil Liberties Today* [New York, 1956], pp. 268–70).

3. American Civil Liberties Union, *In the Shadow of War: The Story of Civil Liberty, 1939–1940* (New York, 1940), pp. 6, 48–50; American Civil Liberties Union, *Crisis in the Civil Liberties Union: A Statement, Including the Basic Documents Concerned, Giving the Minority Position in the Current Controversy in the A.C.L.U.* (New York, 1940), p. 5; Osmond K. Fraenkel, "Extracts from Diaries of Osmond K. Fraenkel Relating to American Civil Liberties Union," 3 vols., 1933–68, vol. I, Manuscript Division, Princeton University Library, Princeton, N.J., pp. 2–3; Corliss Lamont, ed., *The Trial of Elizabeth Gurley Flynn by the American Civil Liberties Union* (New York, 1968), pp. 13–14; Lucille Milner, *Education of an American Liberal* (New York, 1954), pp. 262–68.

4. Roger Baldwin to author, March 6, 1972. In 1976 the ACLU reinstated Flynn (who had died several years earlier) and stated that the 1940 expulsion "was not consonant with the basic principles on which the A.C.L.U. was founded" (*New York Times*, June 27, 1976).

5. American Civil Liberties Union, *In the Shadow of Fear: American Liberties, 1948–1949* (New York, 1949), p. 71.

6. "Proposed Revisions of Constitution and By-Laws of American Civil Liberties

Union, Inc.," June 13, 1951; Board of Directors agenda for September 17, 1951—both in vol. 1, 1951, American Civil Liberties Union Archives, Princeton University Library, Princeton, n.j.)hereafter cited as ACLU Papers).

7. The statement was as follows: "The American Civil Liberties Union is an organization devoted to the protection and expansion of the guarantees contained in the Bill of Rights. Because this proceeding is alleged to involve a member of the Communist Party, we believe that it is pertinent to state our views. The American Civil Liberties Union as a champion of civil liberties is opposed to any governmental or economic system which denies fundamental civil liberties and human rights. It is therefore opposed to any form of the police state or to any single party state and any movement in support of them, whether fascist, Communist, or known by any other name. In opposing these dictatorial or totalitarian systems, the Union takes no position on their economic, social or political practices or politics not affecting civil liberties" (Herbert M. Levy [staff counsel] to Emil Oxfeld, October 6, 1949, vol. 34, 1950, ACLU Papers. Also see Board of Directors minutes, June 26, 1950, vol. 7, 1950, ACLU Papers).

8. ACLU, *In the Shadow of War*, pp. 48–49; Lamont, *Trial of Elizabeth Gurley Flynn*, p. 24.

9. ACLU news release, September 15, 1950, American Civil Liberties Union Papers, ACLU, New York (hereafter cited as New York ACLU Papers); Merle Miller, *The Judges and the Judged* (Garden City, N.Y., 1952), pp. 32–33.

10. Miller, *Judges and the Judged*, pp. 17–26, 29–30.

11. Board of Directors minutes, December 26, 1951, p. 1, vol. 1, 1951, April 14, 1952, p. 2, vol. 1, 1952, and May 12, 1952, p. 2, vol. 1, 1952—all in ACLU Papers. Also see "Complaint before the Federal Communications Commission, Washington, D.C., American Civil Liberties Union, Inc.," April 8, 1952, vol. 38, 1952, ACLU Papers.

12. The minutes of these meetings show Pitzele's presence but record no opposition or comment from him (Board of Directors minutes, December 26, 1951, p. 1, vol. 1, 1951 and April 14, 1952, p. 2, vol. 1, 1952—both in ACLU Papers).

13. Merlyn S. Pitzele, "Is There a Blacklist?" *New Leader*, May 12, 1952, p. 21.

14. Ibid., pp. 21, 23.

15. Special board meeting minutes, May 15, 1952; Merlyn S. Pitzele [to members of the ACLU Board of Directors], May 22, 1952; Board of Directors minutes, May 26, 1952, p. 1—all in vol. 1, 1952, ACLU Papers; Fraenkel, "Extracts from Diaries," pp. 39–40.

16. Merle Miller, "Is *The Judges and the Judged* an Honest Book?" *New Leader*, June 16, 1952, pp. 12–14; Merlyn S. Pitzele, " 'This Book Is a Bad Mistake . . .,' " *New Leader*, June 16, 1952, pp. 15, 18.

17. "Report of Special Committee to Investigate the Charges against Merle Miller's *The Judges and the Judged*," July 14, 1952, p. 7, vol. 1, 1952, ACLU Papers. Special committee members were the ACLU's chairman of the board of directors, Ernest Angell, and board members Whitney North Seymour, an attorney, and William L. White, editor of the *Emporia* (Kansas) *Gazette*.

18. Board of Directors minutes, July 21, 1952, pp. 1–2, vol. 1, 1952, ACLU Papers; Frankel, "Extracts from Diaries," p. 43.

19. Board of Directors minutes, July 21, 1952, p. 2, vol. 1, 1952, ACLU Papers. The vote to renominate Pitzele was a very close one, six to five. Subsequently, Pitzele's reelection votes were just under the necessary total, and almost an entire board

meeting was spent discussing whether or not he should stand elected. Norman Thomas was Pitzele's primary backer for reelection. The final vote was eleven to eight in Pitzele's favor, and one board member, Osmond K. Fraenkel, afterward remarked that he thought the reelection a mistake, "motivated largely by fear that there would be blasts in the *New Leader*" if Pitzele were not elected. Fraenkel, "Extracts from Diaries," pp. 43 and 44.

20. "Semi-Suppression," *New Leader,* November 10, 1952, pp. 30–31; Louis Berg, "How End the Panic in Radio-TV?" *Commentary* 14 (October 1952):315–23; *New York World-Telegram,* October 8, 1952; "Where Is Truth?" *New Leader,* October 20, 1952, p. 31. Board of Directors minutes, October 20, 1952, p. 2; Edward L. Bernays to Alan Reitman, October 10, 1952; Reitman to Bernays, October 27, 1952—all in vol. 1, 1952, ACLU Papers.

21. "Complaint before the Federal Communications Commission, Washington, D.C., American Civil Liberties Union, Inc.," April 8, 1952; "Before the Federal Communications Commission, In re Applications of American Broadcasting Co., Columbia Broadcasting System, Inc., National Broadcasting Co., Inc., WPIX, Inc., for renewal of Licenses. Order," June 11, 1952; "Before the Federal Communications Commission, Washington, D.C., American Civil Liberties Union, Inc., Complainant," July 1, 1952; ACLU *Weekly Bulletin,* no. 1562—all in vol. 38, 1952, ACLU Papers.

22. Board of Directors minutes, June 12, 1950, p. 2, vol. 7, 1950, August 28, 1950, p. 2, vol. 7, 1950, December 1, 1952, p. 1, vol. 1, 1952, and April 20, 1953, p. 2, vol. 1, 1953—all in ACLU Papers.

23. The petition was made on the grounds that the Smith Act abridged free speech and, "even if constitutional, the statute as applied to the eleven is invalid because it was applied in the absence of a 'jury finding of a clear and present danger to carry out the ideas advocated' " ("Justice Department Denies Mass Prosecution of Communists," ACLU Feature Press Service, July 3, 1950, vol. 33, 1950, ACLU Papers).

24. Policy Committee minutes, March 29, 1950, p. 1, vol. 7, 1950; Board of Directors minutes, May 1, 1950, p. 1, and August 28, 1950, p. 1, vol. 7, 1950; Policy Committee minutes, May 9, 1950, p. 2, and November 1, 1950, vol. 7, 1950; executive director to board, June 20, 1951, pp. 12, 14, 16–17, vol. 1, 1951; Board of Directors minutes, July 25, 1951, vol. 1, 1951; ACLU news release, June 28, 1951, vol. 49, pt. II, 1951; [Roger Baldwin] to Palmer Weber, June 23, 1951, vol. 49, pt. II, 1951; [Roger Baldwin] to Patrick Murphy Malin, June 27, 1951, vol. 49, pt. II, 1951—all in ACLU Papers. Norman Thomas, it should be noted, was a strong defender of the Smith Act victims as well as a firm opponent of the Smith Act. See Joseph R. Starobin, *American Communism in Crisis, 1943–1957* (Cambridge, Mass., 1972), p. 12.

25. Board of Directors minutes, December 4, 1950, p. 2, vol. 7, 1950, ACLU Papers; Fraenkel, "Extracts from Diaries," p. 32; American Civil Liberties Union, *Freedom, Justice, Equality* (New York, 1953), p. 103.

26. George Soll [associate staff counsel] to board, July 31, 1950, vol. 7, 1950; Alien Civil Rights Committee minutes, November 29, 1950, vol. 7, 1950; "Positions on the Provisions of the Internal Security Act Section 22: Exclusion of Certain Types of Aliens," January 15, 1951, pp. 1–3, vol. 1, 1951—all in ACLU Papers; Fraenkel, "Extracts from Diaries," p. 33.

27. ACLU, *Freedom, Justice, Equality,* pp. 75–76; Fraenkel, "Extracts from Diaries," p. 31.
28. Alan Reitman [associate director, ACLU,] to author, March 8, 1972; AR [Alan Reitman] to PMM [Patrick Murphy Malin], September 5, 1951, vol. 43, 1951, ACLU Papers. See also ACLU, *Freedom, Justice, Equality,* pp. 9–10. It should be noted that the ACLU returned to active involvement at the trial stage during the 1960s, "when it became apparent that the winning of Supreme Court decisions was not enough to achieve realistic civil liberties gains" (Reitman to author, March 8, 1972).
29. Fraenkel, "Extracts from Diaries," p. 56; [Roger Baldwin] to Palmer Weber, June 23, 1951, vol. 49, pt. II, 1951, ACLU Papers. Malin had been professor of economics at Swarthmore College as well as vice-director of the Intergovernmental Committee on Refugees from 1943 to 1947.
30. Patrick Murphy Malin to [ACLU Corporation], "Reformulation of the Form of Statements 1, 2, 3," January 28, 1954, vol. 1, 1954, ACLU Papers.
31. John Paul Jones, "Statement to be submitted to Board of ACLU," March 15, 1954; Varian Fry to Patrick Murphy Malin, January 20, 1954—both in vol. 1, 1954, ACLU Papers.
32. Lamont, *Freedom Is As Freedom Does,* p. 280.
33. The special committee consisted of Norman Thomas, Morris Ernst, the Reverend John Paul Jones, and James Wechsler.
34. The second section of the statement, on academic freedom and educational and United Nations employment, advocated a United Nations security program and stated that "commitments of any kind which interfere with [the free and unbiased pursuit of truth and understanding] are incompatible with the objectives of academic freedom." The third section, on the proper uses of the Fifth Amendment privileges, stated that "the ACLU recognizes that there are certain situations in which a person's exercise of the [Fifth Amendment] privilege may be inconsistent with his duty of full disclosure toward an employer," particularly in the fields of government service, the United Nations, and education. The statement held that employers in these fields did not violate employees' civil liberties by considering their use of the Fifth Amendment and by giving "such weight to the refusal [to answer] as may be appropriate in the particular circumstances" ("Proposal #1, As Adopted by the Board on April 20, 1953," vol. 1,1953, ACLU Papers).
35. ACLU, *In the Shadow of War,* p. 48. This section of the 1940 resolution read, "The American Civil Liberties Union does not make any test of opinion on political or economic issues a condition of membership. . . ."
36. Fraenkel, "Extracts from Diaries," p. 45; American Civil Liberties Union, *America's Need: A New Birth of Freedom* (New York, 1954), p.128.
37. Contemplating the possibility of Communists controlling ACLU policy, ACLU board member William L. White commented, "As maybe they already have." White to [ACLU], March 15, 1954, New York ACLU Papers.
38. Board of Directors minutes, April 15, 1953, pp. 1–3, and May 4, 1953, pp. 1–2; board to corporation members, May 8, 1953—all in vol. 1, 1953, ACLU Papers.
39. "Affirmative Arguments, Negative Arguments," September 1, 1953, vol. 1, 1953, ACLU Papers; Fraenkel, "Extracts from Diaries," p. 47.
40. Board of Directors minutes, August 31, 1953; Ernest Angell to corporation mem-

bers, September 1, 1953—both in vol. 1, 1953, ACLU Papers; Fraenkel, "Extracts from Diaries," p. 47. Corliss Lamont objected to the impropriety of Angell's action and sent telegrams to each affiliate stating his objections and indicating that the board had only approved the policy statement because its members had become tired of arguing (Lamont to George E. Rundquist, September 11, 1953, vol. 1, 1953, ACLU Papers). One board member, Herbert R. Northrup, a labor economist and member of the National Industrial Conference Board, was so angered by Lamont's action that he proposed censuring him for it; any action was prevented by a quick adjournment of the meeting (Fraenkel, "Extracts from Diaries," p. 47). Edward J. Ennis, an attorney and board member, later proposed a motion to censure Lamont, which the board tabled after Lamont apologized for his remarks to the affiliates (Board of Directors minutes, October 5, 1953, p. 2, New York, ACLU Papers).

41. The ACLU's "general" members, as differentiated from the corporate members, had little formal power in the organization. See Barton Bean, "Pressure for Freedom: The American Civil Liberties Union" (Ph.D. diss., Cornell University, 1955), p. 123.

42. Bean, "Pressure for Freedom," pp. 208–15, 227–31, 239. "Proposed Revisions of Constitution and By-Laws of American Civil Liberties Union, Inc.," June 13, 1951, p. 7; Board of Directors' agenda for September 17, 1951—both in vol. 1, 1951, ACLU Papers; Lamont, *Freedom Is As Freedom Does*, pp. 279–80.

43. Lamont, *Freedom Is As Freedom Does*, pp. 279, 281; "The ACLU's Directors Prepare to Jettison Its Principles," *I. F. Stone's Weekly*, October 31, 1953, p. 2; Corliss Lamont, "Corliss Lamont's Inside Story After 21 Years," *I. F. Stone's Weekly*, March 1, 1954, p. 5. The corporate vote was taken by a weighted voting procedure, a complex arrangement that gave the national committee and the national board of directors a far greater voice than the affiliates in the total vote. I. F. Stone, who analyzed the vote on the referendum, observed that the national committee and national board of directors were three to one in favor of the new policy statement, whereas the affiliates cast all but six hundred of their sixteen thousand votes against the statement ("Convulsions at the ACLU," *I. F. Stone's Weekly*, December 14, 1953, p. 3).

44. Board of Directors minutes, October 19, 1953, p. 2, and November 16 and 30, 1953—all in vol. 1, 1953, ACLU Papers; "ACLU's Directors Prepare to Jettison Its Principles," p. 2; Fraenkel, "Extracts from Diaries," pp. 48–49. Fraenkel noted that at the October 19 meeting those in favor of rejecting the referendum were James Fly, Norman Thomas, Morris Ernst, Ernest Angell, Merlyn Pitzele, Herbert Northrup, Varian Fry, Whitney North Seymour, William Fitelson (managing director of the "Theatre Guild on the Air"), Katrina McCormick Barnes (former publisher of *Common Sense*), James Kerney (editor of the *Trenton Times*), and Norman Cousins (editor of the *Saturday Review*). Those opposed were Osmond Fraenkel, Arthur Garfield Hays, Walter Gellhorn, Corliss Lamont, the Reverend John Paul Jones, Edward Ennis, the Reverend John Haynes Holmes (former chairman of the ACLU board), General Telford Taylor, Elmer Rice (the playwright), Judge Dorothy Kenyon (one of the first persons McCarthy accused of being part of the Communist conspiracy), Dorothy Dunbar Bromley (Scripps-Howard columnist), Richard Childs (chairman of the Council of the National Municipal League), Walter Frank (an attorney), and Judge J. Waties Waring (retired judge of the Federal District Court in South

Carolina) (Fraenkel, "Extracts from Diaries," p. 48). Shortly after the October 19 meeting, several board members who had voted to accept the referendum as final began to change their minds. Five of them (Dorothy Bromley, Edward Ennis, Walter Frank, John Paul Jones, and Judge Waring) circulated a memorandum to the other board members seeking to reject the referendum's results (Patrick Murphy Malin to board members, October 23, 1953, vol. 1, 1953, ACLU Papers).

45. Patrick Murphy Malin to board, November 13, 1953, vol. 1, 1953, ACLU Papers; Lamont, *Freedom Is As Freedom Does,* p. 281.

46. Board of Directors minutes, November 30, 1953, pp. 2–3, vol. 1, 1953, ACLU Papers.

47. "Statement by Special Graham Committee Unanimously Adopted at Biennial Conference, February 14, 1954," New York ACLU Papers; Fraenkel, "Extracts from Diaries," p. 56.

48. Board of Directors minutes, February 15, 1954, pp. 1–2, vol. 1, 1954, ACLU Papers; Lamont, *Freedom Is As Freedom Does,* p. 283.

49. Norman Thomas to board members, March 5, 1954; W. [William] L. White, to [ACLU], March 15, 1954—both in New York ACLU Papers; Lamont, *Freedom Is As Freedom Does,* p. 283.

50. John Finerty to [Patrick Murphy] Malin, March 15, 1954, vol. 1, 1954, ACLU Papers.

51. Board of Directors minutes, March 15, 1954, pp. 1–2, vol. 1, 1954, ACLU Papers; Fraenkel, "Extracts from Diaries," p. 59.

52. *New York World-Telegram,* March 17, 1954.

53. Patrick Murphy Malin to board members, March 18, 1954, p. 1, vol. 1, 1954, ACLU Papers.

54. The committee membership, announced on March 29, 1954, consisted of Judge Waring as chairman with Walter Gellhorn, Dorothy Kenyon, and Norman Thomas from the board. Fraenkel later took Gellhorn's place. The national committee of the ACLU and the affiliates were each represented by two other committee members (Fraenkel, "Extracts from Diaries," pp. 60, 63).

55. The statement also condemned the discharge of an employee from any job, public or private, solely because of that employee's use of the Fifth Amendment: "The use of the privilege against self-incrimination does not justify any inference as to the character of the answer which might have been given to the question." In addition, the statement opposed security probes into the beliefs and associations of United Nations employees other than for connection with possible subversion (Fraenkel, "Extracts from Diaries," pp. 61, 63. Special Committee on Statements 1, 2 and 3, to board members, July 9, 1954; Patrick Murphy Malin to board members, July 21, 1954—both in vol. 1, 1954, ACLU Papers).

56. Patrick Murphy Malin to board members, July 21, 1954, pp. 1–2; Board of Directors minutes, August 2, 1954, p. 1, and November 22, 1954—all in vol. 1, 1954, ACLU Papers; Fraenkel, "Extracts from Diaries," p. 64.

57. See Robert Griffith, *The Politics of Fear: Joseph R. McCarthy and the Senate* (Lexington, Ky., 1970), pp. 212–20, 243–69, especially p. 263.

58. Due Process Committee minutes, April 29, 1952; Herbert M. Levy "to whom it may concern," May 2, 1952, pp. 1, 3; Due Process Committee minutes, June 12, 1952, and September 15, 1952; Herbert M. Levy to Due Process Committee, September

10, 1952, pp. 1–2; Due Process Committee minutes, November 10, 1952; Board of Directors minutes, November 17, 1952; "Statement of the National Board of Directors Regarding Commutation of Death Sentences in Rosenberg Atomic Espionage Case," December 1, 1952; HML [Herbert M. Levy] to PMM [Patrick Murphy Malin], March 3, 1953—all in vol. 51, 1953, ACLU Papers; Fraenkel, "Extracts from Diaries," pp. 41, 44.

59. Patrick Murphy Malin to board, January 14, 1954, p. 1; Board of Directors minutes, January 4, 1954, p. 1, and January 18, 1954, p. 2; Herbert M. Levy to Judge Thurman Arnold, October 28, 1954; Arnold to Levy, October 29, 1954; Board of Directors minutes, November 8, 1954—all in vol. 1, 1954, ACLU Papers; Fraenkel, "Extracts from Diaries," pp. 52, 65.

60. Corliss Lamont to the Senate Permanent Subcommittee on Investigations of the Senate Committee on Government Operations, September 23, 1953, New York ACLU Papers; Lamont, *Freedom Is As Freedom Does*, pp. 33–47.

61. Board of Directors minutes, October 5, 1953, p. 1; Special Committee on Mr. Lamont's Appearance before Senator McCarthy's Subcommittee to board members, October 29, 1953, pp. 1–2; Philip Wittenberg to American Civil Liberties Union, November 25, 1953; Board of Directors minutes, November 30, 1953—all in vol. 1, 1953, ACLU Papers.

62. Those supporting Fraenkel's proposal were Edward Ennis and Arthur Garfield Hays. Those opposed were Ernest Angell, Morris Ernst, James Fly, and Judge Waring (Fraenkel, "Extracts from Diaries," p. 51).

63. Board of Directors minutes, December 14, 1953, vol. 1, 1953; ACLU news release, January 7, 1954, vol. 1, 1954—both in ACLU Papers; Fraenkel, "Extracts from Diaries," p. 52. In March 1954 the ACLU protested to the Senate Committee on Government Operations when that committee voted to cite Lamont for contempt of Congress. The ACLU office contacted the Senate's majority and minority leaders and distributed its memorandum on the case to all members of McCarthy's committee. Nonetheless, in August 1954, the Senate voted for the citation seventy-one to three (Patrick Murphy Malin to board members, March 18, 1954, p. 1; Board of Directors minutes, September 13, 1954—both in vol. 1, 1954, ACLU Papers.)

In October 1954 a federal grand jury in New York City indicted Lamont for contempt of the Senate. In November Lamont filed a motion for dismissal of the indictment, citing a new point: neither the Senate nor the Senate Committee on Government Operations "had ever passed any resolution or minute formally and legally establishing the McCarthy Subcommittee." The ACLU office filed a friend-of-the-court brief supporting Lamont's motion to dismiss the indictment against him. In July 1955 Judge Edward Weinfeld of the United States District Court, Southern District of New York, granted the motion for dismissal based upon his findings that the McCarthy subcommittee had acted beyond the scope of its authority and was not duly empowered by the Senate to conduct the particular inquiry. The government gave notice that it would carry this decision to a federal court of appeals, but it made no move to reindict Lamont, who had won an important victory (ACLU Feature Press Service, November 29, 1954, pp. 1–2, New York ACLU Papers; Lamont, *Freedom Is As Freedom Does*, pp. 46–47).

64. Board of Directors minutes, November 16, 1953, p. 1, and November 30, 1953, p. 2—both in vol. 1, 1953, ACLU Papers; Lamont, *Freedom Is As Freedom Does*, pp. 281–82; "Corliss Lamont's Inside Story After 21 Years," *I. F. Stone's Weekly*, March 1, 1954, pp. 5–6; *New York World-Telegram*, December 11, 1953; Fraenkel, "Extracts from Diaries," pp. 50, 53.

65. Board of Directors minutes, November 30, 1953, p. 2, vol. 1, 1953; Corliss Lamont to the National Committee and Affiliates of the A.C.L.U., January 22, 1954, p. 1, vol. 1, 1954, ACLU Papers.

66. The Emergency Civil Liberties Committee's founders were: James Imbrie, a retired banker; Harold Wilson, professor of politics at Princeton; Henry Pratt Fairchild, professor emeritus of sociology, New York University; I. F. Stone, columnist for the *Compass* and soon to become editor of his own journal, *I. F. Stone's Weekly*; Dr. Paul Lehmann, professor at Princeton Theological Seminary and chairman of the ECLC; and E. Franklin Frazier, chairman of the sociology department at Howard University. Thomas I. Emerson, professor at Yale Law School, and Carey McWilliams, associate editor of the *Nation*, soon joined the ECLC's executive committee ("Emergency Civil Liberties Committee, First Fifteen Years: 1951–1966," *Rights*, December 1966, p. 6).

67. "Emergency Civil Liberties Committee," pp. 4–5.

68. The ACLU's response to the ECLC was far more restrained than was that of the American Committee for Cultural Freedom. See chap. 8 below.

69. AR [Alan Reitman] to GER [George E. Rundquist, field director of the ACLU], April 11, 1952; Rundquist to Loula Lasker, March 5, 1952; "Information on the Emergency Civil Liberties Committee"—all in vol. 33, 1952, ACLU Papers.

Chapter Eight

1. Robert Warshow, "The Liberal Conscience in *The Crucible*," *Commentary* 15 (March 1953):265–71; Irving Kristol, " 'Civil Liberties,' 1952—A Study in Confusion," *Commentary* 13 (March 1952):228–36; Alan F. Westin, "Our Freedom—and the Rights of Communists: A Reply to Irving Kristol," *Commentary* 14 (July 1952):33–40.

2. "The Hards and the Softs," *New Leader*, May 20, 1950, p. 30.

3. Ibid.

4. See the *Nation*'s special editions on civil liberties, June 28, 1952, and December 12, 1953.

5. "The *Nation*'s Fear," *New Leader*, July 14, 1952, pp. 22–23; "Meet the *Nation*'s Experts on Civil Liberties," *New Leader*, July 14, 1952, p. 14; Louis Jay Herman, "The *Nation*: The Ideology of Surrender," *New Leader*, October 25, 1954, pp. 15–18.

6. "How to Beat McCarthy," *New Leader*, September 22, 1952, p. 30; Richard H. Rovere, *Senator Joe McCarthy* (New York, 1959), p. 269; James Rorty and Moshe Decter, *McCarthy and the Communists* (Boston, 1954), especially pp. 1, 125–27.

7. Sidney Hook, "Freedom in American Culture," *New Leader*, April 6, 1953, sec. 2, pp. S5–S6; Richard H. Rovere, "How Free is the Nation?" *New Leader*, July 14, 1952, pp. 12–14; "1952 Can Be Different," *New Leader*, December 31, 1951, pp. 22–23.

8. Special editions on civil liberties, *Nation*, June 28, 1952, and December 12, 1953; "Meet the *Nation*'s Experts on Civil Liberties," p. 14.

9. "Meet the *Nation*'s Experts on Civil Liberties," p. 14; Granville Hicks, "Liberals: Fake and Retarded," *New Leader*, March 22, 1954, pp. 16–19.

10. "The *Nation* Censures a Letter of Criticism," *New Leader*, March 19, 1951, pp. 16–18; "The *Nation* Sues Us," *New Leader*, April 2, 1951, p. 2; *New York Times*, June 9, 1951.

11. Julio Alvarez del Vayo, "A Year of the Truman Doctrine," *Nation*, March 13, 1948, p. 304; idem, "Marshall Plan vs. Socialism," *Nation*, October 4, 1947, p. 339; idem, "The European Opposition," *Nation*, March 19, 1949, pp. 334–35; idem, "Return to Diplomacy," *Nation*, February 3, 1951, p. 101; idem, "Family Fight," *Nation*, July 10, 1948, p. 47; idem, "The Price of Unity," *Nation*, February 11, 1950, pp. 129–30.

12. Arthur Schlesinger to Freda Kirchwey, March 26, 1951, box C-28, American Committee for Cultural Freedom Papers, Tamiment Library, New York University, New York (hereafter cited as ACCF Papers); Reinhold Niebuhr to Kirchwey, April 26 [1951], Reinhold Niebuhr Papers, Manuscript Division, Library of Congress; Norman Thomas to Kirchwey, May 18, 1951; Kirchwey to Thomas, May 23, 1951—both in Norman Thomas Papers, New York Public Library, New York. Robert Bendiner, associate editor of the *Nation*, also resigned from the journal at this time over the del Vayo issue (see Alonzo L. Hamby, *Beyond the New Deal: Harry S. Truman and American Liberalism* [New York, 1973], p. 473).

13. S. M. Levitas to Norman Thomas, September 18, 1951, Norman Thomas Papers; Evans Clark to Reinhold Niebuhr, May 23, 1951, Niebuhr Papers.

14. S. M. Levitas to Norman Thomas, September 18, 1951; Thomas to Max Kampelman, February 8, 1952; Henry Schwarzschild to Thomas, November 15, 1954; Staff, American Committee for Cultural Freedom, to Thomas, November 16, 1954—all in Norman Thomas Papers; "Between Issues," *New Leader*, November 22, 1954, p. 2. The American Committee for Cultural Freedom listed its support of the *New Leader* against the *Nation* under the heading of "combat[ing] Communist influence in the U.S." (Executive Director's report, Executive Committee minutes, September 17, 1954, p. 2, box C-30, ACCF Papers).

15. "Libel Suit Settled," *Nation*, September 24, 1955, p. 272; *New Leader*, September 19, 1955, p. 20; Carey McWilliams to author, February 6, 1970.

16. *New York Times*, March 27, 1949, and June 27, 1950; Sidney Hook, "The Berlin Congress for Cultural Freedom," *Partisan Review*, September-October 1950, pp. 715–22; membership meeting minutes, December 14, 1950, box C-30, ACCF Papers. On the Congress for Cultural Freedom and the ACCF see Christopher Lasch, "The Cultural Cold War: A Short History of the Congress for Cultural Freedom," in *Towards A New Past: Dissenting Essays in American History*, ed. Barton J. Bernstein (New York, 1968), pp. 322–59, and Michael Harrington, "The Committee for Cultural Freedom," *Dissent* 2 (1955):113–22.

17. Executive Committee minutes, April 16, 1952, box C-39; Sol Stein to Elliot Cohen, January 25, 1954, box C-23; Stein to Judge Advocate General, U.S. Army, January 21, 1955, box C-23—all in ACCF Papers.

18. Sol Stein to Milton Konvitz, May 17, 1954, box C-23, ACCF Papers.

19. See the American Civil Liberties Union's assessment of the ECLC in chap. 7 above.

20. *New York Times,* January 20, 1953; Irving Kristol to Reinhold Niebuhr, January 20, 1953, box C-25, ACCF Papers.
21. Rabbi Ira Eisenstein to George S. Counts, January 19, 1953; Fowler Harper to Counts, January 20, 1953; Paul L. Lehmann to Counts, January 19, 1953—all in box C-25, ACCF Papers; *New York Times,* January 20, 21, 1953.
22. William L. Shirer to George S. Counts, January 20, 1953; Lehmann to Counts, January 19, 1953; Roger Baldwin to Irving Kristol, January 22, [1953]—all in box C-25, ACCF Papers; Lehmann quoted in the *New York Times,* January 20, 1953.
23. Irving Kristol to Ben Shahn, February 2, 1953; Kristol to Fowler Harper, January 23, 1953; George S. Counts to Editor, *New York Times,* January 22, 1953—all in box C-25, ACCF Papers.
24. ECLC policy quoted in Corliss Lamont, *Freedom Is As Freedom Does: Civil Liberties Today* (New York, 1956), p. 286; Royal W. France to Norman Thomas, March 31, 1954, J. Robert Oppenheimer Papers, Manuscript Division, Library of Congress.
25. Irving Kristol to Alexander P. Hoffman, January 26, 1953; Karl E. Meyer to George S. Counts, January 25, 1953; Kristol to Meyer, January 29, 1953—all in box C-25, ACCF Papers.
26. *New York Times,* January 20, 1953, and June 12 and 13, 1953.
27. RWJ to Oppenheimer, February 22, 1954; transcript of telephone conversation between Oppenheimer and Mrs. van Gelder for Mr. Leidesdorf, March 5, 1954, pp. 1–2—both in Oppenheimer Papers.
28. Sol Stein to Oppenheimer, March 5, 1954; Stein to Einstein, March 8, 1954—both in box C-25, ACCF Papers; Einstein quoted in RWJ to Oppenheimer, March 9, 1954 (from telephone conversation with Helen Dulcas, Einstein's secretary), Oppenheimer Papers.
29. Norman Thomas to Einstein, March 9, 1954; Einstein to Thomas (translation), March 10, 1954; Thomas to Einstein, March 16, 1954—all in Norman Thomas Papers.
30. "Emergency Civil Liberties Committee," undated; unsigned, undated memo to "Sol"—both in box C-25, ACCF Papers.
31. *New York World-Telegram,* March 11, 1954; *New York Times,* March 14, 1954.
32. Henry Schwarzschild, "The Party Was for Einstein," *New Leader,* March 29, 1954, pp. 21–22; John Ciardi, "Heresy and the High Mind," *Nation,* March 27, 1954, pp. 251–52.
33. Norman Thomas to *New York Times,* March 16, 1954, box C-25, ACCF Papers; "Norman Thomas Letter," *New Leader,* March 29, 1954, p. 22. Royal W. France to Norman Thomas, March 31, 1954; Clark Foreman to Oppenheimer, April 7, May 5, and May 28, 1954—all in Oppenheimer Papers.
34. "Draft Statement for the Congress for Cultural Freedom," January 6, 1955, pp. 1–3, box C-25, ACCF Papers.
35. In an executive committee meeting in 1954, Stein commented that the ACCF should not limit itself to purely cultural activities, because "cultural freedom is a political idea." Daniel Bell remarked that "the ACCF's proper concerns were the political consequences of cultural events, not the cultural consequences of political events" Executive Committee minutes, October 19, 1954, pp. 2–3, C-39, ACCF Papers).

36. *New York Times,* April 27, 1966, and May 14, 1967; Thomas W. Braden, "I'm Glad the CIA is 'Immoral,' " *Saturday Evening Post,* May 20, 1967, p. 12.

37. The Farfield Foundation, a frequent contributor to the congress since the congress's early years, was by the early 1960s channeling CIA funds to the congress (Sol Stern, "A Short Account of International Student Politics and the Cold War with Particular Reference to the NSA, CIA, Etc.," *Ramparts,* March 1967, p. 32). It is most probable that the foundation served the same function in the 1950s, when the congress was also receiving CIA funds. Diana Trilling, literary and social critic and an officer of the ACCF during the mid-1950s, has written that she and others on the board "strongly suspected that the Farfield Foundation, which we were told supported the congress [for Cultural Freedom], was a filter for State Department or CIA money." The suspicion "that the CIA was the source of the congress funds became certainty . . ." (*We Must March My Darlings: A Critical Decade* [New York, 1977], pp. 60–61).

38. Executive Committee minutes, September 17, 1954, box C-30, February 15 and May 16, 1955, box C-39, and December 19, 1956, box C-30—all in ACCF Papers.

39. James T. Farrell to Executive Committee, November 2, 1955, box C-23; Executive Committee minutes, December 19, 1956, box C-30—both in ACCF Papers. Diana Trilling reports that her disagreement with the Congress for Cultural Freedom was with some of its procedures rather than with "the source of its money." The American Committee for Cultural Freedom declared its "independent affiliation" with the Congress for Cultural Freedom "not from the belief that to touch American government money is to be defiled but because there were those of us on the Executive Board of the American Committee who felt that the congress compromised itself and us by some of the attitudes it took in the cultural battle against Communism" (*We Must March My Darlings,* pp. 62–63).

40. Executive Committee minutes, April 16, 1952, box C-39, ACCF Papers.

41. *New York Times,* March 30, 1952; Eastman quoted in Daniel James, "The Debate on Cultural Freedom," *New Leader,* April 7, 1952, pp. 3–4.

42. Richard Rovere to Arthur Schlesinger, Jr., March 30, 1952; Rovere to Norman Thomas, April 5, 1952—both in Norman Thomas Papers.

43. Medford Evans, *The Secret War for the A-Bomb* (Chicago, 1953), pp. v-xvi; Burnham quoted in Norman Thomas to Sol Stein, January 6, 1954, in Norman Thomas Papers. Dan [Bell] to Sidney [Hook], November 23, 1953, box C-23; Executive Committee minutes, December 18, 1953, box C-30—both in ACCF Papers.

44. Daniel Bell to Executive Committee, undated, box C-23, ACCF Papers. See Thomas C. Reeves, *Freedom and the Foundation: The Fund for the Republic in the Era of McCarthyism* (New York, 1969), pp. 178–81.

45. Roger Baldwin to Sol Stein, July 16, 1954, box C-23, ACCF Papers; Sol Stein to Sidney Hook, July 8, 1954, Norman Thomas Papers; Stein to Baldwin, July 22, 1954, and December 22, 1955, box C-23, ACCF Papers.

46. Rorty and Decter, *McCarthy and the Communists;* Sol Stein to James Burnham, September 22, 1954, box C-23; Burnham to Christopher Emmet, July 17, 1954, box C-23; George S. Schuyler to Stein, November 1, 1954, box C-24—all in ACCF Papers.

47. Sol Stein to Michael Josselson, March 1, 1955, box C-23; Stein to Schuyler, Sep-

tember 2, 1954, box C-24; Henry Schwarzschild to Whittaker Chambers, November 8, 1954, box C-23; Stein to Leo Cherne, March 15, 1955, box C-23; Chambers to Stein, November 8, 1954, box C-23; Chambers to Stein, December 15, 1954, box C-23; Stein to Chambers, December 20, 1954, box C-23—all in ACCF Papers.

48. Sol Stein to Harold C. Urey, February 4, 1955, box C-24; Urey to Norman Jacobs, June 14, 1956, box C-24; David Riesman to Stein, March 7, 1954, box C-23; Riesman to Stein, March 15, 1954, box C-23—all in ACCF Papers.

49. Brian Gilbert, "New Light on the Lattimore Case," *New Republic,* December 27, 1954, pp. 7–12. "Is There New Light on the Lattimore Case?" Draft Statement by ACCF, revised, January 1955, box C-27; David Riesman to Sol Stein, January 18, 1955, box C-23; Riesman to Norman Thomas, February 7, 1955, box C-23—all in ACCF Papers; *New Republic,* February 28, 1955, pp. 21–22.

50. Norman Thomas to Richard Rovere, February 17, 1955, box C-23; Sol Stein to Michael Straight, March 7, 1955, box C-27; Stein to Eric Bentley, February 25, 1955, box C-23; Arthur Schlesinger to Jim [James T. Farrell], March 16, 1955, box C-24—all in ACCF Papers.

51. Harold C. Urey to Norman Jacobs, June 14, 1956; Arthur Schlesinger to Jim [James T. Farrell], March 16, 1955—both in box C-24, ACCF Papers.

52. James T. Farrell to Norman Jacobs, August 28, 1956, p. 1, box C-23, ACCF Papers; *New York Times,* August 29, 1956; *New York Post,* August 29, 1956; Diana Trilling quoted in Granville Hicks, *Part of the Truth* (New York, 1965), pp. 274–75; Lionel Trilling quoted in Sol Stein to Michael Josselson, May 20, 1955, box C-23, ACCF Papers.

53. Michael Josselson to Sol Stein, September 22, 1954; Stein to Sidney Hook, June 3, 1955—both in box C-23, ACCF Papers.

Chapter Nine

1. Those voting for the appropriation included liberal Democrats Chester Holifield, John Blatnik, and Abraham J. Multer of New York, and liberal Republican Jacob Javits (*Congressional Record,* 83d Cong., 1st sess., February 24, 1953, 99, pt. 1:1359, 1361–62).

2. Celler, who opposed the 1954 HUAC appropriation, paired his vote. Javits did not vote (*Congressional Record,* 83d Cong., 2d sess., February 25, 1954, 100, pt. 2:2283, 2293–2294).

3. See Richard M. Fried, *Men Against McCarthy* (New York, 1976), pp. 254–92.

4. See Robert Griffith, *The Politics of Fear: Joseph R. McCarthy and the Senate* (Lexington, Ky., 1970), pp. 277–91; Fried, *Men Against McCarthy,* pp. 293–96; *New York Times,* July 17, 20, 1954.

5. Griffith, *Politics of Fear,* pp. 288–91, 294–304; Fried, *Men Against McCarthy,* pp. 296–300; *Nation,* August 14, 1954, p. 123; "Now the Senate," *New Republic,* October 4, 1954, p. 3; "The Watkins Report," *Nation,* October 9, 1954, p. 297.

6. The original co-sponsors of the amendment, with Hubert Humphrey, were Wayne Morse, John F. Kennedy, and Paul Douglas. Of these Morse played the most important role. Additional Democratic co-sponsors were Edwin C. Johnson, Herbert

Lehman, Warren Magnuson, Mike Mansfield, Mike Monroney, James Murray, Clinton P. Anderson (N.M.), Henry M. Jackson (Wash.), Robert S. Kerr (Okla.), John C. Pastore (R.I.), and Stuart Symington (Mo.). Co-sponsors from the Deep South were George A. Smathers (Fla.), Burnet R. Maybank and Olin D. Johnston (S.C.), Lister Hill (Ala.), and John C. Stennis (Miss.).

7. *Congressional Record*, 83d Cong., 2d sess., August 12, 1954, 100, pt. 11:14234–36.

8. *New York Times*, August 14, 1954.

9. Ibid., May 18, 1948, and January 19, 1954; *Congressional Record*, 83d Cong., 2d sess., March 25, 1954, 100, pt. 3:3876–77, and August 12, 1954, 100, pt. 11:14214; *New York Times*, March 19, 1954; U.S., Congress, House, *Internal Security Legislation: Hearings before Subcommittee No. 1 of the Committee on the Judiciary, House of Representatives, Eighty-third Congress, Second Session, on . . .* (Washington, D.C., 1954). For legal scholars' and political scientists' defense of the concept of outlawing the Communist party, see Thomas I. Cook, *Democratic Rights versus Communist Activity* (Garden City, N.Y., 1954), and Charles E. Wyzanski, Jr., "The Communist Party and the Law," *Atlantic Monthly* 187 (May 1951): 29–30. See also the opinions of Justice Robert H. Jackson, who held that the Communist party was a conspiracy rather than a political party, that Congress could legislatively make such a finding (*American Communications Association* [CIO] v. *Douds*, 339 U.S. 382 [1950]), and that the Communist party, as a conspiracy, was subject to the law of conspiracy (*Dennis* v. *United States*, 341 U.S. 494 [1951]). Max Eastman's "Why We Must Outlaw the Communist Party!" appeared in *Reader's Digest* 57 (September 1950): 42–44. See also the writings of James Burnham (especially *The Struggle for the World* [New York, 1947] and *The Web of Subversion: Underground Networks in the U.S. Government* [New York, 1954]), who insisted that the Communist party was a conspiracy rather than a political party; and Sidney Hook (especially *Heresy, Yes–Conspiracy, No!* [New York, 1953]), who called the Communist party a conspiracy to undermine the democratic processes. For general background, see Milton R. Konvitz, *Expanding Liberties: Freedom's Gains in Postwar America* (New York, 1966), pp. 109–57.

10. This bill proposed "to amend the Subversive Activities Control Act of 1950 to provide for the determination of the identity of certain Communist-infiltrated organizations. . . ." See U.S., Congress, Senate, *Amending the Subversive Activities Control Act of 1950: S. Rept. 1709 to Accompany S. 3706*, in Senate *Reports*, vol. 4: Miscellaneous IV, 83d Cong., 2d sess., 1954, p. 1. Senate committee hearings on the bill were titled "Subversive Influence in Certain Labor Organizations." See U.S., Congress, Senate, *Subversive Influence in Certain Labor Organizations: Hearings before the Subcommittee to Investigate the Administration of the Internal Security Act and other Internal Security Laws of the Committee on the Judiciary, United States Senate, Eighty-third Congress, First and Second Sessions* (Washington, D.C., 1954).

11. Quoted in *Congressional Record*, 83d Cong., 2d sess., August 12, 1954, 100, pt. 11:14195.

12. House Subcommittee No. 1 of the Committee on the Judiciary, *Internal Security Legislation*, pp. 371–72; Senate subcommittee of the Committee on the Judiciary, *Subversive Influence in Certain Labor Organizations*, pp. 451–52. After extensive hearings the House Committee on Education and Labor refused to report favorably a bill almost identical to the Butler bill (*Congressional Record*, 83d Cong., 2d sess., Au-

gust 12, 1954, 100, pt. 11:14193). The House Committee on the Judiciary also reported unfavorably on a companion bill to the Butler bill and proposed instead, in a move to kill the original bill, a study commission on security from sabotage and espionage in industry (*New York Times*, July 14 and 16, 1954). Nevertheless, the House Committee on Un-American Activities, in what Senator Warren Magnuson termed an "end around play," reported without hearings a bill almost identical to the Butler bill (*New York Times*, August 10, 1954, p. 41; *Congressional Record*, 83d Cong., 2d sess., August 12, 1954, 100, pt. 11:14192–93), and Magnuson's effort to substitute for the Butler bill a study commission proposal identical to that put forward by the House Judiciary Committee was defeated in the Senate by a vote of fifty-seven to thirty-one (*Congressional Record*, 83d Cong., 2d sess., August 12, 1954, 100, pt. 11:14200). The defeat of Magnuson's amendment was softened only by the passage of an amendment proposed by Republican Senator Irving M. Ives of New York, which provided a presumption of freedom from Communist infiltration for union affiliates in good standing with the CIO or the American Federation of Labor. After Senate floor debate established that the Ives amendment would not prevent the attorney general from proceeding against such unions if he had facts that overcame the immediate presumption of innocence, Butler withdrew his opposition and accepted the amendment, which passed by an overwhelming vote (*Congressional Record*, 83d Cong., 2d sess., August 12, 1954, 100 pt. 11:14200–07). Following the Senate's acceptance of the Ives amendment, the AFL showed little further interest in the Butler bill. The CIO, however, continued lobbying against it (interview with Thomas E. Harris, November 3, 1972, Washington, D.C.).

13. "[The Communist Control Act] was cooked up between Max, the senator and myself at dinner. I don't think anybody else was there" (interview with Harris, November 3, 1972).

14. Max Kampelman recalled that "when we had the bill in shape, Humphrey and I took it over to Wayne, and we talked about it. Wayne looked at it, made a few changes in it, and said, 'I want to be a co-sponsor' " (interview with Max M. Kampelman, October 30, 1972, Washington, D.C.). Kampelman was greatly interested in the subject of organized labor and the Communist party; see Max M. Kampelman, *The Communist Party vs. the C.I.O.: A Study in Power Politics* (New York, 1957).

15. Interview with Harris, November 3, 1972.

16. *Congressional Record*, 83d Cong., 2d sess., August 12, 1954, 100, pt. 11:14211–12, 14222, 14229.

17. Ibid., p. 14234.

18. Interview with Harris, November 3, 1972.

19. *Congressional Record*, 83d Cong., 2d sess., August 12, 1954, 100, pt. 11:14211.

20. Ibid., p. 14212; interview with Harris, November 3, 1972.

21. *Congressional Record*, 83d Cong., 2d sess., August 12, 1954, 100, pt. 11:14222–23.

22. Interview with Kampelman, October 30, 1972.

23. *New York Times*, April 13, 1954.

24. Ibid., April 13 and August 14, 1954; *Congressional Record*, 83d Cong., 2d sess., August 12, 1954, 100, pt. 11:14211, 14222–23, and August 16, 1954, 100, pt. 11:-14564–67.

25. See note 9 above.

26. Kampelman outlined this particular rationale for the Communist Control Act in a memorandum circulated in Minnesota by the Humphrey staff before the 1954 senatorial election, in which Humphrey was running. See Michael Amrine, *This Is Humphrey: The Story of the Senator* (Garden City, 1960), pp. 178–79. Kampelman conceded that the "traditional civil libertarians" did not like the idea of a conspiracy theory, upon which the Communist Control Act was predicated. "But in our preamble," he said, "we deliberately quoted from Judge Learned Hand's opinion, in which he had already, by judicial determination, called the Communist party a conspiracy [*United States* v. *Dennis*, 183 F. 2d 201 (1950)]. So, the whole argument that this was a bill of attainder was simply not the case. The Congress was basing its determination, or its conclusion, by borrowing a conclusion already arrived at by the Court of Appeals" (interview with Kampelman, October 30, 1972).
27. *Congressional Record*, 83d Cong., 2d sess., August 16, 1954, 100, pt. 11:14564.
28. *New York Times*, August 14, 15, 1954.
29. *Congressional Record*, 83d Cong., 2d sess., August 16, 1954, 100 pt. 11:14641, 14644–45, 14653, 14658; *New York Times*, August 17, 1954. The bill before the House was taken to the floor under a suspension of rules, by the terms of which only forty minutes of debate were allowed and a two-thirds majority was required for passage.
30. *Congressional Record*, 83d Cong., 2d sess., August 17, 1954, 100, pt. 11:14726; *New York Times*, August 18, 1954. The only Republican to speak in favor of Humphrey's amendment was Margaret Chase Smith. She, Thomas H. Kuchel of California, and William Langer of North Dakota were the only Republican senators who voted for the amendment. Patrick McCarran was the only Democrat voting against it (*New York Times*, August 18, 1954).
31. *Congressional Record*, 83d Cong., 2d sess., August 17, 1954, 100, pt. 11:14729.
32. Ibid., p. 14851; *New York Times*, August 18, 1954. Ninety-nine of those congressmen voting against the bill as re-passed by the Senate were Republicans, who (with the exception of Usher L. Burdick) presumably supported the administration on this issue. Only one Democrat, Multer (who opposed the bill on civil liberties grounds), voted against it (*New York Times*, August 18, 1954).
33. The House conferees were Republicans Chauncey W. Reed of Illinois, Louis E. Graham of Pennsylvania, and Dewitt S. Hyde of Maryland, and Democrats Emanuel Celler and Francis E. Walter of Pennsylvania. The Senate conferees were Democrats Patrick McCarran and Harley M. Kilgore and Republicans John Butler, Arthur V. Watkins, and William Langer. Of these, Reed, Graham, Hyde, McCarran, Butler, and Watkins opposed the bill as re-passed by the Senate.
34. Telephone interview with J. G. Sourwine, October 20, 1972. Sourwine had no recollection of Langer's role in conference. Langer, a maverick Republican who had ardently opposed the Internal Security Act of 1950, voted for the bill with penalty provisions but said little in its defense during Senate debate.
35. *Congressional Record*, 83d Cong., 2d sess., August 16, 1954, 100, pt. 11:14642–44.
36. Interview with Sourwine, October 20, 1972; *Congressional Record*, 83d Cong., 2d sess., August 19, 1954, 100, pt. 12:15121, 15236–37; *New York Times*, August 20, 1954.
37. Interview with Kampelman, October 30, 1972.

38. *Congressional Record*, 83d Cong., 2d sess., August 19, 1954, 100, pt. 12:15105–6.
39. In 1957 Humphrey stated, "The bill was not perfect and it had its limitations. I recognized that. I've never been wholly happy about all that myself." He seems to have been referring to the act's ineffectiveness, however, not to its threat to civil liberties. In the same interview he stated: "It seemed to me that you had to establish a new law on subversive activity and Communist Party activity that would place these matters in the courts, and thereby anyone accused would be accused in a court of law, where rules of evidence and procedure could prevail" (interview with Hubert H. Humphrey, July 23, 1957, pp. 30–31, Herbert H. Lehman Oral History Project, The Oral History Collection, Columbia University, New York). In 1959 Humphrey told a biographer that "the purpose of the bill—to take Communist-hunting out of headlines and committee circuses, and put it in the courts—was sound" (Amrine, *This Is Humphrey*, p. 180).
40. Amrine, *This Is Humphrey*, p. 180; Winthrop Griffith, *Humphrey: A Candid Biography* (New York, 1965), p. 222.
41. Among those who supported the Humphrey version of the Communist Control Act in the close August 17 Senate vote were the following members then seeking reelection: Thomas A. Burke of Ohio, Allen J. Ellender of Louisiana, Joseph A. Frear, Jr., of Delaware, Guy M. Gillette of Iowa, Theodore F. Green of Rhode Island, Lyndon B. Johnson of Texas, John L. McClellan of Arkansas, Matthew M. Neely of West Virginia, A. Willis Robertson of Virginia, Richard B. Russell of Georgia, and Margaret Chase Smith. All but Smith were Democrats. Gillette, who had chaired a subcommittee investigating McCarthy, lost, although probably not because of McCarthy. Smith had been one of McCarthy's strongest critics within the Republican party.
42. *Congressional Record*, 83d Cong., 2d sess., August 12, 1954, 100, pt. 11:14210, 14215; *New York Times*, August 14, 1954.
43. *Congressional Record*, 83d Cong., 2d sess., August 17, 1954, 100, pt. 11:14718, and August 16, 1954, 100, pt. 11:14577.
44. Johnson played an active role in pushing the Humphrey amendment through the Senate. To prevent any opposition after the close roll call vote (41 to 39) on August 17, he immediately moved that the vote be reconsidered. Democrat Albert A. Gore of Tennessee then quickly moved to table the motion, to which the Senate agreed by a vote of 43 to 39. Johnson then hurried through the vote on the Humphrey-Butler bill, as amended by Humphrey. Following its overwhelming acceptance, 81 to 1—Estes Kefauver the lone dissenter—Butler rose to object that "the only thing we have done here today is emasculate a good piece of legislation." Johnson retorted that Butler himself was "party to that emasculation" (*Congressional Record*, 83d Cong., 2d sess., August 17, 1954, 100, pt. 11:14726–29).
45. Interview with Kampelman, October 30, 1972; *New York Times*, December 27, 1953, and October 14 and November 3 and 4, 1954. Humphrey himself has written: "I did not need to save myself from McCarthy's attacks in the 1954 Congressional elections. I had fought the Communist Party in Minnesota. I had helped organize the ADA which had as its main purpose to differentiate legitimate dissent and liberalism from Communist conspiracy and reaction" (Hubert H. Humphrey to author, January 11, 1973).

46. *Congressional Record,* 83d Cong., 2d sess., August 12, 1954, 100, pt. 11:14210, and August 16, 1954, 100, pt. 11:14577, 14579. See Humphrey to Marvin Rosenberg, who had criticized Humphrey for expediency and illiberalism in presenting the measure. Humphrey wrote, in part: "It has been my position for a number of years now that the Communist Party ought to be outlawed and I have so stated to many of my friends and associates. . . . It is true that I evaluated the political consequences of my amendment before I introduced it, but it is also true that, in my judgment, the factors lent themselves to a conclusion on my part that it would be somewhat of a political liability to introduce the amendment . . . because I anticipated some of the rather emotional reactions from the liberal community . . . because I was hitting somewhat of a 'sacred cow.'

". . . Were I to act politically, therefore, it would have been far simpler for me not to act at all in connection with this Communist issue, because you and I know the people of Minnesota can never be fooled into thinking that Hubert Humphrey is a Communist, because my record of anti-Communism in Minnesota is well known . . ." (August 27, 1954, box 16, Legislative File, ADA Papers).

47. Griffith, *Humphrey,* p. 222. Yet Humphrey continues to defend the Communist Control Act on civil liberties grounds. He wrote in 1973: "There were two reasons for the bill: First to clarify the law as to the purpose and intent of the Communist Party. Secondly, to differentiate between those who sought to overthrow the government by force or violence and those who were engaged in legitimate dissent" (Humphrey to author, January 11, 1973). Humphrey has repeated this explanation at somewhat greater length in his autobiography (Hubert H. Humphrey, *The Education of a Public Man: My Life in Politics* (Garden City, 1976), p. 464).

48. *Congressional Record,* 83d Cong., 2d sess., August 16, 1954, 100, pt. 11:14644–45, 14653.

49. Ibid., pp. 14643–44. A month earlier, during a meeting of the subcommittee of the House Committee on the Judiciary, Celler voted against reporting favorably to the full committee a bill to outlaw the Communist party. He gave as his reasons the fear that such a bill would hurt the effectiveness of the Smith Act and the Internal Security Act, and that it would give the Communists a claim to martyrdom. He added that there were "grave questions as to the constitutionality of the bill," but crossed this last sentence out and omitted it from the final statement he released to the press ("Statement by Representative Emanuel Celler," July 21, 1954, "Outlawing the Communist Party Would Help the Communists," in box 22, Emanuel Celler Papers, Manuscript Division, Library of Congress).

50. *Congressional Record,* 83d Cong., 2d sess., August 17, 1954, 100, pt. 11:14726.

51. Ibid., August 19, 1954, 100, pt. 12:15101–2, 15106–8. Kefauver was cautious on the Communist Control Act perhaps because he, like many among the bill's co-sponsors, was up for reelection in 1954. Kefauver's primary opponent accused him of Communist sympathies.

52. Ibid., August 12, 1954, 100, pt. 11:14216–17, 14232, 14234. John Sherman Cooper's amendment might have had some significance had Humphrey not later amended the measure with the fourteen criteria for determining Communist party membership. Cooper himself did not specify in his amendment exactly what constituted an

"overt act," and in the confusion attending passage of the Communist Control Act, his amendment was never clarified.

53. See note 6 above.
54. Herbert Lehman, *Liberalism: A Personal Journey* (New York, 1958), p. 24; interview with Humphrey, p. 30, Oral History Collection; interview with Kampelman, October 30, 1972. Kampelman recalled that Lehman's assistant, Julius Edelstein, was opposed to the Communist bill and that Morse finally convinced Lehman to vote for it (interview with Kampelman, October 30, 1972).
55. *New York Times*, August 19, 1954; "The Panic of a Mob on Capitol Hill," *I. F. Stone's Weekly*, September 6, 1954, pp. 1, 3; Michael Harrington, "Myths of U.S. Liberalism: A Dissent from Certain Key Tendencies of this Country's Foreign and Domestic Policies," *Commonweal*, December 17, 1954, p. 304; *New York Times*, August 20 and 22, 1954.
56. *New York Times*, August 28, 1954; "Who Should Be Censured?" *Nation*, August 21, 1954, p. 145; *New York Times*, August 21 and 22, 1954. For the ACLU's testimony at congressional hearings, see *New York Times*, April 6, 1954.
57. "Behind the Headlines," *New Republic*, August 23, 1954, p. 3; *New York Times*, August 21 and 26, 1954. For a synopsis of national editorial opinion on the Communist Control Act, see *New York Times*, August 21, 1954.
58. Executive Committee minutes, August 17 and November 18, 1954, box 35, Administrative File, ADA Papers; Arthur M. Schlesinger, Jr., quoted in *New York Times*, August 21, 1954.
59. *New York Times*, August 21, 1954.
60. Ibid., September 30, 1954. This action was upheld in *Salwen v. Rees*, 108 A. 2d 265 (1954).
61. *U.S. v. Brandt*, 139 F. Supp. 367 (1955); *U.S. v. Silverman*, 132 F. Supp. 820 (1955).
62. In re Albertson's Claim, 168 N.E. 2d 242 (1960). In re Albertson's Claim, 169 N.E. 2d 427 (1960).
63. Ibid.
64. "Washington Wire," *New Republic*, December 6, 1954, p. 2; Lehman quoted in Fried, *Men Against McCarthy*, p. 310.
65. *New York Times*, December 3, 1954; Hennings quoted in Fried, *Men Against McCarthy*, p. 313.

Bibliographical Note

Manuscripts

The Americans for Democratic Action collection, located at the State Historical Society of Wisconsin, provides a rich source of information on the ADA's organizational history and on postwar liberalism. The Reinhold Niebuhr collection, Library of Congress Manuscript Division, offers surprisingly little on this topic, although the collection does contain some supplementary material of interest, including a collection of interviews by biographer June Bingham which attempts to establish Niebuhr's influence on a variety of public figures.

The massive American Civil Liberties Union archives are located at the Princeton University library. The New York Public Library has some duplicate ACLU records and many of the ACLU's published materials. In addition, I found several items in the ACLU headquarters archives in New York which I had not found elsewhere. Together, the ACLU records provide a rich account of civil liberties and the left during the years on which I have focused. Another valuable source is Osmond K. Fraenkel's ACLU diary, which is located at the Princeton University library, in the Manuscript Division.

The verbatim transcripts of the CIO International Executive Board Proceedings were, when I found them, located in the Washington, D.C., headquarters of James Carey's International Union of Electrical, Radio and Machine Workers (IUE). Since then, they have been housed in the Wayne State University Archives of Labor History and Urban Affairs, where they are now part of the CIO Secretary-Treasurer [James Carey]'s Papers. These transcripts are invaluable for their revelations of the inner workings of the CIO's upper echelons. Far less helpful were the Philip Murray Papers, at Catholic University of America in Washington, D.C.; Murray's correspondence since 1945 offers few new insights for the historian.

The American Committee for Cultural Freedom Papers are located in their entirety at New York University's Tamiment Library. These contain an extremely revealing collection of letters between some of the most prominent intellectuals of the period on subjects related to the Cold War and McCarthyism. Useful supplementary material is contained in the Norman Thomas Papers (New York Public Library) and the J. Robert Oppenheimer Papers (Library of Congress).

The Herbert H. Lehman Papers, at Columbia University, were helpful on the subject of political liberals, as were the Emanuel Celler Papers in the Library of Congress. Less useful for my research were the Joseph Edward Davies Papers, the Felix Frankfurter Papers, the Theodore F. Green Papers, and the Minnesota Progressive Party Papers, all located in the Library of Congress.

Oral History

Among the interviews and memoirs I examined, the most worthwhile were the interviews with Hubert H. Humphrey and Wayne Morse contained in the Herbert H. Lehman Oral History Project, Columbia University Oral History Collection. Less useful for my research were the Roger Nash Baldwin memoirs, the Felix Frankfurter memoirs, the Ben W. Huebsch memoirs, the Norman Thomas memoirs, and the Socialist Movement Oral History Project, all in the Columbia Oral History collection.

Personal Interviews

Individuals who generously gave me their time and shared both recollections and insights include Justice Arthur J. Goldberg, Thomas E. Harris, Max M. Kampelman, Morris H. Rubin, Miles McMillan, Edwin R. Bayley, William R. Bechtel, Robert Fleming, Willard Edwards, and Alan Reitman. Roger Baldwin, Senator Hubert Humphrey, and Rt. Rev. Msgr. Charles O. Rice answered my questions by letter. Sidney Hook responded to my inquiries in writing, but not for publication. J. R. Sourwine answered my questions in a telephone interview.

Newspapers and Periodicals

Certain periodicals proved especially useful as indicators of the kinds of topics and issues concerning the left-of-center, while also providing consistent patterns of response to these issues.

Of the periodicals which I read systematically for the years 1947 through 1954, most useful were the *Nation*, the *New Leader*, and the *New Republic*. *Commentary* provided some important additions to the anti-Communist campaign waged by former radicals. *Commonweal*, the liberal Catholic journal, was of interest because of its anti-McCarthy position, almost unique among Catholic periodicals. *Progressive*, published in Wisconsin and rooted in the LaFollette tradition, proved valuable (despite its small circulation) because of its respected standing among liberals. Also consulted were the *Partisan Review, American Scholar, Reporter, Atlantic Monthly, Harper's Magazine, Twentieth Century, Saturday Review, National Guardian,* and *Monthly Review. I. F. Stone's Weekly*, founded in 1953, often provided essential information found nowhere else.

Among newspapers, the *New York Times* and its index was an indispensable reference source for the entire period. The *Christian Science Monitor*, now indexed, was also valuable. The *New York World-Telegram* provided clues with which to follow the activities of anti-Communist former radicals, through the articles of its right-wing newsman, Frederick Woltman. Editorials in James Wechsler's *New York Post* were helpful in gauging the mood and responses of the anti-Communist liberal left.

Government Documents

The *Congressional Record* from 1946 through 1954 is an essential although not final source for studying congressional liberals during these years. The *Record* shows the shifting mood of political liberals during the early Cold War as they at first hesitantly and then more confidently embraced the foreign policy of the Truman administration. The *Record* also clearly portrays the rise of red-baiting and "McCarthyism" and documents liberal politicians' frightened and evasive response.

Useful for this study were the bills and hearings on outlawing the Communist party, including: U.S., Congress, House, *Internal Security Legislation: Hearings before Subcommittee No. 1 of the Committee on the Judiciary, House of Representatives, Eighty-third Congress, Second Session, on . . .* (Washington, D.C., 1954); U.S., Congress, Senate, *Subversive Influence in Certain Labor Organizations: Hearings before the Subcommittee to Investigate the Administration of the Internal Security Act and other Internal Security Laws of the Committee on the Judiciary, United States Senate, Eighty-third Congress, First and Second Sessions* (Washington, D.C., 1954); U.S., Congress, Senate, *Amending the Subversive Activities Control Act of 1950: S. Rept. 1709 to Accompany S. 3706,* in *Senate Reports,* vol. 4: Miscellaneous IV, 83d Cong., 2d sess., 1954, p. 1.

The *Public Papers of the Presidents of the United States* for the administrations of both Harry S. Truman and Dwight D. Eisenhower contain helpful background and reference material for the period. The various hearings initiated by or involving Senator Joe McCarthy should be read by any student interested in the postwar left, if only to appreciate the kind of person and movement with which liberals and the left were contending. See especially the Tydings Committee hearings (U.S., Congress, Senate, 81st Cong., 2d sess., Committee on Foreign Relations, *State Department Loyalty Investigation* [Washington, D.C., 1950]); the Subcommittee on Privileges and Elections' investigation of McCarthy, based on William Benton's charges (U.S., Congress, Senate, 82d Cong., 2d sess., *Investigations of Senators Joseph R. McCarthy and William Benton,* Committee Print [Washington, D.C., 1952]); and the Army-McCarthy hearings (U.S., Congress, Senate, 83d Cong., 2d sess., Committee on Government Operations, Permanent Subcommittee on Investigations, *Charges and Countercharges Involving Secretary of the Army Robert T. Stevens, John G. Adams, H. Struve Hensel and Senator Joe McCarthy, Roy M. Cohn and Francis P. Carr* [Washington, D.C., 1954]).

Published Memoirs and Secondary Sources

Although the Cold War and postwar Red Scare were critical factors shaping the development of the postwar left, the left's complex wartime and prewar history remains essential background for understanding what the left had been and had hoped for, as well as why, to a large extent, it failed. Richard H. Pells, *Radical Visions and American Dreams: Culture and Social Thought in the Depression Years* (New York, 1973), and R. Alan Lawson, *The Failure of Independent Liberalism, 1930–1941* (New York, 1971), provide important insights into the dreams and failures of the left-of-center's most influential cultural and political leaders. James B. Gilbert, in *Writers and Partisans: A History of Literary Radicalism in America* (New York, 1968), analyzes the coterie of anti-Stalinist Marxists who clustered around the *Partisan Review* and became the nucleus for the anti-Communist and anti-Marxist former radicals of the Cold War years. Theodore Draper provides a detailed account of the Communist Party USA's origins and early years in *The Roots of American Communism* (New York, 1957) and in *American Communism and Soviet Russia: The Formative Period* (New York, 1960). Irving Howe and Lewis Coser, in *The American Communist Party: A Critical History, 1919–1957* (Boston, 1957), offer a comprehensive history of the party to 1957, and David A. Shannon, in *The Decline of American Communism: A History of the Communist Party of the United States since 1945* (New York, 1959), depicts the party in decline. The most thoughtful history of the party in its later years is that by the former foreign editor of the *Daily Worker*, Joseph R. Starobin (*American Communism in Crisis, 1943–1957* [Cambridge, Mass., 1972]), who explains its failure and decline as a product of its dependence upon Moscow, which never recognized the unique nature of the radical experience in the United States. David A. Shannon has written the standard account of the Socialist party, *The Socialist Party of America: A History* (New York, 1955), while W. A. Swanberg recently has provided a comprehensive biography of Norman Thomas (*Norman Thomas: The Last Idealist* [New York, 1976]); Bernard K. Johnpoll's political study, *Pacifist's Progress: Norman Thomas and the Decline of American Socialism* (Chicago, 1970), remains important. Frank A. Warren focuses on liberals during the so-called "Red Decade" in *Liberals and Communism: The 'Red Decade' Revisited* (Bloomington, Ind., 1966), concluding that the liberal response to Communism during the 1930s was a deeply varied one and that the phrase "Red Decade" was itself a misnomer.

What the left became after World War II is depicted not only by Starobin and Shannon, as well as, briefly and provocatively, Lawson, Pells, and Gilbert; leaders of the postwar left-of-center have provided their own statements through their writings. Most graphic is *The Vital Center: The Politics of Freedom* (Boston, 1949), by Arthur M. Schlesinger, Jr., which provides an appropriate image and description for the Cold War's new liberalism. The interests, fears, and goals of the new liberalism are also sharply delineated in Lionel Trilling's novel *The Middle of the Journey* (New York, 1947), and in Reinhold Niebuhr's many publications from this period, including *Faith and History: A Comparison of Christian and Modern Views of History* (New York, 1949), *The Irony of American History* (New York, 1952), and *Christian Realism and Political Problems* (New York, 1953). Earlier works by Niebuhr which should also be consulted are: *Moral Man and Immoral Society: A Study in Ethics and Politics* (New York, 1932); *The Nature and Destiny of Man: A Christian Interpretation*, 2 vols. (New York, 1943); *The Children of Light and the Children of Darkness: A Vindication of Democracy and a Critique of Its Traditional Defense* (New York, 1944), and *Christianity and Power Politics* (New York, 1940). Gordon Harland, in *The Thought of Reinhold Niebuhr* (New York, 1960), probes Niebuhr's political and theological analysis with particular clarity, while Holton P. Odegarde, *Sin and Science: Reinhold Niebuhr As Political Theologian* (Yellow Springs, Ohio, 1956), is also helpful.

Leslie A. Fiedler, *An End to Innocence: Essays on Culture and Politics* (Boston, 1955), illustrates the remarkable shift in mood among leftist intellectuals from the 1930s to the Cold War, a shift analyzed by Charles Frankel in *The Case for Modern Man* (Boston, 1955) and by Palmer W. Wright in an unpublished dissertation, "The 'New Liberalism' of the Fifties: Reinhold Niebuhr, David Riesman, Lionel Trilling, and the American Intellectual" (University of Michigan, 1966). Intellectuals' break with radical politics may be illustrated in many examples: Richard Crossman, ed., *The God That Failed* (New York, 1949); Granville Hicks, *Where We Came Out* (New York, 1954) and *Part of the Truth* (New York, 1965); Whittaker Chambers, *Witness* (New York, 1952); John Dos Passos, "Reminiscences of a Middle-Class Radical," *National Review*, January 18, 1956, pp. 9–11, and February 15, 1956, pp. 9–12; James B. Gilbert, "James Burnham: Exemplary Radical of the 1930s," in *A New History of Leviathan: Essays on the Rise of the American Corporate State*, ed. Ronald Radosh and Murray N. Rothbard (New York, 1972); Daniel Aaron, *Writers on the Left: Episodes in American Literary Communism* (New York, 1961); and John P. Diggins, *Up From Communism: Conservative Odysseys in American Intellectual History* (New York, 1975).

The new liberalism embraced a pluralist vision, clearly expressed in the political and economic analyses of Max Ascoli (*The Power of Freedom* [New York, 1949]), Irwin Ross (*Strategy for Liberals: The Politics of the Mixed Economy* [New York, 1949]), and John Kenneth Galbraith (*American Capitalism: The Concept of Countervailing Power* [Boston, 1952]). Daniel Bell, ed., *The New American Right* (New York, 1955; revised as *The Radical Right* [New York, 1963]), provides important examples of pluralist thought in its encounter with the pressures of the Cold War world. An introduction to pluralist theory is found in David B. Truman, *The Governmental Process: Political Interests and Public Opinion* (New York, 1951), which should be supplemented with Theodore J. Lowi's incisive analysis in *The End of Liberalism: Ideology, Policy, and the Crisis of Public Authority* (New York, 1969). The desired product of the pluralist society was stability, and a perception of stability and consensus throughout America's history was a common theme in historical studies written during the early postwar years. John Higham ("The Cult of the 'American Consensus,' " *Commentary* 27 [February, 1959]: 93; and "Beyond Consensus: The Historian as Moral Critic," *American Historical Review* 67, no. 3 [April 1962]: 609–25) and Irwin Unger ("The 'New Left' and American History: Some Recent Trends in United States Historiography," *American Historical Review* 72, no. 4 [July 1967]: 1237–63) place consensus historiography in perspective.

The fundamental change within the American left was, to a large degree, the product of the Cold War, which was viewed through the perceptions of the "realist" theory of foreign policy. Any examination of this theory for the Cold War years should include George F. Kennan's *American Diplomacy: 1900–1950* (Chicago, 1951), as well as his *Memoirs: 1925–1963*, 2 vols. (Boston, 1967–72); Hans J. Morgenthau's *In Defense of the National Interest: A Critical Examination of American Foreign Policy* (New York, 1951); and Walter Lippmann's *The Cold War: A Study in U.S. Foreign Policy* (New York, 1947). Robert E. Osgood, *Ideals and Self-Interest in America's Foreign Relations* (Chicago, 1953), is another example of this school of analysis. Important histories of the Cold War from the "realist" viewpoint include Norman A. Graebner, *Cold War Diplomacy: American Foreign Policy, 1945–1960* (Princeton, 1962), and Louis J. Halle, *The Cold War as History* (London, 1967).

A large number of revisionist histories now exist which challenge "realist" assumptions, justifications, and goals for postwar foreign policy. These revisionist histories do not agree on all points, however, and vary considerably in quality; among the best for the early Cold War are Walter LaFeber, *America, Russia, and the Cold War, 1945–1966* (New York, 1967); Thomas G. Paterson, *Soviet-American Confrontation: Postwar Reconstruction and the Origins of the Cold War* (Baltimore, 1973); and Lloyd C. Gardner, *Architects of Illusion: Men and Ideas in American Foreign Policy, 1941–1949* (Chicago, 1970). John Lewis Gaddis, in *The United States and the Origins of the Cold War, 1941–1947* (New York, 1972), has written an exceptionally balanced and useful account of United States foreign policy for these years. Joseph M. Jones, *The Fifteen Weeks* (New York, 1955), and Dean Acheson, *Present at the Creation: My Years in the State Department* (New York, 1969), offer personal recollections of the early development of the Truman foreign policy, while Richard M. Freeland, *The Truman Doctrine and the Origins of McCarthyism: Foreign Policy, Domestic Politics, and Internal Security, 1946–1948* (New York, 1972), provides a revisionist interpretation of this developmental period which links Truman's foreign policy directly with McCarthyism and the Red Scare. The presidential memoirs of Truman and Eisenhower (Harry S. Truman, *Memoirs*, 2 vols. [New York, 1955–56]; Dwight D. Eisenhower, *The White House Years: Mandate for Change, 1953–1956* [New York, 1963]) should not be overlooked, although more often than not they are disappointing for information and insights they do not provide. Two especially thorough histories of the Korean War are Glenn D. Paige, *The Korean Decision: June 24–30, 1950* (New York, 1968), and David Rees, *Korea: The Limited War* (New York, 1964).

The American left changed in response not only to the Cold War, but also to the conservative trend which stemmed from the politics of World War II itself, and to the Red Scare—which by 1950 was identified largely with Senator Joe McCarthy. The origins of McCarthyism have been described by Daniel Bell, Richard Hofstadter, and other historians and social scientists (many of them represented in *The New American Right*) as the product of status anxieties caused by the movements of social groups up or down, which created a radical right backing for McCarthy and McCarthyism. This thesis is challenged in more recent studies, the best of which are Michael Paul Rogin, *The Intellectuals and McCarthy: The Radical Specter* (Cambridge, Mass., 1967), and Robert Griffith, *The Politics of Fear: Joseph R. McCarthy and the Senate* (Lexington, Ky., 1970). Rogin specifically challenges the status-anxiety interpretation of McCarthyism, with all its antiradical implications, and argues persuasively that McCarthy's base of support came not from a radical right but from a traditional and essentially elitist conservative constituency. Griffith's study of McCarthy's political career clearly shows that McCarthy's rapid rise to power was not an aberration of the American political system but the product of normal party politics—in this instance, the decade-long efforts of Republican partisans seeking political power. McCarthy's great achievement, *Politics of Fear* points out, was his ability to make himself into a personal symbol of the Communist issue, which, as other Republican politicians had already discovered, offered an avenue for political success. Earl Latham, *The Communist Controversy in Washington: From the New Deal to McCarthy* (Cambridge, Mass., 1966), provides a detailed history of Communists in American government as well as the Communist issue in politics, and concludes that McCarthyism was the product of frustrated conservatives, who reasserted themselves against the more liberal executive branch through the hearings procedure in the legislative branch of government.

Other historians stress that the Truman administration, in its efforts both to win public support for its anti-Communist foreign policy and to deflect conservative redbaiting through a Democratic loyalty and security program, ended by fostering the atmosphere in which McCarthyism would thrive. See in particular Athan Theoharis, *Seeds of Repression: Harry S. Truman and the Origins of McCarthyism* (Chicago, 1971). This aspect of the history of McCarthyism has led to further investigation of the executive loyalty program itself, and here several studies are important: Eleanor Bontecoe, *The Federal Loyalty-Security Program* (Ithaca, N.Y., 1953); Alan D. Harper, *The Politics of Loyalty: The White House and the Communist Issue, 1946–1952* (Westport, Conn., 1969); Athan Theoharis, "The Escalation of the Loyalty Program," in *Politics and Policies of the Truman Administration*, ed. Barton J. Bernstein (Chicago, 1970), and "The Threat to Civil Liberties," in *Cold War Critics: Alternatives to American Foreign Policy in the Truman Years*, ed. Thomas G. Paterson (Chicago, 1971). Finally, any student interested in the origins of McCarthyism should consult *The Specter: Original Essays on the Cold War and the Origins of McCarthyism*, ed. Robert Griffith and Athan Theoharis (New York, 1974).

While the literature on various aspects of McCarthyism is growing, there is as yet no definitive biography of the senator himself and there may not be one until the McCarthy papers are no longer closed to scholars. Richard H. Rovere's *Senator Joe McCarthy* (New York, 1959) does provide a perceptive study of the man, however, and those interested in McCarthy's Senate career should consult Robert Griffith's *Politics of Fear* and Richard M. Fried's *Men Against McCarthy* (New York, 1976). The latter provides a solid history of McCarthy's political career, focusing on the opposition to him. First-person accounts of encounters with McCarthy include Owen Lattimore, *Ordeal by Slander* (Boston, 1950), and James A. Wechsler, *The Age of Suspicion* (New York, 1953). Other autobiographical accounts from those directly affected by congressional investigations and the Red Scare include O. Edmund Clubb, *The Witness and I* (New York, 1974), and Lillian Hellman, *Scoundrel Time* (Boston, 1976). Also see Philip M. Stern's account of J. Robert Oppenheimer's encounter with the Atomic Energy Commission in *The Oppenheimer Case: Security on Trial* (New York, 1969).

Two important studies of liberalism during the early Cold War have focused on Harry Truman and Henry Wallace. Alonzo L. Hamby, *Beyond the New Deal: Harry S. Truman and American Liberalism* (New York, 1973), stresses Truman's struggle for the hearts and minds of Roosevelt liberals, which took place against a background of Truman's evolving foreign and domestic policy. Hamby regards liberals' break with the popular front and commitment to Vital Center liberalism as a necessary step in the development of a sound postwar liberal movement. Norman D. Markowitz, in *The Rise and Fall of the People's Century: Henry A. Wallace and American Liberalism, 1941–1948* (New York, 1973), portrays both Wallace and the popular front sympathetically and points out that despite anti-Communist liberals' animosity, the Progressive party of 1948 was more clearly a continuation of the New Deal than its opponents were willing to acknowledge.

Any study of postwar liberals leads directly to the study of important liberal organizations. The Americans for Democratic Action has received superficial treatment in Clifton Brock's *Americans for Democratic Action: Its Role in National Politics* (Washington, D.C., 1962), but both Hamby and Markowitz include helpful material on the ADA. Charles Lam Markmann's *The Noblest Cry: A History of the American Civil Liberties Union*

(New York, 1965) is a conventional institutional history, but Donald Johnson has written a solid account of the ACLU's early years, *The Challenge to American Freedoms: World War I and the Rise of the American Civil Liberties Union* (Lexington, Ky., 1963), while Barton Bean's unpublished Ph.D. dissertation on the ACLU is especially helpful in its discussion of the organization's operations ("Pressure for Freedom: The American Civil Liberties Union," Cornell University, 1955). Memoirs and personal accounts by ACLU leaders Corliss Lamont (*Freedom Is As Freedom Does: Civil Liberties Today* [New York, 1956], and *The Trial of Elizabeth Gurley Flynn by the American Civil Liberties Union* [New York, 1968]) and Lucille Milner (*Education of an American Liberal* [New York, 1954]) are hardly disinterested accounts but, if used with care, provide helpful information and insights. Christopher Lasch's study of the Congress for Cultural Freedom ("The Cultural Cold War: A Short History of the Congress for Cultural Freedom," in *Towards A New Past: Dissenting Essays in American History,* ed. Barton J. Bernstein [New York, 1968]) includes the American Committee for Cultural Freedom and is important for its analysis of the cultural context in which the ACCF operated. Thomas C. Reeves's *Freedom and the Foundation: The Fund for the Republic in the Era of McCarthyism* (New York, 1969), provides a detailed account of the Fund for the Republic's early years.

There are few good biographies or political studies of congressional liberals from the decade following World War II. Among the best are: Winthrop Griffith, *Humphrey: A Candid Biography* (New York, 1965); Sidney Hyman, *The Lives of William Benton* (Chicago, 1969); Joseph Bruce Gorman, *Kefauver: A Political Biography* (New York, 1971); Donald J. Kemper, *Decade of Fear: Senator Hennings and Civil Liberties* (Columbia, Mo., 1965); and Allan Nevins, *Herbert H. Lehman and His Era* (New York, 1963). Two recent memoirs by leading liberal senators are Hubert H. Humphrey, *The Education of a Public Man: My Life in Politics* (Garden City, 1976), and Paul H. Douglas, *In the Fullness of Time: The Memoirs of Paul H. Douglas* (New York, 1972).

The topic of Communism and organized labor remains a controversial one. Max M. Kampelman (*The Communist Party vs. the C.I.O.: A Study in Power Politics* [New York, 1957]) and David J. Saposs (*Communism in American Unions* [New York, 1959]) both approach their topics from a strongly anti-Communist viewpoint. Len DeCaux, a Communist and former editor of the *CIO News,* has vigorously defended labor activism and the role of the Communist party in *Labor Radical: From the Wobblies to CIO, a Personal History* (Boston, 1970). Art Preis, in *Labor's Giant Step: Twenty Years of the CIO* (New York, 1964), gives a Trotskyite account of the Cold War struggle within the CIO. Revisionist studies include James R. Prickett, "Some Aspects of the Communist Controversy in the CIO," *Science and Society* 33 (Summer-Fall 1969):299–321; David M. Oshinsky, "Labor's Cold War: The CIO and the Communists," in *The Specter,* ed. Griffith and Theoharis; and Frank Emspak, "The Break-Up of the Congress of Industrial Organizations, 1945–1950" (Ph.D. diss., University of Wisconsin, 1972). Ronald Radosh's *American Labor and United States Foreign Policy* (New York, 1969) is a revisionist account focusing on organized labor's participation in the politics of Cold War foreign policy. Nelson N. Lichtenstein, in an unpublished dissertation ("Industrial Unionism under the No-Strike Pledge: A Study of the CIO during the Second World War," University of California, Berkeley, 1974), offers an innovative analysis of the CIO which stresses the impact of World War II and the New Deal coalition in curbing the CIO's aggressiveness as a trade union federation.

Index

Acheson, Dean, 49

Agricultural Workers, 53. *See also* Food, Tobacco, Agricultural and Allied Workers Union of America

Alsop, Joseph, 80

American Civil Liberties Union (ACLU), 89–107; and blacklisting in the entertainment industry, 91–95, 167 n.17; on civil liberties in U.S., 111; on Communist Control Act of 1954, 142; and Communist policy statement, 97–102, 169 nn.33, 34, 170 n.40, 171 nn.54, 55; on Communists in labor unions, 96; and conflict between board of directors and corporate membership, 99–102, 170 nn.41, 43, 170–71 n.44; and Corliss Lamont case, 104–6, 172 nn.62, 63; and direct involvement in litigation, 96, 169 n.28; and Elizabeth Gurley Flynn, 89–90, 166 n.4; and Emergency Civil Liberties Committee, 106, 173 n.68; files complaint with Federal Communications Commission, 92, 94–95; and Harry Bridges case, 95; and Harvey O'Connor case, 105; and House Committee on Un-American Activities, 89, 166 n.2; on immigration and naturalization policies, 96; and McCarthy, 101; on membership restrictions, 169 n.35; on military conscription, 96; and 1940 anti-Communist resolution, 89–90; and Owen Lattimore case, 103–4; on question of Communist control of ACLU, 169, n.37; resolution on the police state, 90; and Rosenberg case, 103; and Smith Act cases, 95–96,

168 n.23; statement opposing Communism, 90, 167 n.7

American Committee for Cultural Freedom (ACCF), 115–29; and Albert Einstein, 118–21; and anti-Communist coalition, 123–28; and Congress for Cultural Freedom, 121–23, 176 n.39; on culture and politics, 122, 175 n.35; and Emergency Civil Liberties Committee, 116–21, 173 n.68; on *Encounter*, 121–22; and Fund for the Republic, 124–25; and James Farrell, 127–28; and National Lawyers Guild, 116; and *New Leader*, 115, 174 n.14; on Owen Lattimore, 126–27; and Roger Baldwin, 125; sponsors *McCarthy and the Communists*, 125; and U.S. Central Intelligence Agency, 122

American Communications Association, 158 n.21

American Federation of Labor, 179 n.12

American Jewish Committee, 111

American Labor party (N.Y.), 35, 155–56 n.29

Americans for Democratic Action (ADA): bars Fascists and Communists from membership, 7; and the Communist Control Act of 1954, 142, 165 n.30; conception of liberalism, 7, 149 n.12; and the Congress of Industrial Organizations, 17–18, 44, 150 n.40; and Dwight D. Eisenhower, 34–36, 154 nn.6, 8; and foreign policy report, 31–32; founders' goals, 6–7; and future of American liberalism, 87; and Internal Security Act of 1950, 86; liberals' response to, 8–10,

Library of Congress Cataloging in Publication Data
McAuliffe, Mary Sperling, 1943-
Crisis on the left.
Bibliography: p.
Includes index.
1. Civil rights—United States. 2. Liberalism—
United States. 3. Subversive activities—United States.
4. United States—National security. 5. United States
—Politics and government—1945-1953. I. Title.
JC599.U5M2   320.5'3'0973   77-73479
ISBN 0-87023-241-X